Jock McAvoy

"Portrait of a Fighting Legend"

Brian Hughes M.B.E.

Other books by Brian Hughes:
Willie Pep
Jackie Brown
The Tommy Taylor Story
For King & Country

Published by Collyhurst and Moston Lads Club.

Typeset Printed and Bound by
MFP Design & Print,
Longford Trading Estate,
Thomas Street, Stretford,
Manchester M32 OJT.
Tel: 0161 864 4540

Contents

Forward
McAvoy:Portrait Of A Fighting Legend
-a biography from the pen of Brian Hughes M.B.E.

Many experts on the history of boxing consider the middleweight division to be the most competitive of all the various weight categories, and if one looks at the sheer quality of the world champions and contenders throughout the 20th century it is easy to subscribe to that point of view. Champions such as Marvin Hagler, Sugar Ray Leonard and Carlos Monzon from recent times, and Sugar Ray Robinson, Jake La Motta, Marcel Cerdan, Tony Zale, Mickey Walker, Harry Greb, Stanley Ketchel, Les Darcy and Bob Fitzsimmons from the previous eras were all outstanding title holders. In fact, it is safe to say that the middleweight division has supplied some of the greatest fighters the world has ever seen.

McAvoy:Portrait Of A Fighting Legend, by Brian Hughes, focuses on the ring career of one of the 20th century's most formidable yet also unluckiest middleweights. This new biography opens by taking the reader back in time to December 1935, with an imaginative account of a non-title bout between World Champion Eddie (Babe) Risko and British title holder Jock McAvoy. After setting the scene, the one round knockout by McAvoy over Risko - two minutes and forty eight seconds of absolute fistic mayhem - is described in graphic detail. Such a conclusive victory should have gained the redoubtable McAvoy a shot at the title, but the reality was that he had been just too good. Risko's gangster connection made sure that McAvoy was frozen out of the championship picture, consigning the Rochdale based fighter into the ranks of those boxers who might have been world champions had they not been in the wrong place at the wrong time, to coin a phase.

Brian Hughes suggests that Jock McAvoy was the toughest and most destructive of all the British middleweight champions. This book analyses the boxing career of McAvoy with the aid of contemporary journalistic accounts of most of his 147 contests plus the first hand memories of trainers, other fighters, friends, acquaintances and opponents. The consensus of informed opinion is that there can have been few boxers in the middleweight division in the 1930s who relished doing battle with this most hard punching and meanest of opponents - truly a man who gave and asked for no quarter within the squared circle. The reader is left with the impression that McAvoy would have been outstanding in any era, and would most certainly have jointed the illustrious list of world title holders had he lived at any other time and been given the breaks his talent deserved.

Brian Hughes also writes about the turbulent private life of Jock McAvoy, a man who was married three times, was infamous as a serious womaniser and for many brushes with authority throughout his colourful life. McAvoy was also particularly unlucky in contracting infantile paralysis, the much dreaded polio, two years after retiring from the ring. The book details McAvoy's long struggle to come to terms with becoming a cripple, and also his sad decline into depression, committing suicide on his 64th birthday.

The main thesis of this engrossing and carefully documented work is to enlighten the reader about the boxing career of this most fearsome of fighting men. The book is fully illustrated, including many photographs and illustrations which have never previously been published, and also includes McAvoy's complete ring record.

Rob Howard – Editor.

Acknowledgments

I would like to take this opportunity to thank Claude Abrams, the editor of Boxing
News for his help and encouragement in putting this book together. Glyn Leach,
the editor of Boxing Monthly was another who was very supportive in helping in
every way possible. These two men help to keep boxing alive throughout the
world through their excellent publications.

I would also like to offer my apologies to Doreen and Brian Meadows, of Sport
Art. Also to Phil Fitzpatrick, of Phoenix Photo Art. In our last book, 'For King and
Country', Doreen and Brian designed the cover for us, while Phil did all the photographs. Unfortunately, through events beyond our control my acknowledgement
and thanks did not appear. So here goes - A million thanks to the three of you!

Simon Crawford of the Rochdale Observer was another was always on hand with
help and advice. Peter Collins helped in every way possible. There are many people who talk about helping with a project like this, but that is all they do, talk.
Harold Brown the Yorkshire boxing historian, not only helped in every way, but
also supplied a number of the photographs which appear in this book. He was in
constant touch and his help was greatly appreciated.

This book would not have been even started if it would not have been for Bert
Daly's constant badgering. For years Bert and Harold Brown implored me to do
this book on their idol Jock McAvoy. In his younger days Bert was constantly in
or around McAvoy's training quarters. He used to wind McAvoy's old record player up and put the records on the turntable while his idol went through his training
sessions. He was forever telling me stories and incidents concerning his hero. Well
I hope you like the end results gentlemen.

There were many more people who helped with stories, photographs and programmes, far too numerous to mention here. One in particular was a police inspec-
tor from Rochdale, who gave me three rare programmes from the 1930s period.
He declined to leave his name, but I would like to thank him most sincerely. Derek
Bates, the son of McAvoy's trainer, Jack, was extremely helpful. Ray Smith,
whose father Jack, was a famous boxing manager in the 1920s and 1930s also
helped with advice and material. Rob Howard, a school teacher and former
amateur boxer, was a beacon of light in a very dark tunnel. He read and corrected my many mistakes, helped with ideas and was encouraging all the way through.

Rob, I cannot thank you enough. Jimmy Rogers and John Redfearn supplied memorabilia.

A special thank you must go to members of Jock McAvoy's family. Renee Bamford, Jock McAvoy's third wife, and also his daughter, Patricia. Renee and Pat welcomed me into their home and helped as much as they could. I spent many enjoyable hours in Renee's house and I respect both her and her daughter's openness and honesty. We discussed many things about the subject of this book and for my own reasons I have declined not to use certain conversations. Michael Bamford, McAvoy's third son, also helped as much as he could, and I thank him for that.

The Manchester Evening News readers were an inspiration when phoning me and offering advice and help. If there is anyone I have forgotten then please forgive me, it is not intentional I can assure you. Your help was greatly appreciated. God bless you all. Thanks to all the people who supplied me with photographs and written material. Whilst every effort has been made to trace copyright holders, in some cases this has proved fruitless. Anyone laying claim to a copyright not acknowledged should contact the publisher so that a proper arrangement for future editions may be made. If, after all that, I have left anyone out, let me assure you that any such omissions were purely unintentional and I renew my thanks to all who helped in any way.

I hope you enjoy the books we have published. Our main intention is to pay tribute in print to some of our finest fighting men. These boxers were great in their day but might forever be consigned to the back pages of history and forgotten forever to younger generations.

Jock McAvoy: Portrait of A Legend.

Born: 20th November 1907 in Burnley, Lancashire of Irish and Lancashire extraction. Moved to Rochdale while only a schoolboy.

Died: 20th November 1971.

Real Name: Joseph Patrick Bamford.

Nickname: The Rochdale Thunderbolt, because of his ferocious style of fighting. Early management: Joe Tolley of Royton. Harry Fleming of Collyhurst took over as manager and trainer (though Jack Bates was his recognised trainer). At the peak of his career he had American Dave Lumiansky as his business manager. Harry Levene from London also managed him for a spell later in his career.

One word that describes his boxing style: Effective!

Three words that describe his boxing style: Very, very effective.

One word that does not describe his fighting style: Dull. Every boxing journalist who covered his career wrote of McAvoy as being a dynamic fighter with a genius for scoring spectacular knockouts.

What he most liked about boxing: Winning and making money. His record was testament to that with 132 victories from 147 recorded bouts with 91 of his opponents flattened or stopped inside the distance. He loved fighting toe-to-toe and showed nor expected any mercy.

What he liked least about boxing: Losing and being cheated out of even one penny he thought was due to him.

The legacy he left: 11 years undefeated British middleweight champion, also held British Light-heavyweight title. Never knocked out in a ring career spanning 18 years. No middleweight ever hit harder or fought more viciously. Few of his con-

BOXING - JOCK McAVOY

The Rochdale Thunderbolt – Jock McAvoy

tests went the distance. Spectacular at all times, McAvoy was a promoter's and fight fan's dream.

What would he have been if he hadn't taken up boxing: perhaps a speedway rider or the owner of some kind of business. One thing abundantly clear is that he would have had to have been his own boss.

Legends are the backbone of sports. Take boxing, for instance. There would be little to write about the romance and glamour of pugilism if it were not for the legends that have been handed down over the years. There is one particular fighter from the 1920s and 1930s, known as the Rochdale Thunderbolt, about whom more stories have been written and more tales told, many of them are based on pure imagination and speculation but it must be stressed, that the great majority were true. When Bert Daly and Harold Brown asked me to write this book on Jock McAvoy, I hesitated, and told them I would consider their request. When I mentioned that I was thinking about doing this book to old timers, they looked at me as if I had taken leave of my senses. When I contacted people from that period for anecdotes and reminiscences of McAvoy, they were all wary even though the man has been dead for 28 years. What they all told me, and all agreed unanimously, was that Jock McAvoy was the most destructive middleweight this country has ever produced. During McAvoy's halcyon years, he was phenomenal.

A myth that exists in boxing is that Roberto Duran once flattened a horse with one punch and he was said to be the hardest boxer 'on the cobbles' in living memory. There have been many others who have become legends because of their hectic lifestyle. But the hardest of all time? No, that honour belongs to Jock McAvoy, who made his way through the shark invested waters of boxing like a psychotic Colossus. He stood five foot nine inches and weighed eleven stone six pounds of solid Lancashire steel.

When he was a teenager, he was reputed to be the best fist fighter in Rochdale, and this made him a celebrity. He was looked up to by youngsters of his own age for his willingness to take his coat off, roll up his sleeves and have a battle with men much bigger, heavier and older than himself. He was not renowned for his patience, in fact he would soon become exasperated, and then it was no sooner a word than a blow with him. To many folk McAvoy was a flawed maverick who was nevertheless content with his lot. He was at the same time venerated and detested, feared and envied. As a fighter he was unstoppable. Always as fit as the proverbial 'butcher's dog,' he was as awesome as a fighting bull, and one of the most rugged practitioners of the toughest, roughest, and hardest sport man has ever invented. One of his opponents, when discussing McAvoy said: "Defending myself against him was like trying to force a genie back into its bottle!"

Cheering, clapping, and foot stamping were heard wherever the charismatic and controversial Rochdalian fought throughout his 18 year ring career. He brought a level of flair and excitement to boxing not often seen, in British Rings.

However, Jock McAvoy's story is also littered with disputes with boxing officials, and endless controversy in his private life.

Jack Bates, who trained McAvoy through out his peak years, would introduce any conversation about Mac by saying, "Jock McAvoy was a killer in the ring and the greatest fighting machine I've trained. Terrific hooks, fierce jabs, pulverising right crosses - Jock has made a speciality of them all. When he connected, his opponent usually had a sore head for a couple of weeks afterwards." Bates would go on to describe the Rochdale man as a fighter cast in the same mould as Stanley Ketchel and Harry Greb. "Jock attacked all the time, and he had the perfect style. He snorted like a bull with every punch he sent over. And used to bite at the thumbs of his gloves in between rounds and during the actual fighting. Both were just habits. However, neither of them helped to give the fellow he was fighting any confidence!"

Bates' eyes would sparkle at the mere mention of McAvoy's name. The little trainer dispelled any rumours that McAvoy wasn't a genuine middleweight. "Mac could always scale inside 11 st 6 lbs, but truthfully, he never feared anybody at any weight. He gave more weight away to his opponents than any other middleweight who drew breath."

Jock McAvoy seemed immortal. This sturdy, larger-than-life fighter from Lancashire was a legend. Of course, he had a reputation for dourness, but to close

With the boys down at the Belle Vue Gym. To the left of McAvoy is Johnny Cusick and second from the right is Jackie Brown.

friends he liked a laugh and a giggle.

Over the years McAvoy's life was forever filled with incidents of one kind or another. Pat, McAvoy's daughter summed up her father when she remarked: "Every day was an incident, if I was walking home from school, going into a shop, talking to boys, horse riding, something would happen and he would be the main character in whatever it was that took place."

'Atomic Explosion at Madison Square Garden'
World's middleweight champion, Eddie (Babe) Risko goes to the canvas in the first few seconds of the opening round and Jock McAvoy wins a sensational victory

Risko and 'The Mob'

A blinding snowstorm plus a zero charged, bitingly cold wind whipped through the streets surrounding Madison Square Garden, the world famous Mecca of boxing. It was a week before Christmas, the 20th of December 1935, and the whole city of New York had been hit by freak Siberian weather conditions, causing the majority of the population to desert most places of entertainment for the relative comfort of their homes. On a night more fitted for listening to the boxing on the radio, nearly five thousand hardy, intrepid fans were huddled together, braving the snow and plummeting temperature as they made their way into the famous old arena. Although the adverse weather conditions had resulted in a disappointingly low turnout of spectators, the atmosphere inside the stadium was steadily becoming ever more red hot with excitement and anticipation as the minutes ticked away towards fight time. Sitting in the best ringside seats smoking their expensive cigars were many well known New York gangsters, flanked by their bejeweled, glamourous and gorgeous women. Former world heavyweight champion Jack Dempsey was also a keen ringside spectator along with Nat Fleischer, editor of the prestigious Ring Magazine, which was and still is referred to as the 'bible' of boxing. There were many other well-known American journalists present at ringside and, of course, there was also the usual gathering of celebrities from boxing and show business beside a party of America's top politicians.

Once the preliminary bouts were finished, the time had arrived for the eagerly awaited main event. As the ring announcer bellowed his introductions into the microphone, all eyes were focused on the well built, square shouldered British boxer who was standing in his corner biting and gnawing at his gloved thumbs. The spectators smiled and shook their heads at the Englishman's antics, wrongly assuming that he was frightened and acting extremely nervously. Nothing, however, could have been further from the truth. One of the judges for the fight was former world welterweight champion, Jack Britton, who fought our own Ted 'Kid' Lewis at least twenty times. Charlie Cavanagh, the referee, called both fighters to the centre of the ring while he issued his instructions. The men touched gloves and returned to their corners. The Britisher, virtually unknown on this side of the Atlantic, was eager for the bell to sound which would send him into action against his opponent, the reigning World Middleweight Champion, the dark-haired, good looking, Eddie 'Babe' Risko. According to the New York critics, the betting fraternity and the horde of mobsters, the result of this non-title showdown was already a foregone conclusion; they were convinced to a man that this 'Limey' would receive a painful lesson, one that he would not forget in a hurry. Yet another British boxer dispatched back to dear old Blighty with his tail between his legs!

The cigar smoke wafted through the air as the lights dimmed and the sound of the bell brought the two fighters racing out of their corners. Jock McAvoy had obviously not read the script because he immediately unleashed an awesome right hand punch which instantly connected, cracking home on the world champions jaw with a sickening sound. Crash, down on the canvas went the hapless Risko with a terrific thud. Dave Lumiansky in McAvoy's corner was jumping up and down like a puppet and screaming advice to the Englishman. Poor Eddie must have thought the roof had caved in when the Rochdale Thunderbolt struck. There was, momentarily, a deathly silence from the crowd before shrieking and yelling broke out, with the rising deluge of noise drowning out the referee's count. Judging from the look of sheer disbelief on the faces of everyone in the ringside seats, it was hard to imagine who was more shocked, the prostrate 'Babe,' or them.

There were a few isolated shouts of "Good boy, McAvoy" and "Well done England" from a small section of the audience. The Lancashire lad hounded the champion as soon as he regained his wobbly and unsteady feet. Snarling and uttering obscenities as he brushed away Risko's feeble attempts to land a punch, while bobbing and weaving and snorting like a hog, the invader was like a cyclone throwing two-handed blows at his badly shaken and visibly alarmed opponent. It was evidently clear that McAvoy was altogether too fast and much too aggressive for Risko. The crisp thud of the leather gloves on the champions face and body could be heard clearly by the ringsiders. It was an absolutely amazing scene the way the British lad was fighting more like an American style fighter than the champion was. The tough-talking New York reporters couldn't believe what they were watching. This was not what was supposed to be happening, and it certainly was not what they were expecting. An English fighter knocking seven bells out of an American world champion! It was quite obvious that everyone in Madison Square Garden on this unforgettable night had been expecting to see the British boxer performing in the usual upright European fashion. Instead, the Lancashire lad looked like an American fighter.

It was absolute bedlam in the arena: the fans were up on their feet yelling and screaming hysterically at the sheer ferocity of the Englishman's two-fisted attack. It really was an amazing scene, here was a British boxer demonstrating a fighting zest for which the Americans thought only their fighters could display. The hand-ful of English people in the audience stuck their chests out and felt patriotic as only the British can. McAvoy was like a tornado spraying his punches to his opponent's head and body. The Americans had never seen anything like this before from an overseas fighter. The whole place was in uproar as Risko's agitated manager, Gabe Genovese, shouted over to the matchmaker, Jimmy Johnston: "Where the hell did you find this guy?" Johnston was as surprised and shocked as everybody else, looking sheepish and poker-faced as the angry and alarmed manager of the world champion screamed out more unprintable obscenities at him.

The Limey, who only seconds before had been conceived as not having a hope in hell's chance of troubling the Yank, was giving the champion the biggest wallop-ing of his life. Babe Risko tried desperately to grab hold of his tormentor, but like a ferocious dog shaking at a rag doll, the world champion was being treated in a similar manner as he received more thunderous punches from his attacker. The champion was up and down like a yo-yo. This was no longer a competitive fight, it was a massacre, all one way traffic with the Britisher flaying away with fero-cious piston-like punches, and chasing the bewildered Risko round the ring. 'Babe' was taking the shellacking of his life. He had never before had to undergo such a drubbing as he was being forced to take now at the hands of his tormentor, and there was no hiding place for the American on this bitterly cold and unforgettable night.

During one of the knockdowns McAvoy was standing in a neutral corner waiting for the referee to order him to box on. As he stood there he unconsciously started gnawing away ferociously at his thumb, and the fans were highly amused at this mannerism. Harry Markson, a well-known American boxing figure who would later became a world wide respected match maker wise-cracked: "Look at that Limey, biting the hand that feeds him." This would later become a well-known phrase used by many journalists when writing about McAvoy. Three things were evidently plain for everyone to see. The first was that this lightly regarded 'Limey' could most certainly fight and, that he could punch with awesome and devastating power. And, thirdly, the courage of Risko was of the highest order. Battered to a pulp, cut and bruised the American did not know where he was as the British fight-er drilled home punch after punch to head and body. The final blow, a pile-driven right smash which sent him down for the sixth and final time, was delivered with every ounce of the invader's weight behind it and it almost took Risko's head clean off his shoulders. It was a punch thrown from the toes, with the power travelling like an electric current through his knees, hips and shoulders until landing with the full impact of an electric shock on its intended target. "Get up and fight, you bum," urged some of the crowd but the prostrate world champion was oblivious to their cruel taunts. There was complete shock and amazement etched on everybody's face inside Madison Square Garden. Nobody but nobody, the crowd nor the boxing officials could believe what they had just witnessed with their eyes. It had been incredible: an American world champion had been ruthlessly and methodically butchered without throwing a single worthwhile punch in return. He hadn't been allowed to. The lightly regarded 'Limey' had fought sensationally, absolutely breathtaking in his animal-like ferocity. In just under three minutes of mayhem the Lancashire lad had turned the boxing world upside down. He had given English boxing a massive and much needed shot in the arm and, more importantly, he had given British boxing its pride back again.

The power brokers who controlled the world titles breathed a sigh of relief when it was all over. It was very fortunate for them and Risko and his connections that the world championship had not been at stake on this incredible occasion. Though they evidently thought little of the British fighters credentials beforehand, they nevertheless insisted that this non-title match be fought at catch-weights in order to protect Risko's title in case of an accident. At the official weigh-in, Risko scaled 11-stone 7-and-a-half-pounds, while the Britisher came in heavy, at 12-stone and half-a-pound. The reason Mac was a little on the heavy side was due to the liquids he had been forced to take earlier that week while suffering from a bad dose of flu and bronchitis. "We almost called the fight off because of Jock's indisposition," Dave Lumiansky, who was McAvoy's business manager, told the gathering hordes of reporters outside the Britisher's dressing room. "Was you scared?" asked a cigar smoking, button-nosed New York reporter looking directly at McAvoy, who quickly replied between sniffs and coughs, in his thick Lancashire accent: "Neigh lad, neigh." On hearing McAvoy's accent several reporters laughed and asked for an interpreter. The question being asked by everyone interested in boxing world-wide, was: "Would the British fighter now get a return fight with the world champion for his world middleweight championship?" The answer was categorically...No! The Risko connections were part of the American undesirables of that period and they had no intention of taking another chance with the Britisher. They claimed that the English lad was in reality a light-heavyweight and not in fact a middleweight. This was despite the fact that McAvoy was the British 11st 6lb champion and, indeed rated in the middleweight division of the world rankings.

The Americans, nonetheless, loved his style and his punching power. He was welcome back anytime he chose. What was the 'Limey's' name thousands of American
fight fans were now asking? - Jock McAvoy! The Rochdale Thunderbolt! This
fighter was without a shadow of doubt the finest middleweight this small, but
proud little island had ever produced. When news of McAvoy's sensational victory filtered back to England, Jack Bates, McAvoy's trainer, was sitting in his home
in north Manchester, having a cup of tea in front of a roaring coal fire. Nobody
could have been more pleased than Bates who was overjoyed about McAvoy's
success. An inquisitive young reporter called to his house and asked for his views
on McAvoy's brilliant victory on American soil. Jack smiled and told the reporter
he wasn't surprised in the least by Mac's success in the States. Bates stood only
five foot three inches and was the proud owner of a cauliflower ear, the result of
over 400 professional fights. He trained the new British sensation in a dirty, smelly
little gymnasium in the heart of Collyhurst, a poor run-down district of North
Manchester. Jack was one of the few people whom the truculent Rochdale man
respected and genuinely liked. Bates was due to go to New York with McAvoy
whom he affectionately called 'Mac' but had had to pull out at the last moment, due
to domestic reasons. He had always dreamed of visiting America, the country of
his hero Harry Greb, known throughout boxing as "The Human Windmill"
because of his all-action style of fighting. Jack's wife, Sara, was not keen on her
husband being away from home for some considerable time and complained and
implored him not to travel to America. A reluctant Bates agreed to his wife's
request. Sadly, this incident would eventually end with the couple splitting up.

The young reporter worked his way into the Bates household and while having a
cup of tea he questioned the little trainer about McAvoy. He asked Bates what were
McAvoy's greatest attributes. The trainer thought for a few seconds then explained
to the newspaperman that the boxing ring was Jock's domain. It was his kingdom
and he was perfectly at home inside that roped square. The reporter probed further
and asked the little trainer to elaborate. "The boxing ring has been described by
various fighters as the loneliest place on earth, that's perfectly true to some extent.
But McAvoy relishes the confrontation of one-to-one combat. He is the only fighter I've ever trained who really loves fighting. He is a 'one off' and the best middleweight this country has ever produced." Jack went on to explain Mac's determination was at times frightening, even to an experienced trainer like himself. The
reporter asked Bates how he personally rated the new British sensation. Without a
moment's hesitation this time, Jack said: "He's the roughest, toughest fighter ever,
and he is absolutely fearless and the fiercest fighter I've ever set eyes on and,

believe me, I've seen thousands of fighters over a great number of years."

Bates was as pleased as punch about McAvoy's new found popularity with the press and he concluded his chat with the reporter by adding: "I'll tell you something else, he's got the best chin of any fighter I know, and he is always in a hundred percent physical condition."

As this book is primarily concerned with an evaluation of Jock McAvoy's boxing career and, in particular, his record-breaking 91 knockouts and inside-the-distance victories, I do not intend to go into a great amount of detail about his early life or his activities away from the boxing ring. This has already been chronicled and researched to perfection by Jack Doughty in his excellent and highly recommended book the "Rochdale Thunderbolt." However, I feel I must give a brief picture of his roots, his upbringing and his family.

McAvoy (left) sparring with Glen Moody at Hollingworth Lake in the early part of his career.

Joe Bamford - The Best Fist Fighter In Rochdale

Jock McAvoy's real name was Joseph Patrick Bamford. He was born in Burnley on 20 November 1907. His mother, Mary Ellen Ginty, known as Nellie to friends and family, came from Irish ancestry, was born in Salford then raised in Pendleton. While working as a weaver in one of the thousands of cotton mills of that time, Nellie met a man named George Hardacre, and in 1893 gave birth to a daughter named Rose Ellen. Nellie and George never got married and later went their separate ways. A few years later Nellie met Joe Bamford, a Burnley man, and settled down with him and gave birth to a powerful ten pounds baby boy. His parents christened him Joseph Patrick. The family moved to Barnoldswick, near Burnley. Shortly after the First World War the Bamford family moved from Burnley back to Manchester in order to find work, scarce during this period. Nellie had relatives and the family stayed with them. Rose, now in her twenties, had married and had two children of her own, and though widowed, she remained in Barnoldswick. After being unable to secure work or decent living conditions in Manchester the Bamford family quickly moved again, this time to Rochdale where they settled down for good. At this period Joe was about twelve years old.

Few of life's luxuries came knocking at the door of the Bamford household. They lived in the poorest, toughest and roughest part of the old mill town that was later made famous by Gracie Fields. Joe's life as a schoolboy was probably no different to most youngsters of that time, although he was never afraid to have his say. Though being the only son young Joe was spoiled to an unhealthy degree by both parents, and there was a distinct lack of discipline in the household. His mother absolutely worshiped the ground he walked on and could never see any wrong in her son, while his father, a powerfully built man known for his feats of strength and love of animals, rarely chastised him. Young Joe had a wicked temper, even as a child, and at times seemed uncontrollable. He would rant and rave, always wanting his own way. This in a period when children didn't dare open their mouths, the "children should be seen but not heard" era. It was very much the case in most households of "Speak when you're spoken to." Neighbours described the youngster as an arrogant, bombastic and spoiled brat whose vile temper would land him into trouble as he got older. In his later life this would be highlighted for all to see. The average family in those days was usually six or seven. Young Joseph went to St. Patrick's Roman Catholic School in Rochdale, a typical Victorian two-storey edifice. Joe Bamford remained at this school until leaving at the age of fourteen.

In the 1920s the cotton mills, the mines and engineering were the source of regular employment for Lancashire folk and Joe tried his hand in the various mills around his neighbourhood. However, he soon decided that this type of work was most definitely not the life for him as he hated the deafening, incessant noise coming from the hundreds of looms together with the cotton stench which hung heavily in the air. Joe's mother and father pleaded with him to get a trade for the sake of his future. It was, moreover, a status symbol to have a tradesman in the family, especially in a predominantly industrial town like Rochdale. Their pleas though fell on deaf ears. Their son tried several other jobs over the following three or four years such as labouring on building sites and working in an iron foundry, but he didn't seem able to settle into any kind of steady employment. His biggest problem was that he hated being told what to do by people in authority such as a foreman or supervisor, and he was fired from several jobs after arguing and on occasions brawling toe to toe with those in charge. New acquaintances found him to be a dour, sullen-faced young fellow with hardly any sense of

McAvoy, a glutton for hard training, uses a sledgehammer while preparing for one of his early fights.

humour. He had no time for debating any issue and would boorishly never listen to the other person's point of view, as many found out to their cost due to his violent temper, and it was no sooner a wrong word than a blow with him. His reputation soon spread and his workmates tended to give him a wide berth. There were a lot of hard, tough men living and working in the Rochdale area during this period, and tales of young Bamford's bare fist fights are legendary. He could occasionally be seen having a 'bundle in' with workmates and men in charge.

There is one particular story that typifies Bamford at this time. It was an incident that occurred while he was working for Rochdale Corporation laying tramlines. Over the years the story has become folklore in Lancashire. In those days if an argument occurred and the two men arguing felt strongly enough about whatever was the cause of their friction, it wasn't uncommon for them to step outside on to any spare ground, a back entry or a street, roll up their sleeves and have a fist fight. There would be no weapons used, unlike today's society. Anyhow, on this particular day the heavens opened and rain came down in sheets. Joe and his workmates naturally took shelter in a cabin. The foreman was a huge, robust, overbearing fellow, known affectionately to his labourers as "that big bastard," rushed in and was fuming because the men had stopped working without his permission. He started abusing the workers, calling them softies and lazy so and so's. Turning to Bamford he smirked, and in no uncertain terms told Joe he was not pulling his weight and called him a lazy so and so. Joe, even though only a young man, nonetheless had strong opinions, and it not being in his nature to be downtrodden and also being the fiery tempered fellow he was, answered the foreman back. "Don't you get lippy with me, I'll put your lights out," snarled the foreman whereupon he moved menacingly toward Bamford and, in no time, the two men were going at each other as if their very lives depended on it. It was a violent affair with both men falling into the holes that had been dug earlier that day and splashing about in the pools of water which had formed after the deluge of rain. Blood and hair were flying all over the place as the two men punched, butted and kicked away at each other, and soon both were covered in mud from head to toe. It was a vicious fight. No mercy was asked nor given. Eventually after what must have seemed like hours of fighting, the younger Bamford smashed his right fist onto the foreman's jaw and it was all over. Word of Joe's fight with the foreman travelled fast, and he became a minor celebrity in Rochdale.

Just to digress for a moment. Johnny King, the former British and British Empire bantamweight champion and a member of the Collyhurst stable, of which Jackie

Brown and Jock McAvoy were members, remembered Joe Bamford in the 1920s. Many years later while discussing McAvoy's early days King said: "It wasn't just his workmates who steered clear of Joe, his neighbours were extremely wary of him and kept well out of his way. Many of them expressed the opinion, not in his presence I must add, that he was a conceited devil, foul mouthed and a lazy so-and-so who hated work."

Joe had a voracious appetite, and his friends used to say he could eat for England. He was always hungry and would regularly polish off a full loaf of bread and dripping and two or three meat pies. He was a tough robust lad, and liked sport, especially rugby and speedway. He was also often spotted playing soccer with some of his old school friends on spare ground or the park. Many times they would play against blokes from the mills or factories. They all played in their shoes or working boots with their trousers tucked into their socks. They were hard matches with no quarter asked or given and, needles to say, Joe would be in the thick of the action. In those early teenage years, participation in boxing did not hold much attraction for him, unlike Jackie Brown and Johnny King, who would later become his friends and stablemates at Collyhurst. In contrast to Joe Bamford, both had considerable fistic experience while still at school, and by the time they reached sixteen were already professionals.

Joe liked reading about famous sporting personalities. His favourites were the magazines or books about boxing, and he read everything he could lay his hands on concerning Jack Dempsey. Dempsey was his favourite sporting hero. The Manassa Mauler seemed to inspire him and spark his imagination. He loved reading about Dempsey, one of the most colourful characters in ring history. Kid McCoy, Stanley Ketchel and Harry Greb were also among his favourite boxers. These Americans were middleweight champions who were also renowned as first class characters. After devouring every bit of information about Dempsey and his other favourite fighters, Joe decided to give boxing a try himself.

Wherever Joe Bamford went, controversy was sure to follow. He was a fearless character in every sense of the word, entering a highly competitive world which called for nerves of steel. Many former boxers will tell you that taking those first steps into boxing are the hardest. They will readily admit they were frightened and more than a little apprehensive at what would happen to them once they laced the gloves on. This however, was most certainly not the case with Joe Bamford. As a youngster Johnny King lived in Rochdale for a period, and he clearly recalled his first meeting with Bamford. "How could I ever forget my first glimpse of Joe," he said whimsically. "I was a couple of years younger than him, and one night while I was training in a gym in Rochdale that I often frequented, in walked this sturdy, well-made young fellow. It was Joe Bamford. I paid no attention to him and went about my training in a different part of the gym. All of a sudden I heard this commotion and I looked into the room where all the noise was coming from and I saw three hefty blokes having to restrain my future colleague."

What transpired was that Bamford had put the gloves on with a man who had some ring experience and things got out of hand and Joe was steamed up, and he had to be restrained by several people. King often smiled when telling stories of Joe Bamford's early beginnings in boxing, but he added: "Joe could handle himself all right, though I must confess that when he was in one of his rages he was quite frightening. Many folk thought he was nothing more than a bully. Many times I would watch him arguing with someone on the street or wherever, and in a flash he would end the argument instantly by belting the unfortunate person or persons in the mouth. I have to say in fairness to him, that if he was ever on the receiving end of a walloping, he never complained. Though he would seek retribution and revenge as quickly as possible over whoever it was that had got the better of him at that particular time, and he would sulk until he extracted full revenge."

If there ever was an English born fighter who fought in the true American tradition that man must surely have been young Joe Bamford. He had purchased a Jack Dempsey boxing instruction book and he devoured every morsel of information there within. And he fought like his hero, out of a crouch, bobbing and weaving. After a few weeks of intense training he felt he was ready for a competitive fight. He was nineteen and there was, as yet, nothing really exceptional about him apart from the fact that he was very powerful and determined in whatever he put his mind to doing. Joe was still playing soccer and amateur Rugby League, but he knew that these sports would not make him into a rich man like his heroes of the boxing ring.

One day after labouring on a building site in pouring rain and a cold, bitter wind, he was in a foul mood. Navvying was backbreaking work, even for a tough, strong youngster like Bamford. He seemed to realise that if he were to make his fortune in life it certainly would not be achieved being a navvy laying tramlines. He decided to give boxing his undivided attention from then on, encouraged by two brothers, Charley and Stan Hall, both of whom had some experience of professional

An unusual shot of 'the Rochdale Thunderbolt' as he exercises in the gymnasium.

boxing and had the use of an old basement in their home in Holland Street in Rochdale in which to train. Joe was a regular attender and put his heart and soul into his workouts. But, like the other gyms where he later trained, friction and resentment soon surfaced as Bamford could not hold back in sparring against the two brothers and other boxers who used the basement to train.

His problem was that he never knew how to pull his punches and take it easy while sparring. It is common practice for boxers generally to hold back in training, preferring to save their efforts for the actual contest. Bamford, however, because he was just starting out in boxing and not having anyone to advise him, never learned to hold back and continued like this throughout his career. Every time he laced on the gloves he gave his full commitment and many times he had to be physically restrained when things got out of hand. Bamford, cocky and confident of his own ability, became unbearable to the other members who used the premises. In fact he terrified them and he was told in no uncertain terms that he was no longer welcome to train in the basement and, after being turned away from other establishments, he rented an old house for a couple of shillings a week. It was at this time that he showed true dedication and a fierce determination to succeed that would put many modern-day boxers to shame.

It was often said nostalgically that the 'good old days' of the 1920s and 1930s were the best times. But many people disagree and refer to those bleak times as the 'bad old days.' The unemployed went on hunger marches. Such conditions caused professional boxing to boom as men fought as often as they could in order to make some kind of living. Fighters were a dime a dozen; there were scores of hungry fighters at every weight in those austere times and to reach the top rung of the ladder a fighter had to have that little something extra above and beyond the others. Joe Bamford really was, as we will see, something special!

Joe, full of enthusiasm and self-belief, rigged up his own makeshift gym in an old derelict house near to his home. In one of the bedrooms he nailed pieces of wood into the wall with six inch nails which he used as ring posts, old orange boxes and tattered ropes were hastily put together to make a ring. His home - made improvised punch bag was an old sack stuffed full of paper and old clothing and whatever else he could find to fill up the bag. He would set his alarm clock ticking, and here on his own he would commence training in complete solitude. He had no trainer, no sparring partner, nobody whatsoever to help him. What he had in plenty though, was total dedication.

In these formative years he used a great deal of psychology on himself, and this caused him to progress. For instance he would tell himself that there was nobody in the world at his weight that could beat him, inside or outside the ring, and this fierce determination remained with him throughout his career. He would let his imagination run wild, pretending he was Jack Dempsey and remembering what a tough upbringing this famous champion had undergone, and what hassles he had to overcome before he became a world champion. He also admired the all-action style of Jack "Kid" Berg, telling himself that if these two champions could do it, then, he could also achieve fame and fortune. A lesson here for all would be boxers!

He would shadow-box and while he was going through the motions he would imagine that an opponent was in front of him trying to knock him out, and snarling, he would put plenty of venom into his punches. He worked himself into such a fury that had there been any onlookers present they would probably have thought he was demented. Joe would skip away for minutes at a time until he had completed the equivalent of ten - three minute rounds non-stop. He studied what great fighters like Dempsey had for their meals, cutting out starchy and fried food. At dawn he would drag himself out of bed and run eight miles without letting up for a walk or a jog. He trained, very possibly, like no other boxer before or since. Johnny Cusick, the former British featherweight champion was a great admirer of McAvoy, though in retrospect Johnny believed that the Rochdale lad trained much too hard. Johnny's opinion was that on many occasions Mac had over-trained for many of his epic battles in the ring.

Mrs Bamford, though happy Joe was keeping himself fit and out of trouble, was not keen on her son actually boxing and pleaded with him to forget the idea of fighting, and urged him to find a nice steady job and settle down. He was intrinsically lazy and was not keen on the idea of getting up at the crack of dawn as most workers did in those days. Moreover, he was a free spirit and working regular hours and taking orders from foremen was certainly not for him. The older he got, the more self-centred and bombastic he became and, at times a very obnoxious person as we will discover later, with a mind of his own. Like most young men he didn't know what he really wanted to do with his life. He certainly did not fancy the discipline of an apprenticeship or stuck in one of those noisy cotton mills. His friends told him he would do well in boxing, though at first he wasn't certain. But, after a few weeks of turmoil, he decided to give boxing his full commitment.

He had thought deeply about the situation and after deliberating on whether he should or shouldn't make boxing his chosen profession, he decided that he would take the plunge and have a go at fighting for money. Having had no amateur experience whatsoever, his first recorded fight took place at Royton Stadium in Oldham. However, before continuing it should be pointed out that local legend has it that Joe Bamford did actually fight professionally on several un-licensed tournaments before actually joining Joe Tolley. In later years McAvoy himself claimed he had taken part in many more contests than his record officially stated and although there are no details available of these contests, it was almost certainly no idle boast.

Mrs Vera Wilson a Rochdale resident, was a teenager in the early 1920s. Her name then was Veda Gragg, and she was living with her mother and father above Joe Heywood's undertakers at number 1 Court which was near Lomax Street and Yorkshire Street in Rochdale. She remembers quite vividly that the Bamfords lived at the back of the undertakers, and their families were very close. "No working class folk had a telephone in those days," she said. "Because we lived in the undertaker's, my father used to look after the horses for Mr Heywood, and we had a telephone. It was one of the really old fashioned types which was fixed on the wall. I still remember the number, Rochdale 396." Vera remembers Joe calling to speak to her mother and father, asking them if they would tell his mother the results of his fights if he phoned their number after he boxed. "My mother and father readily agreed to his request," added Vera. "I would run around to his mother's house and give her the news. When he won, which was always, she would give me a block of chocolate. If he had been marked up he would say 'tell my mother I won't be home for a couple of days until my face looks better.' He thought the world of his mother and father, though he and his mother had a special kind of rapport. He made a terrific fuss of her. His father was an unassuming man who enjoyed simple pleasures."

Joe Tolley was a well-known manager and promoter of the 1920s, especially in the Lancashire area, and it was he who gave Bamford his official start in professional boxing. There were a great number of venues in those days with tournaments taking place every day of the week as well as Sunday afternoons. There were scores

McAvoy training with a run.

of hungry fighters in every town, village and city - Manchester, Salford and Royton being among the most prominent breeding grounds for pugilists. In those days it was often the accepted thing that any unknown aspiring pugilist would have to box in a trial contest in order for the promoter and matchmaker to see if he was worth a spot on their promotion. Young Joe Bamford's illustrious boxing career started on a cold, brisk Sunday morning on the 6th November 1927 when he travelled the short distance from Rochdale to Royton.

A friend asked Joe Tolley if Bamford could have a trial and the answer was 'Yes.' The Rochdale lad found himself facing Mickey Maloney, who was a relation of Tolley's and though lighter than Bamford was much more experienced. After four rounds of what can only be described as a baptism of fire in which the lighter man's punches, though not particularly powerful, had plenty of sting in them and constantly found Joe's face. He was greatly surprised when the promoter offered him a fight on his tournament that was being staged that very afternoon.

This story highlights just how tough it could be in those good old, bad old days. Having gone hell for leather Joe was required to go back to the stadium a few hours later and engage himself in an official contest in which there would be no quarter asked nor any given. It would send shivers down the spine of present day fighters. Several tournaments were staged on Sunday afternoons in the 1920s and 1930s. While getting dressed after the hectic trial, Tolley, who beside being the manager, promoter, matchmaker and ticket seller, was also the Master of Ceremonies and a referee, was writing the programme out and not knowing Joe's name, he asked the youngster what he called himself? Not wishing to upset his mother, the lad was flustered and called out..."Jack McCoy." This was after one of his favourite fighters, the legendary American, Kid McCoy. Imagine Bamford's face later that afternoon as he was standing in the ring and Tolley announced him as "Jock McAvoy from Rochdale." The promoter had that many jobs to undertake he was bound to get things like a name mixed up. Nobody apart from Bamford bothered, but poor Tolley's ears must have been red-hot! From that moment on the name McAvoy stayed with him. Obviously, to his friends and family, he would remain Joe Bamford. However, to boxing followers he was simply known as Mac!

Enter Jock McAvoy

Somebody had to pay for this error of Tolley's, and his first professional opponent Billy Longworth of Royton, the unfortunate recipient of Bamford/McAvoy's flash of pique, was flattened inside two rounds of storming action. The McAvoy legend had begun. The crowd loved his tear-away tactics and the place was in uproar. He had gone like a bull at a gate from the opening bell, throwing wild punches for all he was worth, finally decking the lighter local lad for the full count. He was gloriously delighted with himself but was brought back down to earth when Tolley paid him his purse which was a pound, and remarked: "The fellow you fought was a lot smaller and lighter than you. You can please yourself if you come back next week. It will not bother me either way." At these remarks, McAvoy fixed Tolley with an icy stare and was about to give the promoter a few choice words, but using discretion he declined to reply, though he never forgot Tolley's remarks and would have a sort of love-hate relationship with him over the coming years. At this point Mac was fighting as a welterweight, (10st 7lb), although it was only a short time before he grew into a fully-fledged middleweight (11st 6lb).

Fighters were paid a pittance early in their careers because the promoters could virtually pick and choose who fought on their tournaments. It was obvious that a man who fought tooth and nail would receive regular work and if the crowd liked his style of fighting, so much the better. When McAvoy commenced his career there were plenty of good welterweights and middleweights in the north alone. It was little wonder that so much brain damage was sustained in this period. Nobody was particularly to blame, it was more a sign of the times.

Delighted with his victory, but even more pleased with his money, Mac made his way home to Rochdale and was more determined than ever to become a big name celebrity like his heroes Dempsey and Kid McCoy. He felt like a big time celebrity himself later that night as he sat in his four shillings and sixpenny seat in the Champness Hall in Rochdale, listening to the popular well-known tenor singer, Tom Burke, known at that time as "The Lancashire Caruso." It was reported that thousands were unable to get in when Burke had sung at the Royal Albert Hall in London only a couple of weeks before. Another form of relaxation he enjoyed was going to the cinema.

It would be three weeks later before he fought again, having trained religiously throughout that period. In the opposite corner for his second fight was Bert Hilditch, another local lad who hailed from Shaw, and came from a family of three fighting brothers. Bert, though only seventeen, had plenty of experience and quite a number of victories to his credit. Hilditch was lighter than Mac and started in sprightly fashion, making a bright enough start. However, his good start soon came to nothing as he was facing a man possessed in McAvoy, an opponent who simply would not be denied. Young Bert's neat boxing could not contain the human dynamo in front of him. In the sixth, Hilditch was put on the canvas several times before the referee rushed in and rescued him. Mac was shattered from his exertions and breathing rather heavily, but as proud as punch with his second victory. He was already being spoken about as a 'prospect,' and he strutted around Rochdale like a peacock, loving all the adulation.

At this stage McAvoy did not have his own trainer, although Charlie and Stan Hall and other close pals from the Rochdale area were helping him in his makeshift gym. He trained long and hard and nobody could fault him on this issue. What he needed more than anything else though, was regular sparring work, because being a very late starter in the boxing business he had not learned the fundamental basics of the sport correctly. For example, though he was an awesome puncher even at this early stage of his development, he was not delivering his blows in the correct manner, and suffered badly from injuries to his knuckles and various other bones in his hands, injuries which would plague him throughout his career.

He needed plenty of sparring but there was nobody at Joe Tolley's gym big or heavy (or willing) enough to give him a decent sparring session and Tolley couldn't find suitable sparring partners for Mac to box against. The other fighters in the gym knew that even in sparring McAvoy never eased up, it was all out war every time he put the gloves on, and they wanted paying if they were going to get treated in this manner. It made no difference to Mac how big or small the man facing him was, he would fly at them with a savage vengeance and he could be very spiteful in every respect in or outside the ropes. Other fighters gave him a wide berth and avoided him at all costs.

Mac was keen to learn the business of boxing and he devoured every morsel of information in his Jack Dempsey boxing and training manual that he had purchased from a book shop a couple of years earlier. He treated this book like a bible. Disaster, however, struck in his third fight which was staged in the Lancashire village of Haslingden in January 1928. He was matched over ten rounds with the vastly experienced Billy Chew of Darwen. Chew was a teak-tough miner. After going hammer-and-tongs for seven rounds, Mac was absolutely fatigued and it took all his will to rise off his stool and go out for round eight. After a few seconds McAvoy very reluctantly raised his hand in surrender. It was his first loss and he was devastated. He need not have felt too badly about it because Chew was a very good fighter and young Mac was clearly overmatched and should never had been allowed to box ten rounds at this early stage of his career.

The irony of it all was that he didn't know how to pace the fight or conserve his energy in order to last the ten round distance. Not having the services of a trainer had cost him this fight. Because it was a ten round bout, Mac mistakenly had the idea that he needed extra stamina. On the afternoon of the fight he and a friend went up on the moors above Rochdale and hiked three miles across the moors in heavy snow. Coming home, he then took part in a strenuous game of football on some spare ground which was full of snow. This took its toll disastrously later that night. On returning home after the fight, his mother was visibly upset at the state of his face and pleased with her only son to give up this foolishness of fighting for a living. Chew, the gritty Lancashire miner had given him a pasting.

Years later, Billy Chew smiled as he reflected on his fight with the young McAvoy. "McAvoy told people I was too heavy for him," remarked Billy, "but my normal fighting weight was usually 10st 6lb. In those days most men in Lancashire were on the small side. Flyweights, bantam, feather or lightweights, anything above that was considered big. I fought lots of bigger men, full middleweights even. Times were tough and we couldn't pick and choose our opponents." Billy explained how the match with McAvoy came about. "I fought a lad named Joe Heywood at Haslingden. As I was getting dressed the promoter and matchmaker, Harry Barlow, walked up to me and asked if I fancied topping the bill on a show he was staging at a new venue called the Public Hall in Blackburn. Jack Strahan, my manager and trainer, asked Mr Barlow the name of the chap I would be fighting and was told - Jock McAvoy. 'Get your posters out, my lad will box McAvoy,' Strahan told the promoter."

Chew did his training at the Copperfield Street Gymnasium, near his home in Darwen, and worked harder than ever for this contest against McAvoy. Billy Chew was another person who was certain that McAvoy had actually more contests than his official record stated, especially prior to his fight against the Rochdale lad. "McAvoy was supposed to have had only two fights prior to fighting me," stated

Chew. "Well, I can honestly tell you that he most definitely had fought more than twice before meeting me, you can take my word on that. There were several halls and venues littered all around Lancashire where boxing took place every night of the week. It was near impossible for anyone to keep an accurate check on records." It is quite true what Billy Chew stated. In those days proper records were never kept. Talking further about his first fight with McAvoy, Chew said: "I knew McAvoy could hit, because he had flattened a mate of mine with the first punch of the fight. My pal told me I would get the same treatment but I lost no sleep I can assure you."

Talking about the day he fought the Rochdale man, Billy said he worked a full day down the coal pit, rushed home when his shift finished, had a good wash and after his dinner he fell asleep on the sofa for an hour. Afterwards, along with his second, George Yates, he made his way to the venue. While getting ready in his dressing room the door suddenly opened and in walked McAvoy complaining that he,

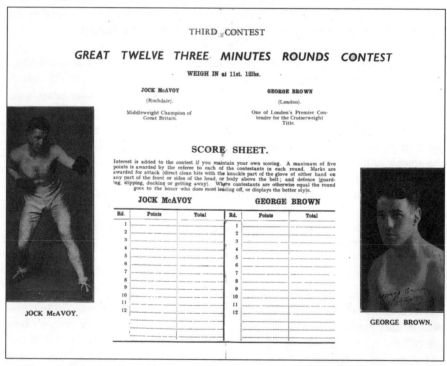

This early fight card from 1932/33 pits McAvoy against the Londoner, George Brown.

(Chew) had not weighed in and was much too heavy. Jack Strahan asked Harry Barlow to bring the scales into the dressing room. Billy stepped on the scale and weighed just under 10st 6lb. Mr Barlow then asked McAvoy to step on the scale. McAvoy was livid, uttered some remark and refused to step on the scale.

Despite his mother's pleading Mac fought again in March of the same year. Teddy Cox was his opponent, and the fight was on Cox's own patch at Todmorden Drill Hall. Mac was like a human dynamo on this occasion, winning by a seventh round count out. This victory gave McAvoy the boost he needed after the disastrous Billy Chew fiasco. However, after his victory over Cox, McAvoy suddenly vanished from boxing for almost eighteen months. Many gossip mongers around the Rochdale area said he was in prison, but this certainly was not the case. Though he was a tear-away on the cobbles, McAvoy was not a criminal in the accepted sense. Later, the rest from boxing would show it had done McAvoy no harm at all, and if anything, it had developed his physique and his strength.

Speedway was a very popular sport in this period and quite a lot of glamour was attached to it, the Belle Vue Aces being particularly high profiled. Mac had always fancied riding motor bikes but did not have the money to indulge in this expensive hobby. "My mother hated boxing," he said many years later when recalling his early life. "But I had this burning desire to be a star at something, anything really. I fancied speedway and bought an old bike to practice on. When I thought I was good enough I set off on the twelve miles journey to Belle Vue. I was hoping the Belle Vue team would give me a trial or something. When I eventually got to Belle Vue Stadium, the bike literally fell to pieces outside the gates. I was so disgusted and disappointed that I left it there on the road and walked it all the way back home to Rochdale."

Marriage - The First Time Around

A womaniser from his early teens, Mac was attractive to the local ladies with his well brylcreamed dark-hair, parted in the middle, and his strong rugged features. He was a regular visitor at the many dance halls around the Rochdale area. He had several lady friends, but in November 1928, he married Eliza Jarman, at St Patrick's Church in Rochdale. He was just 21 while his bride was barely 18, and the new Mrs Bamford was expecting a baby, hence the marriage. The responsibility of being a married man had no favourable effect on Mac, he was more fiery than ever outside the ring and his temper had a short fuse. Violence was never far from the surface and at times he thought nothing of giving his young wife a back hander, or anyone else for that matter who happened to upset him for the slightest reason.

Early in 1929 the McAvoys' celebrated the birth of their baby son whom they called Joseph, after his father and grandfather. Mac knew he had to start earning some money, and he could not or would not hold down a steady job. After being unemployed for a few weeks Mac secured a job at the Breda Visada silk mill in Littleborough, not far from his home. He was given a job on the mill's 'heavy gang,' whose job it was to do all the repairs, odd jobs and anything else which cropped up at the mill. He liked this kind of work because it was mostly outside and he wasn't stuck in one place. Outside, facing the works was a billiard hall, and every lunch time a group of the workers would go across and play a game of billiards. It was only twopence for a game and Mac became a regular visitor and he was quite a useful player. The men would place little bets on the games and this of course caused arguments. It was nothing serious, but Mac would have many a heated argument with workmates, especially when he was playing for money.

Albert Woolfenden, the foreman in charge of the 'heavy gang,' stood well over six foot tall and had the weight to go with his size. He was known as a likable sort of fellow but, like Mac, he was a man with a hair-trigger temper when roused. Albert would stand for no nonsense, or put up with any idleness or excuses from his gang. Mr Woolfenden's gang was expected to work some weekends when the rest of the mill would be closed down. The men were delighted when he told them they would be required for weekend work as it meant extra 'brass' for them. One particular weekend the 'heavy gang' were doing overtime, which meant all day Saturday and Sunday. Mac turned into work on the Saturday, but failed to show up on Sunday. Albert was annoyed at Mac's absence. Monday morning dawned and Mac made his way to work he walked toward the shed where the 'heavy gang' congregated in readiness for the day's work. Suddenly a rasping voice barked out. "Where were you yesterday Bamford?"

It was Mr Woolfenden. Mac turned round and explained to the foreman that he had been out on the Saturday night with some friends, and he had had a good time but felt a little tired and bilious on the Sunday morning so did not bother turning up for work. Mr Woolfenden was red-faced and furious at Mac's feeble excuse, and he curtly shouted at Mac. "Oh, is that so, well you're sacked, get to the office and pick up your cards." Mac tried to reason with him but to no avail. He then became agitated at the remarks made by the foreman, then without saying anything else McAvoy placed his parcel of sandwiches on a wall and strode over to where the foreman was standing and walloped him flush on the whiskers with a shattering right hand. He then went to collect his cards and walked home. This was, in all probability, his last manual labouring job.

After not being able to get another job for one reason or another, McAvoy went for talks with Joe Tolley regarding making a comeback into boxing. Tolley suggested they sign a boxer-manager contract. Having done this Mac was soon back in action. It was July 1929, to be exact, when he faced Frank Ormerod of Nelson in the New Market Stadium in Burnley. To get to the venue by the cheapest route, Mac travelled on the back of his friend Len Collinge's motor bike. Len agreed to let Jock ride on the iron carrier of his machine as there was no pillion seat. Mac had a small bag containing his canvas shoes, his shorts and a towel tucked under his arm. Collinge was rewarded for his help by getting into the hall free.

Waiting for the bell to send him into action, McAvoy had to be held back in his corner. Fighting like a demented demon, he stalked forward and pole-axed his rival in the first round. A terrific right cross that connected on Ormerod's jaw did the damage. His manager Joe Tolley was the referee, but he wouldn't have to bother his conscience if the contest went the full distance because it was all over in twenty seconds of round one. McAvoy's punching was dynamic, and he seemed like a man possessed. He hit poor Ormerod so hard that he was out like a light and so badly concussed that Mac thought he had killed him.

"I had waited a long while for a real fight and this fight which was scheduled for ten rounds of two minutes duration was just what I needed. I wanted to feel the sting of leather and the satisfaction of burying my knuckles into the flesh of my opponent," said Mac later. Though Mac was delighted at his speedy victory the promoter, Mr Heyes certainly wasn't. He stormed into the dressing room and gave McAvoy a rollicking for not giving the spectators their money's worth. In this period promoters did not like quick endings it meant they had to put another contest on the bill to satisfy the customers. McAvoy couldn't have cared less what the promoter wanted. He wanted to end the fight as quickly as he possibly could.

His next opponent, Jack Ogden, the Chadderton stylist, lasted three rounds by virtue of his ring savvy, though he had been down a few times during those nine minutes. It was that pulverising right hand punch which again caused all the damage. "Get me Billy Chew," growled Mac and Tolley obliged. On this occasion, Chew was guilty of over confidence, believing that what he had achieved so easily once, he could repeat again. As the gong sounded to start the proceedings Chew was disdainful of the Rochdale fighter, and it showed in his boxing. This suited McAvoy who was in superb physical condition, unlike on the previous occasion when he had unwisely over-trained. The Darwen fighter threw caution to the wind and elected to fight rather than use his undoubted superior skill. He played right into Mac's hands and the fans were hysterical with excitement at the slugfest. The roars of the crowd could be heard all over Burnley as the two boxers went at it like two alley cats, with blood and sweat flying all over the place. Mac was a clear winner after the ten rounds. He had exacted his revenge for the only blemish on his record so far. In the changing room later a small squabble broke out and the smirking Rochdale man was quite willing to oblige Chew and his companions to a bout of fisticuffs on the cobbles. Fortunately, for all concerned this offer was immediately defused by worried boxing officials. In later years, McAvoy always said that he had the greatest of respect for Billy Chew and said Chew was one of the hardest fighters he ever fought.

Seven days after his convincing victory over Chew, Mac was fighting at the Winter Gardens, Morecambe. This would be his first fight for the legendary Harry 'Kid' Furness. Furness, who stood under five feet, was the busiest matchmaker in the country and organised tournaments seven days a week all over Lancashire, Yorkshire and Cheshire. A very diminutive fellow, Furness was a known hard task master and anyone fighting on his tournaments had to earn their money or else they wouldn't get paid. The Kid had done Mac no favours when matching him against Eric "Basher" Bargh, a local fighter with a fearsome knockout reputation and a big following. The hometown supporters drowned out the introductions as their man was being announced. This was another fabulous encounter for the punters with action galore from both men, hard punches were given and taken and courage above and beyond the call of duty was displayed by both fighters.

The two fighters took turns in rocking each other down to their toenails, so ferocious was the power of their punching. After four rounds the referee humanely stopped the slaughter in McAvoy's favour. It had been a contest devoid of the science of boxing but full of raw-blooded excitement. The diminutive Furness was jumping up and down with glee and rubbing his hands. "What a scrap, what a scrap," he was shouting to everybody. The fans had been treated to a truly fabulous fight and Mac would be welcome on the Kid's promotions any time. In fact a fortnight later to be exact, at the same venue, Jack Jukes of Tyldesley was the chosen opponent.

On the afternoon of the contest, Mac threw a pair of canvas shoes, a pair of faded old shorts and a towel into his battered old attachè case and caught a bus into Manchester. Once in the city centre, he caught another bus to Chapel Street near Victoria Bridge in Salford. Once there he made his way to Alf Heywood's little cafe which was the meeting point where Kid Furness would pick up fighters who were appearing on his tournaments outside of Manchester. Alf Heywood was a character in every sense of the word, and a top-class referee into the bargain. When Furness eventually arrived at the cafe, there were quite a few boxers waiting. The matchmaker piled everyone into a taxi and headed for the Winter Gardens in Morecambe. During the journey Mac hardly spoke a word. He was suspicious of everybody and Kid Furness in particular. He had heard various unsavoury stories about Furness. "He is very cunning and mean," said his friend Martin Gallagher, who had experience of the Kid's way of conducting business. "Keep your eye on him, and watch he doesn't try and pull any kind of strokes on you about your purse money."

After six absorbing rounds, in which Jukes hit the canvas several times, the fight was stopped in the Rochdale lad's favour, though Mac suffered a very badly swollen right fist as a result of hitting his opponent on top of his cranium. It was a bad injury and another example of Mac never having been taught to deliver his punches properly.

I will digress again. Shortly after he joined the Collyhurst camp, McAvoy was having his fists massaged by Jack Bates. When Bates expressed concern about the
condition of his knuckles; "Lord above Joe," said the little trainer in a worried
tone. "How on earth have your hands got into this state?" Bates was amazed to be
told by Mac that during his early fights with Joe Tolley, he never once had his
hands bandaged or taped. He did have constant problems with both fists throughout his entire career as we shall find out later, but he also told Bates that he neither used a foul proof protector or a gum shield during that period.

"Hard times produce great fighters," said Tommy Fynan, one of the old-time
Collyhurst fighters. "And none came rougher than this fellow McAvoy," he concluded.

Why was Mac allowed to fight without the usual requirements of having his hands
taped properly, not wearing a protector and more importantly, no gum shield? Well
during this period there was no official controlling body to supervise tournaments
and medical supervision was almost non-existent. However, Mac should have
known he required his own gum shield and protective cup, though it should be
pointed out that many boxers of this period went through their careers without the
aid of gum shield or protector. Len Johnson, the famous Manchester middleweight, was an example as was the great Len Harvey. Many of the fighters were
only paid a few shillings and could not afford their own protector so borrowed one.
Many boxers prefer to tape their own hands. However, normally the bandages and
tape are usually provided by the chief second or the man in charge of the boxer for
that evening. Joe Tolley was a busy man and in constant demand to referee fights
all over the British Isles, thus on many occasions he was not in Mac's corner.

Sceptics said Mac was being his usual truculent self when stating nobody had ever
bothered bandaging his hands. Even in these early days, it was a known fact
around boxing circles that he was a very moody and awkward person to reason
with, and Tolley and Mac were often at loggerheads with each other. No one who
witnessed their arguments at various tournaments would have believed they could
ever actually work together. "It must have been exasperating for Joe Tolley," said
Harry 'Kid' Furness, who saw McAvoy from the beginning of his career to its conclusion. "Their arguments often degenerated into slanging matches, though Tolley
stood up to McAvoy's pontificating. Mac was a hard person to get to know and
though he could be an awkward so and so I often witnessed plenty of good deeds
that he did. However, he was infuriating at times." One thing is quite clear. Mac

would seldom listen to advice if he did not wish to do so. He had a stubborn streak. It is conceivable that Tolley did not make the journey to places like Morecambe, so McAvoy's hands would be the responsibility of whoever was seconding him that night.

McAvoy was most probably the only boxer Joe Tolley's son, Albert, found almost impossible to get along with because of his moods and nasty temper. To Albert, Mac was the sort of fighter whose behaviour drained the enthusiasm from a manager or trainer. He found it difficult to handle McAvoy, and he loathed him. Many boxers tend to be moody, but Mac was a class apart, being likely to explode at any minute and spend the rest of the trip sulking. "He had a stubborn streak which made it difficult for anybody to advise him," said Albert. Though only eighteen, Albert sometimes accompanied the fighters on trips out of Rochdale. But though Albert was a friendly young man and well respected by the many fighters managed by his father, he detested the task of looking after McAvoy or having anything to do with him. He was no match for the volatile Rochdale man and often told the other fighters he disliked going with him. Over the couple of years or so McAvoy was with the Tolley stable, there was an air of unpleasantness and intimidation between Mac and young Albert. Albert liked to join in the banter, although he never felt at ease in Mac's company. Poor Albert nervously feared the wrath and the smirking, scathing tongue of McAvoy and knew the violence Mac expressed so awesomely inside the ring was never far from the surface in ordinary everyday life.

With having such a large stable of fighters to look after, it was not unusual that on some nights Joe Tolley would have several of his boxers appearing at different venues in various parts of the country. At these times Joe would quite often delegate Albert to take several fighters to where he had booked them to appear on tournaments. Tolley senior would usually be officiating in another part of the country. Albert would drive the fighters to their destination in his father's car. After the weigh-in he would take the fighters into a cafe, and with money his father had given him he would buy meals for everyone. Mac was a prodigious eater and exceedingly greedy whenever someone else was paying. He would eat enough food for three or four other boys. He did this, it was said, because he believed somehow or other he was being cheated out of his purse money. McAvoy had a suspicious nature which verged on paranoia about anyone involved with the business side of boxing, and he reasoned that if there was anything going free, he would make sure he would be first in the queue for any handouts.

Three weeks after the Jukes victory McAvoy was in action again, demolishing Tiger Bob Ennis, a fighter from Halifax who was much bigger and heavier than Jock, in one sensational round. Ennis, a lookalike for Desperate Dan, the famous comic strip character, came into the fight with a three day growth of beard and he really looked fearsome. Mac looked at bit concerned at the beginning and decided to toss a right hand straight away. Ennis threw a similar blow but Mac's landed first. The punch caught the Halifax boxer on the right eye, splitting it wide open, and knocked him senseless. This sensational victory was achieved by McAvoy, despite still feeling the effects of his still tender and bruised right fist. This was remarkable under the circumstances. Whose responsibility was it? There is every possibility that Tolley advised McAvoy to rest the injured hand but was overruled by the aggressive attitude of the frequently argumentative fighter. Nothing can be discounted.

In the early 1960s, this writer got to know Bob Ennis well. Bob coached amateur boxers in Halifax as I myself did at Collyhurst. Ennis was a big amiable fellow and because I came from Collyhurst he assumed that I knew of McAvoy, though Jock had not joined the Collyhurst camp at the time of his fight with the Halifax man. However, he spoke in reverence about McAvoy.

"He were a villain were that McAvoy," remarked Bob in his deep Yorkshire accent. "Could he punch, somebody once asked me? I'll say he could flaming well punch. They told me he had a damaged right hand when I fought him. Well, I knew nowt about that. He could bloody pulverise you with either hand. He were a killer, he really were," concluded Bob. What surprised me was the advantage in height Ennis must have had over McAvoy, because he stood over six feet in height, while Jock was only 5ft 9inches tall.

McAvoy loved dancing to the sounds of the big bands. In fact he was quite a snazzy dancer when twirling a young beauty on those polished dance floors. There is simply no contest between today's so-called bands and the big bands of yesteryear. The folk of McAvoy's era were spoilt, growing up in an era when you could hear the finest and best musicians and instrumentalists of the century. There were numerous bands in every city, town, or village, and they were mostly extremely good. On many occasions, while out socialising or dancing, Mac could be extremely truculent and arguments would arise over trivial matters. It was in these situations that his spitefulness would rise to the surface and his face would change colour as he would go into an uncontrollable rage and hammer the daylights out of whoever he was arguing with. He was tolerated by a few close friends, but given a wide berth if he started his moaning and arguing.

Sidney W. Auckland, the editor of "Boxing" the weekly paper for boxing fans, had heard about the young McAvoy while on a refereeing engagement in Portsmouth. Mr Auckland had been the referee in a contest featuring Martin Gallagher of Rochdale. On the train journey back to London, Gallagher was in raptures over the young welterweight from the Lancashire mill town. He was telling anybody who would listen. "This lad will wipe them all out," said Martin. "He's got the lot, and he's as tough as old clogs." Pricking up his ears, as usual, for a good story, the editor was told a compelling and chilling tale of the teenager whose real name was Joe Bamford, but who fought under the name of Jock McAvoy. Many years later, Mr Auckland said: "I heard Mac was a fighter with a knockout punch in either mitt, who would compel the best in the country to treat him with respect. And has Mac done it? He sure has!"

In 1929 the British Boxing Board of Control, was formed and many changes were taking place. Every boxer, manager, trainer, second, M.C. referee and official involved in professional boxing had to be licensed by the new body. Joe Tolley and others held too many licenses and this was considered a conflict of interest. And rightly so! It was pointed out that in Tolley's case he was also refereeing fights in which boxers whom he managed were participants. This, the stewards pointed out, would most certainly have to cease. Joe was earning quite well while receiving offers to referee across Great Britain. He loved these engagements and the travelling, and was very reluctant to give this job up. He quickly found the solution. He relinquished his own manager's license, and applied for a manager's license for his son, Albert who was only eighteen. Tolley senior was a founder member of the B.B.B. of C. and Albert duly received his manager's license. No doubt his father had pulled a few strings and called in a few favours.

Once Tolley relinquished his manager's license the forty or so boxers under his jurisdiction were free to seek new management if they wanted. However, Tolley, virtually instructed them to sign up with Albert as their new manager. They willingly consented. It was no secret, though, that all the fighters knew full well that Tolley senior would still be in charge and young Albert was manager in name only. McAvoy, not surprisingly, proved the only problem. He kept delaying signing the contract despite several pleas from Tolley senior. Mac was being his usual obstinate, argumentative and truculent self. Though only a beginner in boxing terms,

McAvoy was already perceived as a damn good prospect, and the Tolleys, especially Joe, certainly did not wish to lose his services. After several promises and delays, Mac eventually agreed to put pen to paper and sign the contract.

Albert Tolley was not overjoyed at the prospect of being McAvoy's manager, despite the fact that it was in name only. He told the rest of his father's fighters that he detested even seconding Mac. Tolley senior got to hear of his son's reluctance and impetuosity and Albert received an ear bashing from his irate and worried father. Joe didn't wish to upset Mac in any way, fearing to do so might result in the surly fighter going elsewhere. He suggested that Albert should have a laugh and a joke with McAvoy, and try to jolly him along. Poor Albert was bemused, He wondered if he had heard his father correctly. Have a laugh and a joke with McAvoy? Young Tolley couldn't believe what is father was saying, knowing that Mac barely acknowledged him at the best of times.

However, Albert did as he was told and he made his way to McAvoy's house in Rochdale. He went on the pretence that he had been in Rochdale on some business for his father and as he was passing thought he would call and see how his (McAvoy's) injured hand was progressing. Knocking with a certain amount of trepidation on the door of McAvoy's small cottage, he heard Mac's booming voice shout: "Who's that?" Young Tolley wished the ground would open up and swallow him. He was told to enter. As he went into the front room, Mac was sitting in an old easy chair looking directly into Albert's eyes. Albert froze! He soon detected a hostile atmosphere in the home. It seems that Eliza had been smoking in the house which was something McAvoy hated. Anyhow, Mac was looking very menacingly at poor Albert and Eliza, and scowling. Albert was fidgety and felt very uncomfortable and was hoping and praying that McAvoy would not offer him a cup of tea, which he didn't. Albert got the impression that Eliza was relieved that he had called, possibly saving her from getting a further rollicking for daring to smoke in front of her husband. Or possibly something worse. Albert wanted nothing more than to get out of that house and into the fresh air and head straight for home. After what seemed an eternity and without uttering a word, the boxer finally spoke. He told Albert his hand was fine and that Tolley senior had better get him some fights quickly. Albert was relieved and told Mac he would tell his father immediately he got back home. "I'm not bloody well paying you as well as your father," Mac shouted after Albert.

The Mean Machine

McAvoy continued destroying opponent after opponent in an orgy of licensed mayhem. He was remorseless in his pursuit of his opponents, hitting them with sledge-hammer punches, and his amazing fitness saw him outlasting all opposition placed in front of him. He wasn't adverse at whacking them with his head, elbow, knee, and he often threw punches at his opponent's wind pipe. He was rapidly outgrowing the welterweight division and though not quite a fully-fledged middleweight, he took on and hammered tough fighters much bigger, heavier and vastly more experienced than himself. For all his complaining and cynical ways, he wasn't afraid to fight anybody. Though tall for his weight, he fought out of a low crouch, with his chin resting on his chest and looking through his eyebrows. As we know he could score explosive knockouts, but he was no slouch either when it came to boxing skill, throwing his punches with fluidity and plenty of variety. He could also feint to perfection, but it was Mac's body punching which was his real forte. His movements were done with speed and agility, and he gave the distinct impression he could fight all night long. And as Jack Bates often said, he must have possessed the best chin in boxing, being seemingly oblivious to punishment.

After demolishing Tiger Ennis on 17 September 1929, McAvoy had a further nine contests. Seaman Douglas retired after six rounds. In a return match he met old rival Billy Chew in Burnley at the New Market Hall. As Chew walked into the venue he bumped into McAvoy, they shook hands and chatted about various things. Later, Joe Morris the referee, called the two fighters together, gave them their instructions, the bell sounded and both men had the crowd yelling with excitement as they stood toe-to-toe. For seven rounds the pace never relented, it was a tremendous battle. Both men were putting plenty of force behind their punches, suddenly someone in McAvoy's corner drew the referee's attention and pointed to the gloves, which had burst with the sheer power they were putting into each blow. The fight was held up for several minutes while the gloves were changed. Chew wanted to continue but the referee refused telling him they could blind each other. When the rivals resumed boxing, Mac surged forward and with the crowd standing, stamping and cheering he won a fifteen round points victory. What A fight!

Less than 24 hours after battling for 15 rounds against Billy Chew, Mac outpointed Jack Ogden over ten rounds in Fleetwood. The date was the 30 September.

After beating Jack Ogen, Mac didn't fight again until December, when he had six contests, starting with Jack Harrison who he forced to retire on his stool after four hectic rounds. His next contest saw him travel to Rhyl in North Wales where he opposed the local favourite, Soldier Jones. Jones was a popular character around the Welsh seaside resort. He had won the heavyweight championship of the Indian Army. He looked massive compared to McAvoy, but in those days giving away weight was normal for Mac. The crowd were rooting for their man and the atmosphere was quite hostile. In the first round Mac used his speed and kept out of the big Welshman's reach. The second saw the Rochdale fighter leap up in the air and connect on Jones's jaw with a jarring right hand. The Soldier hit the floor with a resounding thud. He was visibly hurt, but amazingly staggered to his feet and walked unsteadily into a neutral corner.

There was no way he could recover and box on, his seconds sensed his plight, and not wanting McAvoy to score a knockout over their man threw in the towel of surrender. Mac however, didn't see the towel and attacked his big, opponent unmercifully. The crowd were furious at the Lancashire fighters act of unsportsmanship and jumped to their feet, booing and screaming insults. Poor Jones was on rubber legs taking a frightful hiding from Mac and was defenceless. The referee looking concerned at the crowds reaction pulled Mac off the badly beaten Welshman and stopped the massacre. Spectators were livid at McAvoy for continuing punching after the towel had been thrown into the ring. There were a lot of bad feeling and ugly remarks shouted as McAvoy hurriedly made his way to the dressing room. He was advised to throw his street clothes over his boxing togs and leave as quickly as possible through the back exit. The following evening, Mac fought Doncaster's Ted Abbot, who retired after going six rounds; a Norwegian named Lud Gresvig lasted just two rounds; Billy Horner lasted only four with the wrecker from Rochdale, while in his final contest of the year, Mac was unlucky to only receive a ten round draw against Griff Williams.

January 1930 saw Mac notch up two knockouts over Marine Davies in six and Sid Aldridge in four. He was moving along nicely and in February he had four bouts scoring three knockouts while going the twelve round distance for a points verdict against Doncaster's Fred Oldfield. McAvoy liked it when he was busy and fighting regularly. March saw him engaged in five contests. He continued his knockout ways when he disposed of Bill 'Shocker' Bowman in three rounds; Fred Blything took him fifteen rounds before Mac was declared the winner.

When McAvoy fought Bowman it must have been the only occasion when the promoter wanted his drawing card beaten. The promoter was a man named Mr Edwards. He owned a grocery business in the little market town of Penrith, where 'Shocker' Bowman was the local celebrity and drawing card. It appears that Bowman was getting a bit big for his boots and the promoter wanted him bringing down a peg or two. When McAvoy stepped from the train in Penrith, Mr Edwards was there to meet him. "Oh dear, you're nowhere near big enough to trouble Bowman," he said disappointedly. "He is a big man and weighs thirteen and a half stone. You only look a welterweight." McAvoy had travelled alone and could visualise a pay day going out through the window. "Don't worry, I look bigger when I'm stripped and in my fighting togs, he told the dejected promoter. It was much too late for Mr Edwards to get a replacement so he grudgingly accepted Mac. The contest was staged in the Market Hall and the ring was pitched on flagstones, with a wooden board across. There was no canvas covering, and the board was covered in bloodstains. To make it more difficult the ringside spectors were so close to the ring that they could touch the fighters. In his dressing room McAvoy while getting into his togs had the door partly open, he saw Bowman almost running to the toilet. McAvoy smiled, he knew this was a sure sign of nerves. He's running scared, and halfway to being licked, he reasoned. This was a ritual he had tried to observe from the beginning of his career. Mac was in the ring first and was greeted by booing and nasty remarks. The whole place erupted when the local favourite entered the main hall. Mr Edwards had certainly not exaggerated, Bowman was big, he looked a fully-fledged heavyweight. Straight away McAvoy decided there was no way he was going down on the rock hard floor.

The first couple of rounds saw the Lancashire fighter moving around the ring like a greyhound in reverse. He was figuring out a way to bring the big fellow onto his punches. The crowd were giving him some terrible stick and with them being right on top of the ring things looked intimidating. In the third round Mac stood his ground and through some nifty head movement made the Penrith man miss time and time again. Mac feinted a left jab and Bowman fell for it, the Rochdale man immediately fired a tremendous right hand which caught 'Shocker' full in the face and really 'shocked' him. There was a loud crack, and the local sensation slowly fell to his knees. Blood poured from his nose which had been broken from the impact of the punch, and his mouth was also gushing with blood. The fans were dumbstruck and poor old Bowman looked a picture of absolute despair. The referee started counting and the crowd were shouting for their hero to rise. But he couldn't, he remained in a kneeling position looking dazed and bewildered as the referee counted him out. He had to be carried back to his dressing room. Mr Edwards had got his wish, though he later admitted he only wanted his star fighter to get beaten on points, not flattened.

Three days later, Mac travelled to Stourbridge and outpointed Wolverhampton's tough Fred Blything over the 15 round distance. Six days later he was back on home soil in Royton where he knocked out Jack Wilkinson the Warrington scrapper in two rounds. Five days later he appeared at Haslingden. The local fight fans who crammed into the little hall witnessed one of the finest action packed contest they had ever seen. For the entire eight rounds Mac and his opponent Doncaster's Fred Oldfield, gave and took punishment, stood toe to toe, whacked each other with murderous punches and had the sell-out audience drooling with excitement. This was a 'war.' In the seventh round Mac landed a powerful right hander that caught the Doncaster fighter directly under the heart, Fred let out a gasp. The punch had broken a couple of his ribs and he couldn't continue. Back in his dressing room the veteran referee, Mr W.J. Farnell, walked over to where McAvoy was getting dressed and shook his hand. "Look after yourself son," he told Mac. "You are the best prospect I have ever set eyes on."

Around about this time it was the view of the cognoscenti of the local boxing establishment that Joe Rostron a young boxer from Heywood was considered a much better prospect than the lethal-fisted McAvoy. They reasoned that at 19, Rostron had everything, a good temperament, speed, footwork, boxing ability, sound defence, a good chin and a knockout wallop in either hand. The Heywood warrior was certainly developing into a really excellent craftsman. Many boxing followers were already starting to build up a Rostron versus McAvoy fight into a grudge match, and they had not even been matched at this stage.

Both fighters were with different organisations. Mac of course, was with Joe Tolley, while Rostron was being groomed by Tolley's arch-rivals, the Chapman family from Chadderton near Oldham, which was almost on Tolley's doorstep. Tom Chapman was the official promoter though the whole family was involved with the promotions. The Chapmans were doing a wonderful job in directing the Heywood boxer's progress, getting him the right kind of matches and looking after his welfare. Rostron received acclaim when matched at Manchester's Free Trade Hall against the wily, experienced Jim Pearson of Bamber Bridge. He fought the perfect fight and gained a momentous fifteen round draw with a middleweight few in the British Isles could defeat, according to popular opinion.

By a stroke of fate, Pearson was McAvoy's next opponent. Jock was originally down to box Salford's Hal O'Neill, in Preston. The Salford lad pulled out and Jim Pearson replaced him. For his part Mac wanted to do a demolition job on Pearson which would prove more convincing than Joe Rostron's draw with the Preston man. This was without doubt McAvoy's most formidable task up to this point of his 29 fight career. Jim was much taller and a great deal heavier than the Rochdale fighter. He could also 'dig' and had flattened his share of opponents. Though Mac fought tirelessly he could not fathom out Pearson's straighter punching and bleeding heavily from the nose, he was adjudged a clear and decisive loser on points after twelve hard and brutal rounds.

The Chapman camp were absolutely delighted at this result and made their claims that Joe Rostron was a much better prospect for honours than the man from Rochdale. This setback for McAvoy made their claims all the more feasible. For his part, McAvoy couldn't care less about the feud going on between the rival promoters. His only concern was this second blot on his record. Though he accepted the defeat like a true sportsman, once he got back home, he was like a bear with a sore head for a few days afterwards.

Within a couple of weeks of his defeat Mac was back in action stopping Ted Lewis in six and Dai Beynon in five rounds. Eleven days later came the showdown with arch-rival, Joe Rostron, though it came about quite unexpectedly as we shall see. Tolley, despite the gossip and feeling under pressure from folk in boxing circles telling him that everyone wanted a Rostron versus McAvoy confrontation as soon as possible, was taking no notice. He did not want to do business with his rivals, the Chapmans. Tolley had been promoting Sunday afternoon tournaments at his Royton Stadium venue for years, and thanks mainly due to McAvoy's popularity with the paying customers he was having to turn spectators away. The Chapmans decided they would also start promoting on a Sunday, in direct competition to Tolley. Obviously Joe Rostron was featured on these tournaments. Local fans were often in a quandary, they had to decide who they were going to watch - The all action, fierce punching McAvoy, or the smart boxing stylist, Rostron?

Mac was scheduled to box a return with his recent conqueror Jim Pearson at the Majestic Theatre, Preston. Mac claimed in later years that he himself arranged this contest without Joe Tolley's knowledge. Be that as it may, for some inexplicable reason he travelled on his own to the Lancashire venue. His sole intention was to destroy the classy and cagey Preston boxer. While undergoing the usual medical procedure he was informed by the matchmaker that the medical officer had declared Pearson was not fit to box on that evening's tournament for some reason or other. It was suggested afterward that this had all been a ploy to catch McAvoy unaware and certainly unprepared for a much sterner test. Disappointed at not having the opportunity to erase the blemish on his record by Pearson, he shrugged his shoulders and declared he was willing to box a substitute. In those days, fighters who were not down to fight on certain bills, took their boxing togs with them in the fervent hope that someone on the programme would pull out and they could step in as a replacement and earn much needed cash for their families. So promoters were not unduly concerned if an arranged fight fell through at such short notice.

Joe Rostron was a bit special as a boxer. Born in Heywood a cotton town with a population of 25,000. "It was just one long main street with other streets branching from it, situated between Rochdale and Bury," said Joe when describing his hometown. It was 1922 when he first took up boxing and he never boxed as an amateur. Joe got his early tuition from two Manchester trainers, Sam Hunter and Joe Goodwin, and what these two didn't know about boxing wasn't worth knowing. After a few months under these two gentlemen, Joe felt he was improving leaps and bounds. After several early contests he had his first big break at the Free Trade Hall in Manchester in 1923. Rostron was slightly different than the every day fighter of those times in that he worked in the Co-operative Society, Gents' Outfitters department.

He lost only two bouts from 1926 to the end of 1929, most of his fights being staged in Manchester. During the afternoon on the 25th of April 1930, Joe was contacted by the promoter in Preston requesting his services immediately. Rostron hastily gathered his equipment and jumped into a taxi and arrived at Preston later that night. Joe Tolley, of course, had not got a clue as to these new arrangements regarding his drawing card. Needless to say, the fight with Rostron would not have been accepted under these circumstances. However, McAvoy would not hear of pulling out, certainly not against a man of whom he was a little envious, because Rostron had been getting much more publicity than himself. This was another case of his single-mindedness and bull-at-a-gate approach to certain situations. Without another word he fought the boxing stylist from Heywood. Mac was determined to hammer his neighbour and put an end to the comparisons between them once and for all. But at the end of twelve blistering rounds of entertaining boxing, the skilled stylist from Heywood was a deserving winner. Mac had been out-boxed, out-foxed but more importantly, out-manoeuvred by the political side of the fight game. Tolley was hopping mad when he found out and accused the promoters of dirty work, but the damage was done.

McAvoy rarely let a defeat bother him unduly, not that he lost that many contests of course, the loss to Rostron being only the third time he had been defeated in 33 bouts. He sulked and moaned and blamed everyone bar himself, then get on with his career, more determined than ever not to be beaten again.

Mac's next fight was against fellow Rochdale middleweight his chief rival, Eddie Strawer exactly a month to the day of the Rostron fight. The Rochdale fans were falling over themselves to see this genuine grudge fight. Tolley promoted this outdoor tournament on a warm and sunny Sunday afternoon, which proved a sell-out at his Royton Stadium. The doors were closed a couple of hours before the two Rochdale lads entered the ring and the atmosphere was electric. Strawer was one of the best and hardest hitting middleweights in the British Isles, and like Mac he was a 'character' he was certainly no slouch, in fact he was a highly dangerous opponent with a record the equal of any other middleweight fighter in the country.

It was said that Mac received his largest purse for this fight though the amount varies from £6 to £30 and another estimate is that he received 60 per cent of the gate, which seems highly unlikely. Jack Dare of Liverpool was the referee, a strong disciplinarian type of official. And he needed to be. As the two fighters waited anxiously for the announcements to finish and the bell to sound, they both looked rather tentative and slightly nervous. Mac though supremely confident as always, was a little edgy until the first bell rang. He was in his corner shadow boxing, being extremely impatient for the bell to ring and send him into action.

Eddie Strawer's father, a portly-looking figure with a ruddy complexion was a well-known character in Rochdale. Mr Strawer had caused a great deal of friction and animosity because of his bragging and boasting on the virtue of his son's prowess as a fighter. Eddie was a damn good fighter and could well have done without his father's antagonistic baying. Along with a large party from his local public house he was at ringside and nobody could be mistaken as to who he was cheering for. He was going much too far with his disparaging remarks about McAvoy, most of which could be heard by Jock despite the huge volcano of noise from the massive crowd. Mac looked down at the man and his face turned into a scowl.

Once the fight got going McAvoy was in a spiteful mood as both fighters gave each sets of supporters exactly what they wanted to see action, and plenty of it! McAvoy went onto the attack from the start but Eddie knew how to tuck-up and ride punches. When he was driven against the ropes Strawer nifty used all his cunning and know-how to confuse Mac by twisting, rolling, and pulling back from punches. He was nice and neat. It was a humdinger of a battle with the crowd screaming and yelling themselves hoarse. The conclusion came about in the tenth

One of McAvoy's adversaries, the formidable Jack Forster

round, when after landing some wicked, rib-bending blows to the solar-plexus which took the wind out of Eddie, Mac then switched his attack and connected with a thumping right cross on the point of Strawer's jaw. It was all over, and McAvoy had scored a decisive and cracking clean-cut knockout victory over his fellow 'townie.' The huge crowd were roaring their heads off. They were thrilled and in good humour having seen a brilliant fight. Afterwards they headed for the pubs in Rochdale to discuss the fight further.

During all the excitement there was a brief scurry at the ringside when Mr Strawer senior began verbally accusing McAvoy of foul tactics and many other rule infringements. Mac was fuming and was more than ready to sort out the problem then and there, being quite willing to add Strawer senior to his knockout list, but he was quickly hustled back to the dressing room by friends and boxing officials. Later that night, McAvoy while out on the town with a few friends, was milking his victory for all it was worth. People were coming up to congratulate him and he was beaming.

Three weeks after dismantling Eddie Strawer, Mac dispatched Billy Green, a robust Welshman in round fourteen in a promotion in Preston. Then he was again matched against his local rival, Eddie Strawer. Mac was fed up with the taunts of Eddie's father which were going the rounds in Rochdale, and he was determined to annihilate young Strawer once and for all. When Mac and Eddie faced each other it was staged once again at Royton, and once again there was a great deal of animosity between McAvoy and the Strawers. Once the opening bell rang he proceeded to administer a shellacking to his fellow townie. Dropped for nine in the first round, Eddie rose and fought with valour until the fifth when a powerful body blow nearly tore him in half and he sank to the floor. Upon rising he was knocked from pillar to post and was fortunate to last out the remainder of the round. The body punch had hurt the courageous Strawer and he could hardly get off his stool for round six, but he was a proud fighter and so he forced himself forward and Mac met him head on. A ferocious well-timed left hook whistled onto Strawer's head and the power of the punch dumped him out of the ring unable to beat the count. Afterwards, the two Rochdale lads shook hands and the past animosity was forgotten. A few days after the fight Eddie's father approached McAvoy shook his hand, and asked if his son could train with him in future. So much for the feud between Mr Strawer senior and McAvoy. Eddie was a capable fighter but lacked that special ingredient which all great fighters possess the so called "killer instinct." You either have it or you haven't. Mac had it in abundance.

Revenge

In September 1930, Mac got the chance to reverse his loss to the classy Preston man, Jim Pearson. They were matched at the Stadium in Royton and the fans were expecting to witness a terrific fight between the two highly regarded middleweights. By this time Mac had developed into a full middleweight. The Rochdale Thunderbolt's fight plan was to surge forward and blast away at Pearson's mid-section and wear him down. From round one this is exactly what he did though it is fair to say that he was forced to take a few counter punches in return. He was enjoying himself, grunting and snorting as he stalked forward. Once in range of his opponent he would bend side-to-side and bang home the body punches which landed with a resounding thud on the Preston boxer's body. After the opening couple of rounds, Pearson, realised that this was a different McAvoy than the one he had clearly outpointed a few months previously. The crowd were thrilled by this wonderful contest and voiced their pleasure loudly and enthusiastically. Mac wanted revenge and he was first off his stool as the bell sounded for each round, bobbing and weaving while digging those scything hooks to Pearson's body. The audience sometimes doesn't appreciate the weakening effect such a body attack has on a boxer, because the effects are not instantaneous, but fighters on the receiving end of these blows would vouch for their strength sapping quality.

By round seven, Mac was in complete control and it was just a matter of time before he landed with the final blows. Slipping inside Pearson's lead, Jock crashed home a pile-driven right to the Preston man's heart, the colour drained from Pearson's face and he looked like a sailor stranded at sea. Immediately McAvoy switched his attack to his opponents face and a volley of well aimed punches resulted in Jim going face down to the canvas. Jack Smith, the referee, could see that Pearson was out to the world and shouted over to Pearson's seconds who frantically rushed into the ring to aid the stricken boxer but it was quite awhile before he could leave the ring.

Mr Smith, the referee, was also the matchmaker for the Free Trade Hall promotions in Peter Street, Manchester. He was suitably impressed by what he had just witnessed and a couple of weeks later Mac found himself having his first fight at the famous hall. Up to this point McAvoy had fought mainly in places such has Haslingden, Blackburn, Morecambe, Preston, Rhyl and Royton so he was delighted to have made the break through into this major Manchester venue. There were promotions every night of the week throughout the entire country but, just like today with different organisations calling the shots, of course this all depended on the commodity, which was the fighter. If he sold tickets and was an outstanding pugilist so much the better. Manchester was no different and there was a great deal of wrangling and boxing politics taking place around this period.

At The Free Trade Hall Mac's unlucky opponent Billy Delahaye, a Welsh fighter from Pontypridd, lasted barely two rounds with the dynamic Rochdale man. Three days, yes, three days after demolishing the Welshman, Mac was fighting in Preston at the Majestic Ice Rink, and he hammered Patsy Flynn from pillar to post. The end came in the third round, when Flynn was ducking Mac smashed him with a terrific right hand that landed on the point of the Lambeth boxer's jaw. Flynn was out cold and what made it appear worse was he caught the back of his head on the boards as he dropped, to be counted out. Mac then heard the news he had been eagerly waiting for and that was he was matched against Joe Rostron at the Free Trade Hall. Mac was beside himself with glee. As we have already gathered, he hated losing, and whenever he lost he would badger the life out of Joe Tolley to get him a return. Since their first meeting McAvoy had filled out physically and gained experience with a varied assortment of opponents. Rostron, though, had also matured as a boxer and was on a nine fight winning streak with his victims being of an exceptional high quality, though he had lost a fifteen rounder against the Welsh champion, the teak-tough gypsy from Newport, South Wales, Ben Marshall.

While getting ready for this fight, McAvoy was bristling with confidence and really fancied doing a job on his near neighbour from Heywood. It was rumoured just prior to their fight Rostron had suffered a badly bruised right hand in his losing contest against Marshall. The sensible thing to do would be to pull him out of the McAvoy fight until the injury healed. However, Joe, was told by people close to him, that he had too much boxing knowledge for the robust Rochdalian and could beat him with one hand tied behind his back if necessary. This, of course was foolish talk and an act of bravado by those not actually getting into the ring to face McAvoy. Whatever the reasons, the fight went ahead.

By the time the two boxers walked to the centre of the ring for the referee's instructions, Joe Rostron was declared 100 per-cent fit. After treatment his right hand was as good as new - but was it? Once the fight started it was quite plain to see that the

Heywood battler was holding back from using his right, and facing such a dangerous assassin as McAvoy required two sound mitts. The Rochdale Thunderbolt surged forward throwing punch after punch and was in total command throughout the entire bout. He was like a human tidal wave as his punches never ceased landing on their target, and Mac was really enjoying himself. It was to his eternal credit and cleverness that the Heywood boxing stylist managed to stay out of really serious trouble until taking a full-blooded punch to the body in the 14th round. This was a pulverising right-hand wallop which ringsiders felt sick watching it land-it was like somebody pricking a balloon. Joe gasped, and sucked air into his lungs and tottered on unsteady legs. Later, he admitted that this blow was the hardest he had ever been hit with, and only for the bell sounding he did not know what would have happened.

He lasted the full course of the contest because he used his excellent ring technique and his determination. It was a hard fight for Joe and he admitted in later years that McAvoy was like a tornado and was a much better boxer than he had previously been given credit for. "He was so formidable," said the sporting Rostron. Yes, Jock had answered all the questions regarding his temperament and his ability. He had avenged the other set back and was gloriously happy with his win, so too was Joe Tolley who knew that in Mac he had the greatest fighting machine seen in the ring for a long, long time.

During the war years, Rostron was a Physical Training Instructor in the Army, and at one stage was asked to box an exhibition with a young Royal Air Force corporal named Freddie Mills in aid of the RAF Benevolent Fund. Joe had been retired from active ring fighting for a number of years but he and the future world light-heavyweight champion put on an exhilarating contest which brought a standing ovation from everyone present. Later while both men were getting changed, Freddie as jovial and chatty as always, and knowing Joe had fought Jock McAvoy started talking about Mac. "I beat McAvoy quite easily," he said. Joe looked at Freddie and replied. "Not the McAvoy I fought, he was an old man when you fought him. I'm afraid he would have beaten you if you had met when both of you were in your prime." Joe went on to say that McAvoy's body punching was terrific. "He didn't have a great variety of punches, but what he had were all killer punches, I can assure you," said Rostron.

Eight days after his victory over Joe Rostron, Mac was in action again. This time in the Morecambe Winter Gardens, and he was facing the reigning Northern Area middleweight champion, Joe Lowther, the canny Leeds fighter. McAvoy was upset when told it was a fifteen round contest but Lowther's title would not be at stake. It must be remembered that in those times being a champion of any description carried with it a great deal of prestige, honour and admiration, also being champion meant receiving a bigger purse. Area champions were heroes to the men and young boys who followed the fight game. Joe Lowther was an experienced boxer of the highest calibre. He came into boxing when the North resounded with a glut of top-notch middleweights. Joe won the Northern title and championship gold and silver belt at this venue on 16th August 1930. At one point during his career, in which he fought a galaxy of talented fighters, he engaged in 54 bouts in a twelve-month period of which he won 50 and drew one. This was a remarkable sequence of contests in such a short space of time. Anyhow Mac beat Lowther on points, cutting the champions right eye and bruising him badly. It was a clear cut victory for the Rochdale fighter. McAvoy stopped two more victims before the year was out when he hammered another Welsh boxer, Tate Evans from Maestag in the 15th round at the Free Trade Hall, then he flattened a Geordie boxer, Jim Johnson in the second.

Farewell To The Tolley Stable

1931 was to be McAvoy's farewell to the Tolley stable. He took part in fourteen more contests under the Royton promoter's banner before moving on to bigger and better feats. The frustrating thing from Mac's point of view was that he only scored seven stoppages from those fourteen bouts, though he eventually relieved Joe Lowther of his Northern Area middleweight crown in his last fight with Tolley. After sampling the likes of Liverpool Stadium, where he outpointed Charlie McDonald over fifteen very dull rounds, Jock was eager to display his talent in other such big venues which created a tremendous atmosphere. The fight with Joe Lowther took place in the King's Hall, Belle Vue. Mac grew to love fighting in the marvellously atmospheric King's Hall arena where he became idolised on his progress up the boxing ladder, and where he had many unforgettably exciting nights.

Johnny King was topping the bill against Pat Gorman, a 21-year-old from Wheatley Hill in Durham. This was billed as a final eliminator for the Northern Area bantamweight championship. Hundreds had travelled to Manchester from the small mining village. Though sickened when their hero was stopped in round six on a technical knockout, they were agog with excitement while watching McAvoy, who, with his three-day growth of beard and closely cropped back and sides haircut, looked somewhat like a smaller version of Jack Dempsey. Joe Lowther, slightly balding, was a scientific boxer but on this occasion he was completely steamrolled and hammered to the canvas in round eight. When he regained his feet, he was wobbling around the ring like a drunken man, and when his seconds saw that referee Tom Gamble, was about to count him out they threw the towel into the ring. Mr Gamble then waved Lowther's seconds into the ring to attend to the stricken fighter.

The following day this action caused a caustic comment from Norman Hurst. "Last night, both Johnny King and Jock McAvoy were robbed of clean-cut knockout victories because their opponents' corners threw in the towel. Lowther had been reeling around the ring helpless for a couple of rounds but not a move from his seconds. It was only when the referee indicated the fight was all over that they tossed in the towel." This didn't bother either King or Brown, both knew they had won decisively. They were thrilled especially McAvoy, who had the added satisfaction of being crowned the Area champion. It is hard to believe this level of excitement nowadays, when this sort of title (and, very sadly, often even the once highly esteemed British title) is virtually meaningless today. Mac was treated like a conquering hero in Rochdale and feted wherever he went. John Kay, a prominent cricketer, and chief sportswriter for the Manchester Evening News, remarked: "McAvoy was like a cat that had cornered a mouse and was cruelly taking it to pieces bit by bit. The sound of his punches hitting poor Lowther flush to his head and body could be heard ten rows back from the ringside. He certainly made a mess of the gallant Leeds man and he left an indelible impression on me."

In one of his other six stoppages he accounted for Dick Burt, in front of the Belle Vue fans. Mac was brutal in this fight. He handed out a thrashing to a very game but totally outclassed opponent, before stopping him in the eighth round after the gutsy Plymouth fighter had been on the deck several times. The red headed Plymouth fighter was certainly no mug, in fact he was one of the best known figures in the West Country. His colourful style of fighting gained him engagements all over the British Isles. During his career which he had approximately 230 fights, he fought Joe Lowther, George Rose, Archie Sexton and 'Cast Iron' Jack Casey, being one of only a handful who managed to deck the redoubtable Sunderland man before losing on points. So highly thought of was Burt that he had been to America where he won three out of his four fights. The Americans loved his all-action style and booked more fights for the Plymouth lad. But Dick left the States after coming to the conclusion that everyone but he, himself, was making money out of him. When he retired from active boxing he became a manager for a while, then a class A referee. Years later recalling his fight with McAvoy he said: "I consider Jock McAvoy the hardest hitter of the lot. He was the only man who ever really hurt me."

The knowledgeable King's Hall crowd had grown to like Mac's exciting style of fighting. At times he took chances and left himself open, but he was rough and tough and he joined Jackie Brown and Johnny King as one of their favourites. His next bout though, was back at Royton, and he treated Nottingham's Charlie Keeling with complete disdain for three rounds, dropping him in the third for a count of eight with a crunching, beautifully delivered right cross. He then applied the finisher with the same punch, but on this occasion switching the punch to the solar plexus. Mac was brutal in this bout, sending body blows in forbidden areas

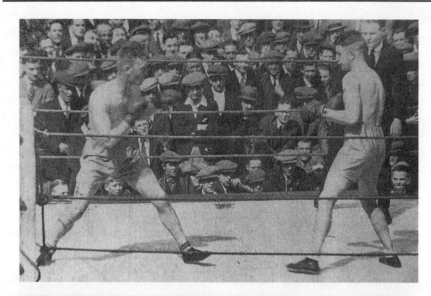

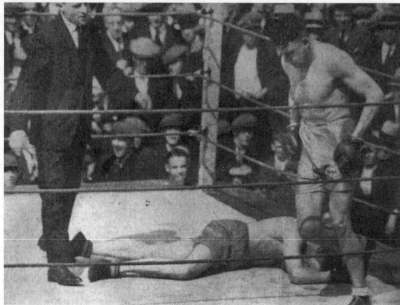

Top: Look at McAvoy's stance and 'Jack Dempsey' hair style in this 1931 open air fight with Jack Bottomley at Rochdale Hornets Rugby Ground.
Below: 5.5 seconds after th opening bell, Bottomley was spark out, with McAvoy looking down on him. Note the crowd, wearing flat caps.

and roughing up the Nottingham fighter in no uncertain terms. Joe Tolley was the referee. Sitting at ringside for this contest was an immaculately attired American named Dave Lumiansky. He was suitably impressed by the fighting fury. Lumiansky would later play a large part in the McAvoy story.

Johnny Seamarks of Bedford was flattened in three rounds, again at Royton. Con Van Leowen, was on paper a worthy opponent and had boasted that he had already beaten three British fighters in Tom Stribling, whom he knocked out in four sessions, then he accounted for Jack Thomas, from Wales, who was also a heavyweight. He had also beaten former speedway rider, Ian Ritchings. Armed with these impressive credentials the big Dutchman entered the Royton ring very confident indeed. Five rounds later he was a wrecked man. McAvoy had battered him so badly that when the bell rang to end the fifth round the Dutch fighters cornermen hurriedly called the referee over and retired their man.

McAvoy's next contest would be his first and last in his hometown of Rochdale. At one time, Rochdale was one of the best sporting towns in the North. However, in 1931 there had been no boxing there since the days when the late Jimmy White staged charity tournaments at the Theatre Royal, at which all the various champions appeared. Rochdale, nevertheless, had turned out many good fighters, but the trouble was the town had no suitable venue in which to stage professional tournaments. Joe Walsh, a local, who fought all the best lightweights in the game a few years previously, had secured Rochdale Hornets Rugby League ground at Milnrow. The first show under Joe's direction was to be staged on 11th July, 1931,when his main attraction was the contest many Northern promoters had been hankering for some time to feature, i.e. a match between two explosive punchers, Jock McAvoy and Jack Bottomley of Leeds. Rochdale Observer stated in the preview of the fight that Mac had scored 57 knockouts from his 93 fights, however, these figures are misleading and possibly included McAvoy's unlicensed fights which do not show on his official record. His official record at this time showed him having 58 fights before the Bottomley contest and scoring 36 inside the distance victories. His pal, Martin Gallagher, another Rochdale lad was also appearing on the bill, meeting the clever little Oldham boxer, Willie Walsh (this fight ending in a draw).

McAvoy's father, Joe, who rarely attended his son's fights, made an exception on this occasion and was a ringside spectator at this event. There were over five thousand fans inside the ground when Mac and the big Leeds fighter faced each other.

Mac desperately wanted to look good and please his dad. In the dressing room while waiting to be called into action, he got himself into a savage mood and within fifty-five seconds the fight was all over. Mac rocked Bottomley down to his toe-nails with the first punch he threw. It was a straight left jab, he put his shoulder into the punch in order to generate more power, and it landed with a crack, knocking big Jack's head back on his shoulders. The Leeds boxer seemed to freeze as he stood perfectly still in an upright position. Like a panther, McAvoy sprang after his prey and smashed home a potent left hook, which made the Leeds fighters eyes open like saucers. Within a split second he followed through with a right cross that spread-eagled Bottomley on the floor. Jack was as game as they come and tried to rise from the canvas, but he was dazed and obviously concussed and he fell back into a prone position where he was counted out. McAvoy senior, though, missed his son's dramatic victory. He had bent down to pick something up from the floor that his grandson had dropped, and when he straightened up the fight was over!

A trip to Ireland and an outdoor tournament at Tolka Park, Dublin, followed for McAvoy's next ring outing. Mac fought Belfast fighter, Jack O'Brien. The weather was atrocious with heavy rain pouring down while the fight was in progress. Within no time the old horse-hair gloves the fighters were using were soaking wet and, must had been extremely heavy, thus making the impact of receiving a punch have an added effect. The Irishman gave it a damn good try in front of his home fans and forced McAvoy into making a few mistakes. By round three though, Mac had decided that he was wet enough, and growling, he tore into the Irishman and belaboured him with stunning two-handed punches, water spraying from Mac's gloves when landing on his target. O'Brien fought back determinedly but, as he went to throw a punch, he slipped on the wet canvas and fell off balance. Within a split second McAvoy, with cool precision countered with a terrific right hook, which lifted the Irish fighter completely off his feet and dumped him on the canvas, his head thudding loudly on the boards. Up at four, O'Brien was now a standing target and Mac showed no mercy when moving in for the finishing blows. He whipped a couple of left hooks at the statue-like Irishman and when O'Brien's seconds realised that their man would be left unconscious if the Lancashire fighter threw another punch, they immediately threw the towel into the ring.

To achieve what he had accomplished in such a short space of time was indeed a feather in McAvoy's cap. And to advance to the status of one of the hottest prospects in the country, without the benefit of a recognised trainer was remarkable to say the least. He was at this time training himself in Rochdale, helped by

Three of Jock McAvoy's children from his first marriage.

Benny Sutcliffe, a Rugby League star for Rochdale Hornets. Though he was fighting on a regular basis perhaps two or three times a month, the money was by no means fantastic. For example, he was averaging £5 or £10 a fight now, perhaps a little more when he fought the likes of Eddie Strawer and Joe Rostron, compared to the few shillings he received when first starting out.

Though a married man with a young family to care for, he still often went his own way. He would be out whenever he felt like it, and this would usually be at weekends, because he was a disciplined fighter and always kept himself in good condition. He would dress impeccably, in the modern style. The American gangster style of dress was the "in" thing then, and Mac and his friends would walk through Rochdale's town centre. He was by now a well-known celebrity and as he walked by onlookers would stop and stare at him. Mac was a sort of hero to many in the area and sometimes he was ready for a laugh and a joke with down to earth folk. He would visit the well-known pubs of the town, listening to a good old-fashioned singsong. And later perhaps he and his pals would go to a dance hall. Though he neither drank nor smoked, he did like the ladies and being a big shouldered, well-groomed fellow, they liked him a great deal.

At times he would seem very placid and laid back, always ready for a giggle with people he knew, like some of his old school chums. He was proud of his roots. Nonetheless, at these times there was puzzlement about his behaviour. Was the violent moodiness in him extinct or merely dormant? Deep down he was like a time bomb waiting to go off. The least thing that upset him would bring forth his violent temper.

"I wouldn't bet a brass farthing on his behaviour," said one old chap from Rochdale who watched McAvoy's rise to fame and fortune. "He was a strange type of man, he always was. I'm surprised he kept out of trouble with the law for so long. I'm not saying he was a burglar or anything of that nature, not at all. What I mean is because of his violent temper and the way he would set about someone who upset him I felt sure he would land himself into trouble. There were a lot of big, tough Irish navvies about Rochdale in the 1920s and 1930s, and a lot of Polish workers, all genuine hard men who after a few pints would step outside onto the cobbles, roll up their sleeves and fight like two dogs. I've seen Mac in plenty of these kind of situations and he was merciless, yes, he thumped quite a few. Mind you I've got to say that if the fellow he was arguing with was on the small side, Mac would merely give them a stiff back-hander. But if they were big fellows, wow, beware because he would lay into them with both fists flying."

The Collyhurst Connection

1931 saw a change in McAvoy's career for the better. Though he had done remarkably well under Joe Tolley and had gained a tremendous amount of prestige while being acclaimed as a genuine prospect, he had reached this status mainly through his own natural fighting instincts. It is fair to say that he had hardly been groomed for stardom, having had no formal coaching in the finer points of boxing. In the main he had been left to his own devices. It's also a fair point to make that McAvoy was a very stubborn and obstinate fellow who wouldn't listen to well meant advice from Joe Tolley. This is open to speculation. McAvoy claimed he had several more contests   which never appeared on his official record. However, Mac, had fought 61 times while under Tolley's guidance and had only been beaten on four occasions, while scoring 39 inside the distance victories. Today, this would be regarded as incredible, he would be hailed as a star, and this sort of record would catapult him to fame and fortune. But in those days there were several really good fighters in his weight class who could both box and punch so in reality, McAvoy was only on the first rung of the boxing ladder.

Norman Hurst, the doyen of boxing writers of this period, had seen a number of Mac's fights and was suitably impressed by what he had witnessed. The newspaperman had seen enough of the Rochdale lad to know he had developing potential. Hurst also knew that left without the proper schooling and tuition, the Rochdale lad would never fulfil his undoubted potential. He needed guidance and the right kind of matches. Hurst was intrigued by Jock's cold-eyed "killer-instinct" and impressed by his total commitment to boxing and his incredible will to win attitude.

There were and are many fighters all over the world who have the ability to become champions, but lack the will power to overcome all the odds and be successful. In professional boxing, the major factor in ultimate success if a man has above average boxing skills, durability and power is the ability to persevere. Just as we can't dodge all the raindrops in life, in boxing it is expected that setbacks of some kind will crop up. It may be a defeat because of an injury, a bad decision by a referee or judges in an opponent's home town or there might be off nights when his form deserts him; he might even get caught cold and get knocked out. Champions and the really great fighters are not those who avoid setbacks, they are the fighters with the greatest ability to handle them, learn lessons from them and be able to bounce back resiliently still chasing those big dreams. It is determination and will power which are every bit as important in the making of a champion as the physical skills. Many fighters after suffering a few losses became disillusioned and quit. McAvoy's slogan could well have read: 'Fortune favours not so much the brave as more often those who stick at it.' This fellow McAvoy had the will to succeed all right as he would prove over the coming years.

Norman Hurst was part of what was and is still referred to as the Belle Vue Syndicate, along with Jack Madden, Henry Isles and Harry Fleming. Isles was the promoter while ex-fighter Madden, who was closely related to the notorious American gangster, Owney Madden, was the live-wire matchmaker. Fleming was the manager of a brilliant stable of fighters that included Jackie Brown and Johnny King amongst many others. It was Hurst though who was the undoubted "Mr Big" behind the organisation.

In the late 1920s through to the outbreak of the war, Collyhurst was a hot-bed of boxing in Manchester and, under Harry Fleming and Jack Bates, had produced brilliant and successful fighters who regularly appeared on tournaments all over the British Isles. However, over a number of years Fleming had watched many of his brightest prospects disappear into oblivion, mainly through having to constantly travel and fight in their opponents' back yards, thus rarely getting the breaks so necessary in boxing. Harry decided to throw in his lot with the so-called syndicate at Belle Vue. And in future his proteges would have their own 'home' fighting ground which was the fabulous King's Hall in Belle Vue, situated in the Gorton district of Manchester and destined to become part of Manchester's history.

When exactly McAvoy joined the Collyhurst stable is anyone's guess, depending on who is telling the story. Tommy Fynan remembered Mac training with the Collyhurst team long before he signed a contract with Harry Fleming. Be that as it may, what is certain is that when the time came for McAvoy to officially change managers, Norman Hurst was behind it. He organised a meeting between himself, Harry Fleming and Jack Madden, and decided that they would sign McAvoy. Joe Tolley was sounded out about the prospect of releasing Mac from his contract. It was no secret throughout boxing circles that Tolley and McAvoy didn't always see eye to eye with each other, there was certainly no love lost between them.

When the Royton man expressed his willingness to discuss terms, he was called to a meeting with the Belle Vue Syndicate, and it was amicably agreed that McAvoy would sign a contact with Harry Fleming as his new official manager. In return Tolley would receive a substantial amount of money as settlement of his remaining contract with Mac. Sitting in the room where the meeting was being held, McAvoy was excited and full of optimism about his future. After listening to Hurst's exciting proposals and plans for the Collyhurst stable, Jock could not wait to put pen to paper and sign with Fleming. He visualised what he could achieve with such a powerful and influential organisation behind him. Hurst, Fleming and Madden could get him the right opportunities and more importantly, the right kind of money. Hurst would also make sure that McAvoy's team would receive plenty of publicity, which was a very important factor at that time.

It has been stated since that the contract he signed was based on the American boxer-manager style of contract that stated that earnings were split fifty-fifty. With the management paying all expenses from their percentage, such as managers and trainer's fees, sparring partners, accommodation, meals etc. At first Mac winced, moaned, groaned, and was less than happy with the details of the arrangement. However, he eventually signed the contract, albeit reluctantly. Over the years there has been speculation about the contract McAvoy signed when he officially joined the Collyhurst stable. Many people of that time stated that the standard British Boxing Board of Control contract stated that a manager was only entitled to 25 percent of a boxers earnings, (which is still the case today). However, McAvoy was on the American style contract as stated above which called for a 50-50 split. It was said that only Mac was tied to this kind of contract and the other Collyhurst boxers were on the standard Boxing Board of Control contract. But this was most certainly not the case.

Paddy McGrath, a rising heavyweight prospect at the time, was already a member of the Collyhurst team when McAvoy joined. Recalling events of that time he said: "I vividly remember Mac joining the team and he certainly wasn't happy about the issue of the contract and the implications of it. He thought the 50-50 split was a bit much and often said so. But, I'm sure all the Collyhurst fighters were on the same kind of contract. I know I was, and I was only a kid." Paddy showed me a copy of his contract and it clearly states it was the same agreement that McAvoy signed. It can be assumed that Norman Hurst and Dave Lumiansky, who was on the scene even at this early stage of McAvoy's career, were behind this deal. Furthermore, it is a known fact that Jackie Brown was also on a similar contract.

There were hundreds of fighters in Lancashire alone who looked upon Belle Vue as the Mecca of boxing and would gladly have fought there for nothing given the choice. Though having had in the region of sixty one professional contests up to this point, McAvoy had only appeared at the Kings Hall on a couple of occasions. This, of course, would all change once he joined the Collyhurst stable. Some of the greatest nights of boxing were in store for the Lancashire fight fans as McAvoy settled into his new environment. It was to prove a fruitful and nostalgic relationship with the district for Mac.

In the Collyhurst gym, McAvoy impressed everyone with his keenness and total commitment to hard training, though it did not take him long to start his characteristic moaning and groaning. He was a persistent hypochondriac and poor Harry Fleming and Jack Bates were forever looking for different remedies and potions for his various illnesses. They were very fortunate in having the likes of Dr Graham and Dr Driscoll to call upon for help and advice, and on many occasions one of the doctors would call to the gym to help out with McAvoy's various maladies.

The Collyhurst gym under the Fleming team was invariably full every session with good class fighters who were all straining at the leash to get a break through to the higher echelons of boxing. In truth, the gym itself was a disgrace with hardly any equipment whatsoever. Yet surprisingly, it was in this dump of an establishment that several really great fighters and three exceptionally wonderful champions were spawned. Harry Fleming was delighted at his latest acquisition and visualised more titles coming his gym's way. Though Henry, as Fleming was known to everyone, was as pleased as punch with Jock McAvoy, other fighters in the stable were not so happy. One such man was Ray Robertson, from Failsworth, who had spent a number of years in the Collyhurst stable. Ray who had won several schoolboy and junior championships before turning professional under the name of Ray Wood, saw the writing on the wall.

"I joined the Collyhurst team because that's where all the best scrappers were," he vividly recalled. "I was put with Jack Bates, what a lovely man he was. He was a wonderful teacher and always encouraged all the youngsters. He would go in my corner for schoolboy fights and, as I advanced and got older, he would still be in my corner. The Paley Street gym was a disgrace, though I never heard any of the fighters ever complain about the conditions. Mind you, those were extremely hard times. Henry (Fleming) was constantly on the look out for good fighters. Lads like myself, and other youngsters were just filling up the bills on small promotions. I wanted to advance my career in order to get bigger purses, but Henry spent all his time with Brown, King and McAvoy. These three were really great fighters, make no mistake. They were the best! But that wasn't helping me or my chances of climbing up the fistic ladder. I stuck it for a few months after McAvoy joined and then I left. Over the years many folk have asked me what he (McAvoy) was like? Well, as a fighter he was thrilling and superb, but as a person he and Jackie Brown were selfish, big-headed and abusive people. I couldn't stand the pair of them. They were obnoxious. There was an atmosphere in the gym when McAvoy was training - it was as if he didn't want any other boxers around."

Ray Robertson wasn't the only disgruntled member of the Collyhurst team. Paddy McGrath said that after McAvoy settled into his new environment a few other lesser lights of the stable expressed their displeasure and joined other camps. Talking about what McAvoy was like while training, Paddy said he was full of enthusiasm "Sparks flew many times when Mac was sparring," said Paddy. "Mac was a blunt man and his abrupt tone of voice was very intimidating. His language was course to say the least. And he didn't seem to know the meaning of taking it easy and often the gym would erupt during one of his sessions. Many folk said he was a liberty taker and deliberately went out of his way to be spiteful when sparring."

In the fights that followed Mac's change in management, the improvement was quite evident for all to see. When he was with Joe Tolley, McAvoy was renowned as a merely heavy puncher. But Jack Bates and Harry Fleming changed his style completely. This wasn't too difficult to achieve because up to this stage of his career he had virtually trained himself, and had never been coached by a regular trainer. At Collyhurst he learned to take the initiative as soon as the first bell sounded. Jack Bates said that when Mac joined the Collyhurst stable he was a slugger. "He paid next to no attention to the finer points of boxing. He just waded in and fired away in all sorts of directions with all sorts of punches. His stamina and love of a fight was amazing. We taught him how to judge distance. And how to get close up to his opponent without getting picked of, then we taught him to shorten his punches," he said, adding "and once he was on top he had to remain there until the opposition had wilted and been swept away. Fighting out of a crouch, the bow-legged, snorting, scowling Jock, with his crucifying punch would

Jack 'Cast Iron' Casey.

go on to prove that he was a match for anyone in the world. He was perpetual motion, and the most savage and devastating body-puncher this country has ever seen."

There is an old saying in boxing that fighters are born not made. Jack Bates believed that Jock McAvoy destroyed that myth by copying his idol's fighting style to the 'last T.' Bates explained that McAvoy studied everything about Jack Dempsey that he could lay his hands on: books, magazines and newspapers. They described everything about Dempsey and other well-known fighters in every minute detail. In those days there were no televisions, videos or film projectors, the only visual experience was via the newsreels which were shown on the thousands of cinemas throughout the British Isles. McAvoy told Bates that whenever Dempsey's fights were shown on the silver screen he would visit the cinema every night. "Mac was a student of Dempsey, almost a clone," stated Bates. "Remember, the majority of British fighters fought in the typical English style of straight up stance, straight left jab. They were stiff as Grenadier guardsmen. Mac was the exception. He was the first English fighter to my knowledge who fought from a crouch, bobbing and weaving while throwing short punches. He fought like Dempsey, with an American style. That's why he was so popular with thousands of spectators."

Boxing followers are fascinated when reading accounts of past middleweight champions such as Stanley Ketchel, Harry Greb and Rocky Graziano. The latter of these three's autobiography was a huge success and a film based on the book 'Somebody Up There Likes Me,' starring a young Paul Newman is now a classic. Also Jake LaMotta, known as the 'Bronx Bull' and whose life story was made into a best selling movie which saw Robert DiNiro, playing the part of LaMotta in the film, receive an Oscar. Then a fighter of a more recent vintage with a terrifying reputation was Roberto Duran. But compared to McAvoy these fighters were little angels.

What did Harry Fleming really think of Jock McAvoy? A couple years after Mac retired, Fleming, the man who helped steer him to glory and immortality, glowed with pleasure as he reminisced about his years with the Rochdale man. Harry often said that he had many headaches and his blood pressure would jump to bursting point because of McAvoy's behaviour. "I had more trouble from him than from all the other fighters I managed," said Fleming, though he was quick to point out it was nothing very serious. Merely petty things that bothered Mac as he was getting into peak condition for a fight. "He would complain that the punch bag was hung too low," said Fleming smiling. "He would moan that the sparring partners were late, too slow, or too soft. His skipping rope had been used by someone who had tied a knot in it, his bandages were either too loose or much too tight. But the headaches, blood pressure and worries were all forgotten when the bell rang and McAvoy left the corner for a fight. There was no need to tell him to watch out for this or be careful of that; all the worrying was transferred to the other corner. He was the finest middleweight this country has ever had."

McAvoy's first fight under the new regime came in Leeds at the end of August, 1931, when he fought Jack Hyams a good-looking Jewish fighter from Stepney, winning by disqualification in round eight. It was not the auspicious start the eager-to-please Rochdale lad wanted, but he could do nothing about the Londoner's clutching tactics. Hyams, once known as 'Kid Froggy,' was a wily experienced fighter and, having sampled Mac's ferocious punching, decided that this was not his night and held on for all he was worth. Mac called him some unprintable names.

From the commencement of their relationship, Harry Fleming had been horrified at the condition of Mac's fists. He asked Dr Graham, a Collyhurst doctor, and a member of the area boxing council to examine his knuckles. All kinds of remedies were diagnosed until Fleming devised a special method of bandaging and taping McAvoy's badly mauled hands, and it became a ritual over the ensuing years, help-

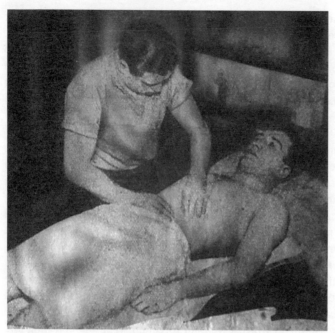

Massage helps Jock McAvoy to fitness – Jack Bates on the Champion after another work out.

ing the Rochdale man considerably. But the lasting damage was done and was never properly corrected. Yet, what a remarkable achievement of Mac's to fight and gain the honours he did with two badly injured 'paws.' Jack Bates was not surprised that McAvoy suffered with his hands. "His idea of winning a fight was to blast the daylights out of his opponent. And as he never cared where his often wild haymakers landed, so long as they were above the belt, I was always worried about his hands." Bates remarked that in many fights, Mac would put every ounce of his weight behind a punch and hit his opponent on the top of his head and bust up his hand! Jack was forever treating the damage to McAvoy's fists.

Taking part in a further six contests until the end of 1931, Mac showed marked improvement and scored six resounding stoppage victories. A week after the Hyams fight he was featured in the chief support of a Belle Vue tournament in which one of his new stable companions, Johnny King was topping the bill against Petit Biquet. McAvoy butchered the Welsh middleweight champion, Jerry Daley, in two rounds. His next Belle Vue appearance saw him again as the chief support but this time to his other stablemate, Jackie Brown, who was fighting Ottavio Gori from Italy. Mac was matched with Alfred Pegazzano, a French fighter with plenty of experience. After a tame first round, McAvoy while sitting in his corner awaiting the bell for the second round heard several ringside spectators remark that the fight would probably go the distance because he, (McAvoy,) was too cautious. Seething with anger at these remarks, Mac stormed out and punched the Frenchman from pillar to post, decking him three times for long counts. Mac was awesome in this mood and the crowd rose to him. Pegazzano would have been forgiven if had chosen not to contest the third round, but as brave as they come, he was out and trying to fight back in the third session. McAvoy walked into his opponent and bombarded him with ferocious two-handed punches that quickly had the Frenchman down and out.

Blackpool Tower was his next stop and it was a fight that McAvoy had besieged Harry Fleming to obtain for him. He had a grudge against Paul McGuire, ever since he had lost by disqualification to the Sunderland boxer over a year previously. Mac had even thrown out a challenge to McGuire, with a hundred pound side-stake, but the fighter from the North East had never replied. Losing was never pallettable for Mac. However, he was sincere with his congratulations when beaten fairly and squarely. But in the case of McGuire, McAvoy always claimed he was easily winning their previous fight when McGuire went down clutching his lower region, claiming a foul. What really annoyed Mac, though, was that the Sunderland lad had been going around telling one and all that he had clearly beaten this 'great' prospect named - McAvoy. Paul however, omitted to say how he had gained the victory. Anyhow, the scene was set for revenge.

Harry Fleming, knowing that Jock was riled and eager to fly at his opponent, told him to concentrate on throwing head punches. This McAvoy did with precision and just before the first round ended, Mac caught his man with a booming right hand, sending McGuire to the boards with an almighty thud. Despite what McAvoy said about the Sunderland boxer, there was no disputing his fighting heart. That punch would have finished almost any other fighter, but he got up on shaky legs and made it back to his corner. Groggy but unbowed, McGuire came out to meet McAvoy for the second round, who was in no mood for feeling his man out. Mac snarled, and immediately took the initiative, swarming all over his by now helpless opponent, knowing he had McGuire at his mercy. Fleming and Jack Bates prayed and hoped their fighter would not do anything foolish. But Mac took aim and directed a tremendous right hand punch at McGuire. It was one of the hardest punches he had ever hit anybody with and the Sunderland boxer staggered round the ring yet wouldn't go down. Everyone in the Tower held their breath, hoping McAvoy wouldn't crash another punch at this ever so game fighter.

Instead, McGuire held out his hand in surrender.

Back at Belle Vue for a battle against Billy Adair, the blond-haired Bethnal Green tough-as-teak brawler, McAvoy launched body attacks from the beginning and a vicious smash landed under the Cockney fighters heart sending the Londoner down for the full count. McAvoy was now becoming a big box-office attraction. This was what Harry Fleming and Norman Hurst had envisaged when bringing him into the fold. His last two fights in 1931 were at Royton, not on Joe Tolley's promotions, but for Tolley's rival, the Chapmans at the National School of Boxing, which became known to everyone as simply the N.S.B. The former tramway depot was packed to capacity as Mac jumped through the ropes to tangle with old rival, Sonny Doke, from Battersea. Doke, a tough and rugged southpaw had taken Mac to fifteen and twelve round points decisions earlier that year having achieved this by messing him around and using his wrong way round style to confuse the Rochdale lad. This time though, it was a new McAvoy, as the London fighter was soon to find to his cost. After three spirited rounds where both fighters threw caution aside, and blasted each other with dynamic punches from both fists, round four saw McAvoy move up a couple of gears and as a result, Doke took three long counts before being saved by the bell. In no mood to waste time Mac was off his stool sharpish, and as round five started he fired a power-packed left hook at the Cockney and down tumbled Sonny. The Battersea man was badly hurt and his seconds tossed the towel into the ring.

It was about this time that newspaper reporters and fans were referring to Mac as The Rochdale Thunderbolt' and this became his nickname. For his last fight of the year, McAvoy was again at the same venue, only four weeks after disposing of Sonny Doke. His opponent this time was the popular Cardiff middleweight, Ernie Red Pullen. Within seconds, this contest became a toe to toe confrontation and within one minute and forty-five seconds of the fight commencing Jack Bates was throwing McAvoy's dressing gown over his shoulders. Poor Pullen was starched out on the canvas, out to the world, courtesy of a right cross which landed with such ferocity that the audience were praying for the Welshman's welfare. There was no doubt that McAvoy was on his way to the British title and the big purses he so desired.

After a brief honeymoon period, Mac had settled into his new environment in Collyhurst and become his usual moody, bombastic, and argumentative self. Jack Bates was detailed to work with him and iron out a few of his fighting wrinkles.

Though a great deal smaller than McAvoy, Bates would often put the gloves on and get in the ring with Mac in order to get his point across more forcibly. They didn't spar as two boxers would normally do, it was more a learning process. Jack would teach the Rochdale lad little moves such as how to fight better on the inside and how to pull an opponent onto his punches. Bates also showed his pupil the art of tugging, side-stepping, and how to cover up then quickly launch a counter attack, plus all the other little tricks only a master of in-fighting like Bates could teach a willing pupil.

"What impressed me about him," said Bates many years later. "Was that this fellow could really punch. He was a natural hitter. That doesn't mean that a fighter can get by on this one aspect of his fighting make up, certainly not, you have to practice at anything to become more proficient. Joe was great at close quarters where his little 'digs' were hurtful. Straight away we could tell he was from a different mould than other fighters. His natural love for fighting was there. What we also noticed, was his capacity for hard work and his almost total dedication to keeping himself in tip-top condition. His floor work (calisthenics) were an integral part of his workouts and were largely responsible for the abnormal toughness he later showed. He skipped for nimbleness, did neck bridges to strengthen his neck, which would make him less vulnerable to head punches. He stood on his tiptoes for long periods to improve his balance. He could do sit-ups and push-ups all day long."

Tommy Fynan was Collyhurst born and bred. He had fought numerous ring battles, and his rubber face, semi squashed nose and cauliflower ears were his legacy. However, despite his looks, Tommy was a very intelligent man. His brothers had also boxed and the whole family loved boxing. They were part of the Collyhurst establishment. Tommy was a wonderful warm-hearted character who became well known in Collyhurst for the way he walked. He would walk down the road as if he owned it, a woodbine cigarette in his mouth, proud as a peacock, straight backed and his shoulders would sway, and parents would say to their children when going somewhere in a hurry or coming out of the cinema. "Come on now, put your Tommy on." They meant walk like Tommy Fynan! He helped Bates and Fleming in the Collyhurst gymnasium and was a great admirer of McAvoy's fighting ability, though indignant at Mac's attitude outside the ropes. Remembering Mac's early days Tommy said: "People were sceptical about him. He was a villainous character inside and outside the ring. However, having said that, I noticed a big change in Mac's overall style of fighting. He soon responded to the schooling he was getting in our little gym. You could see how much he had improved in a short space of time. He became the best puncher I ever saw. And like Dempsey, he had that touch of spitefulness that all great hitters possess. Even in sparring he was awesome. Oh my God, I saw him poleaxe fully-fledged heavy-weights, then shout at them to get up while he hit them again."

Joe Burke lived in Collyhurst, just around the corner from Harry Fleming's Whitley Street home. Joe a lean, lanky, sallow-looking fellow was a boxing fan who followed Fleming's fighters to many of the tournaments, and was a gym regular in Collyhurst, Belle Vue and Hollingworth Lake. During the war he was Jackie Brown's sergeant while serving in the Pioneer Corps. Joe has many recollections of McAvoy, some good and some horrid. "It's no good beating about the bush. He was an arrogant and odious fellow," said Burke. "He had a very cruel and sinister streak. I was always wary of him and while he was training I personally would try not to go anywhere near him. He would look at you with those cold, piercing eyes of his, and you would automatically feel intimidated and uncomfortable in his company. He would sneer at my tall, bony figure. In those days I stood about six foot three, but only weighed around ten stone soaking wet. Many a time he tried to get me to put the gloves on and get into the ring, but Bates and Fleming would tip me off by giving me a look or a wink which I knew meant, don't be stupid. I didn't particularly like him as a person, but as a fighter, I take my hat off to the man. Christ, he could fight, and I do mean fight. I am not being nostalgic because I still like watching modern fighters and the middleweights intrigued me. Terry Downes and that boy Minter were very courageous lads, but he (McAvoy) would have destroyed both of them. Truthfully, I haven't seen a British middleweight since his time who I genuinely believe could have lived with him."

The Collyhurst gym was always busy. Indeed, it was a hive of activity. Various fighters would be preparing for forthcoming tournaments so with the different characters and personalities it can be imagined that there was a tremendous amount of leg pulling. Mac, however, liked nothing better than to train alone. On many occasions Jack Bates and Harry Fleming would have to train him in solitude. McAvoy would put his wind up record player on and train to music. He must have been one of the first boxers to ever train with music blaring away in the background. On these occasions there was none of the usual bluster and laughter like there was when Jackie Brown was training. But both Fleming and Bates patiently adhered to McAvoy's whims and request to train in solitude.

When McAvoy became a member of the Collyhurst team, Jackie Brown and Johnny King were already well established celebrities. Brown was the British and European flyweight champion and a huge attraction wherever he appeared, and King was already in line for a shot at the British bantamweight title. Though King knew Jock from their Rochdale days they didn't socialise together. It was the charismatic, flamboyant Brown to whom Mac became close. He laughed and joked with Jackie and would often be found playing billiards in various pubs and clubs around Collyhurst. Besides playing billiards they loved dancing and were often seen at Belle Vue, The Ritz and other well known dance halls in Manchester. These were of a similar breed, always out looking for a good time. Over the years these two kindred spirits, distinguished themselves with some late night carousing. Because of their high-spirited behaviour and their court appearances for indiscretions, they offended and outraged the public.

After McAvoy had appeared in court for some infringement or other, Brown would invariably defend his stablemate to folk who were critical of his behaviour. "He's a good bloke, Mac," said Brown as if condoning McAvoy's outlandish behaviour, "He's misunderstood." On the occasions when Brown found himself in trouble with the police, Mac would similarly come out in defence of him. "Jackie's a great fellow. He would always do you a good turn," McAvoy said. "Folk don't realise what fighters have to put up with. We get all kinds of idiots trying to pick a fight, because they are after a reputation."

Derek Bates, Jack's son, remembers McAvoy with a great deal of affection. The fighter often visited the Bates' household for a chat and to let his trainer give him a rub down. "When the Paley Street gym had to close down, I cannot remember the reason why, but Henry Fleming moved all his fighters to his brother John's gym. This was situated on the bottom of Collyhurst Street, near the Oldham Road end. Funnily enough, it was actually over another coal yard like the Paley Street gym was situated. And it was at the side of the White Heart Public House," recalled Derek. "In the middle of the floor of this gym, John Fleming had erected a big round steel base, about three foot in diameter. In the centre of the base were a series of springs an inch in diameter and drilled into the thick joists by huge bolts. Also, on top of the base, to give it extra weight, were placed several old coal yard weights. In the middle of the base stood an iron rod that stood a foot high. On top of this was a ball, something like a stand ball which is used in modern gymnasiums, but this one had been specially constructed by some workers from Carey's Steel works in Red Bank. The other fighters would attempt to hit this piece of equipment but found it hard to budge it. McAvoy though, would thump it viciously making the floor vibrate from the impact of his punches and while he was slugging away at the ball, he would be cursing at some imaginary opponent. He hit this thing with such power that he lifted the bolts from the floor. Gee, could he punch."

The year of 1932 was to prove a disastrous one in some respects for McAvoy. He had 18 contests and though he scored 12 inside-the-distance victories from his 16 wins, he lost the two most important fights up to that stage of his career. In January he was matched against the taller and heavier Accrington scrapper, Jack Marshall. The Lancashire cruiserweight fancied his chances against Mac so much so that he backed himself that McAvoy could not knock him out. When he entered the ring in Royton, Jock knew nothing about the side - stake. It was as well under the circumstances, because in round two Marshall lost his wager when he was flattened by a sizzling short right cross which put him into dreamland. It was a tremendous punch thrown with great ferocity.

A couple of weeks later in front of the Belle Vue crowd who had come to hero worship him, Mac, fought and won a laboriously dull 15 rounder with the canny and awkward former Royal Navy champion, Seaman Albert Harvey from Plymouth. Four weeks later he boxed another bigger and much heavier opponent in Manchester when he faced the Belgian, Jack Etienne. London boxing scribes were forecasting a rough ride for the Rochdale man on account of the fact that Etienne had forced the great Len Harvey to pull out all the stops before forcing the giant Belgian to retire in the 13th round. In the early rounds it looked like the London scribes would be proven correct with their forecast as Etienne's vast advantage in height, weight and reach would be too much of a handicap. Though this contest went the full 15 round distance, it was a thrilling encounter with Mac's over-eagerness costing him the chance of a stoppage victory.

On 21st March 1932, McAvoy challenged reigning champion Len Harvey for the latter's British and Empire middleweight titles at the King's Hall, Belle Vue. An account of this closely fought contest in which Mac was adjudged the loser is told in a chapter which deals specifically with the various McAvoy - Harvey encounters. After the disappointment of losing to Len Harvey, McAvoy knew he would have to keep going in order to get a second chance for the middleweight crown. In May he stepped into the Belle Vue ring and was in no mood for going the distance. The boxer opposing him was poor Edwin John, who was in for a rough night's work. John's father, Augustus, was a famous artist from Chelsea. On this night, Edwin frustrated the Rochdale Thunderbolt until round six. It was obvious from the first couple of rounds that the spectators sensed that Mac's sharpness and punching power were not functioning at full throttle, because he was missing with far too many punches and unable to follow through when he gained the advantage. John, as it happened, was a very astute boxer with his guardsman like stance. He was quite happy to keep the bout at long range and last the distance. But in round three, he was on the floor hearing the referee, Jimmy Wilde, counting eight over him. After he got to his feet, he quite rightly moved around the ring as if on roller skates, with Mac chasing after him. The spectators though showed their displeasure, and Jock knew he had to open up. The sixth proved to be the fatal round for the classy London boxer. He hit the Collyhurst based fighter with a stinging left swing that caught McAvoy and stung him. He spat out some obscenities and moved menacingly toward the Chelsea boxer. As he reached him, Mac brought a tremendous right cross into action. The blow hit John flush in the face and blood came gushing down, and straight away Wilde stopped the fight.

McAvoy's next two bouts were held at N.S.B. Royton. Bill Hood, of Plymouth, was his opponent for this Sunday afternoon contest, and an interested spectator was Jack Casey, of Sunderland. Casey had been named as McAvoy's next challenger for his Northern Area middleweight title. It is worth remembering that these championships were prestigious titles to have at that time. The Sunderland fighter was a cocky fellow and McAvoy didn't want him to go home thinking that he, Casey had an easy task in front of him when they were due to cross gloves. Mac's opponent, Bill Hood had just returned from a successful tour of America and was feeling confident. After exchanging heavy blows in the first, from which the Plymouth fighter took an eight count, the crowd was really warming to this slugging dual. As the second started, Hood punched rapidly with his left, though Mac ignored the blows and went "downstairs" with effective smashes which had Hood wobbling. McAvoy stepped straight in and smashed a solid right that put the Plymouth boxer down for the full ten seconds. He was still out to the world as his handlers helped him back to his corner. When the referee raised McAvoy's hand, Casey, sitting at ringside, was looking straight at the Rochdale lad. Mac gave him a look enough to freeze an Eskimo.

Both Casey and McAvoy were billed to appear on the next Royton show three weeks later. It was another complete sell-out. Both were out to gain quick, decisive victories in order to impress each other as to who was the better man, before

McAvoy walks away after pulverising Archie Sexton.

they eventually fought each other. McAvoy was first into the ring and Sandy McKenzie, a Glasgow boxer with an estimated 200 fights behind him, was his opponent. The crowd could feel that this wasn't going to last very long by the way Mac was pouncing up and down while the introductions were going on. He wanted to fight. It was quite obvious. For the short time the fight lasted the fans were on their feet. The Scottish hard - man drove the Rochdale fighter back against the ropes as they swapped vicious punches. They stood toe to toe slugging it out in the best manner of an American Western film. Then quite suddenly, the bombs from McAvoy ended the proceedings. Mac fired home a perfect right cross that had every once of strength that he possessed behind it. There was a huge gasp from the audience as they waited the outcome. The reaction of McKenzie after the punch hit him needed to be seen to be believed. The crowd now fell into a hushed silence, as time momentarily seemed to stand still. The Scot's arms fell limply to his sides, and his eyes went to the top of his head. For what seemed an age, but was in fact a few brief seconds, he stayed upright. McAvoy looked puzzled. "Should I go in and hit him again?" He seemed to be asking himself. Then in that very instant McKenzie fell face first on the canvas, not moving a muscle as the referee, Gus

Platts, counted him out. The crowd had never seen anything like it before. The sheer ferocity of that dynamic right cross must have been absolutely awesome. McAvoy's performance screamed out: "What about that then, Mr Casey?"

Later, on the same bill, Casey fought a Welshman, Billy Thomas, who had quite a reputation, and had spent some time in New Zealand, staying long enough to win the national middleweight title. Casey stopped his foe in a couple of rounds. McAvoy soon got a chance to see if he could better Casey's performance, when nine days after demolishing McKenzie, he fought Billy Thomas in Blackpool. It was the holiday season and over three thousand fans packed into the stadium. McAvoy was vicious. He decked Thomas twice in round one with heavy hooks to the head and body. Round two saw the game Cardiff lad take a further thrashing, being on the floor on two other occasions. And finally in the third, after going down three times the referee stopped the one-sided fight.

Marcel Thil, the extremely tough, hairy-chested French fighter had just beaten the black American fighter, Gorilla Jones, for the National Boxing Association's version of the world middleweight championship. Thil had agreed to defend his title against Len Harvey at the White City Stadium, in London, on 4 July 1932. To Jock's delight, promoter, Jeff Dickson, offered him a fight on the bill's undercard. His opponent was the leading French middleweight, Carmello Candel. It would be a ten round bout and labelled an eliminator for the world title. This would be McAvoy's first ever trip to London and he was deliriously happy. When Mac stepped off the Manchester train in London, he was met by Charley Rose, a well known boxing man who would later manage Len Harvey. Rose took Mac to a hotel and the hotel staff looked after him until Harry Fleming arrived. In his room, to pass the time, Jock read his favourite detective novels. Later that evening, Mac beat his French rival easily, though it was only by a points decision. And sadly, Harvey lost to Thil. McAvoy watched the Harvey versus Thil contest and believed in his heart that he now knew how to defeat Harvey when the opportunity arose, and in the meantime, he now set his sights on his forthcoming contest against Jack Casey.

When genuine grudge fights are made such as Zale-Graziano, Pep-Saddler, Ali-Frazier and here in England who can forget King-Brown, Boon-Danaher and more recently Eubank-Benn, to mention but a few, boxing followers look forward to it with a great deal of excitement. Well, McAvoy versus the 'Sunderland Assassin,' Cast Iron Jack Casey was one such event. It was a must!

Before his contest with Eddie Peirce, Jock McAvoy put all he knew into his work-out so that he would be fit to take another step towards a World Title fight. This action shot shows him throwing a right at the jaw of sparring partner Harry Bliers of St. Helens.

In September 1931 Casey publicly issued a challenge to the Rochdale Thunderbolt but because of boxing politics it was not until 18th July 1932 that these two genuine hard men faced each other in the King's Hall ring at Belle Vue. Casey's manager, Walter Russell, told the newspapers that McAvoy, far from being the best middleweight in the North, was way behind his fighter, Cast Iron Casey, in the pecking order when it came to title challenges against Len Harvey. Mr Russell stated his man would fight the Lancashire fighter anytime, and further more he deposited a sum of £25 with the Newcastle promoter of the St James' Hall as a guarantee of Casey's sincerity. John Jacob Paget, the Tyneside impresario, confirmed the offer and stated he was quite willing to give each fighter percentage terms if McAvoy was in agreement. Casey himself got in on the act and told reporters that Mac couldn't call himself the champion of the North until he had fought him. He stated that he was willing to back himself to beat McAvoy with a £100 side bet thrown in for good measure. The only stipulations were that Mac's Northern Area title was on the line and the fight took place wherever the top purse bid was made. The truth was that Casey had in fact been offered £100 to meet the Rochdale man earlier but he had turned it down flat, saying he received a much better offer for his services from another source and said that as a professional he accepted it.

Jack Madden the Belle Vue matchmaker offered the two fighters £250 to be divided: £150 to the winner and £100 to the loser. McAvoy was furious, and said he would not accept this offer pointing out that when he won the title from Joe Lowther he only received 40 per cent of the purse. "I am the champion," he said, "and Casey will have to accept similar terms."

When all the arguments had finished the match was finally signed and sealed, Belle Vue having secured the fight against strong bidding from Tyneside. The Casey fans converged upon Manchester in droves on special excursion trains, which had been laid on by the railway companies, from Newcastle and Sunderland. A few days prior to the fight, Casey moved in with some relations in Ashton-under-Lyne on the border of Manchester. This was the most important fight of his career so far and he was leaving nothing to chance. He fancied "doing McAvoy good and proper," and so did his supporters because they bet heavily on their man. Mac thought Casey was a cocky fellow and secretly believed he could "do a number" on the iron man. There was a huge throng of people in Belle Vue on the afternoon of 18 July 1932. The occasion was the official weighing-in ceremony for the 15 round contest that night between the two toughest, roughest, meanest and hardest punching middleweights in the British Isles. This was a genuine "grudge" fight. Casey was first on the scale making the weight limit with over three pounds to spare. He was extremely cocky, and when he stepped of the scale he bellowed: "I will stop McAvoy tonight." He was smirking and confident and his Sunderland followers were equally confident. The place went silent and everybody in the room looked straight at the Rochdale man who was putting his clothes on after successfully coming inside the weight limit. Mac didn't say a word: he just gave the Sunderland fighter a look that was enough to turn most folk into tablets of stone. Casey laughed, and turning to the crowd he boasted: "If there is any counting needed tonight, it will be McAvoy who the referee will be counting over, I assure you."

The tough-as-teak Sunderland middleweight intended relieving McAvoy of his Northern Area title when he challenged the Collyhurst based champion in their fight at Belle Vue. Casey, known as the 'Sunderland Assassin' and also the 'Iron Man,' was no ring scientist but an all-out aggressive fighter who, like Mac, carried a knockout wallop in both his fists. He showed no pretence for setting his opponent up for openings for his dynamite laden punches, he just stormed forward, head down and blasted away for all he was worth. He was no shrinking violet either, as his pre-fight boasting testified. He was something of the same ilk as McAvoy; in fact many observers said that as a man, he was just up McAvoy's street. Though Mac never openly boasted about what he would do to his opponents, those inside his Collyhurst camp would discretely tell you that Jock fancied hammering the living daylights out of Casey.

Casey was the idol of the North East fight fans because of his exciting, attacking style of fighting and his toughness. Like McAvoy, it didn't bother him how big or heavy his opponents happened to be. He would take on all-comers. To show how tough a fighter Casey was, today he would be classed as only a light-middleweight, which was basically what he was during his hey-day. Yet, incredibly, this fellow fought and defeated three men who would win the British heavyweight championship: Jack London, Reggie Meen and the legendary Welshman, Tommy Farr. Enough said about his impressive capabilities, you must agree.

The King's Hall was packed to capacity for this eagerly awaited showdown between the two toughest, roughest and hardest-punching middleweights in the British Isles. There was a special buzz of excitement in the air as the fans waited for the bell to clang and send these two fearsome fighters into action. Fight time came at around ten o' clock when referee, Tom Gamble, called the two lads into the centre of the ring while he issued his instructions. McAvoy looked menacingly in Casey's direction but never uttered a word. However, everyone at ringside was left in no doubt that these two fancied 'chinning' each other.

It proved to be one of the greatest slugging matches in British boxing history, with Mac throwing away the contest and his title by a punch that left the referee little option other than to disqualify him. Why the Rochdale lad lost his head to such an extent everyone present was at a loss to understand, because without any exaggeration, bar him getting knocked out, which seemed highly unlikely given the circumstances, he had this fight won convincingly. The crowd was caught up in the whirl of excitement as the fatal 14th round got underway. Women as well as men

All smiles at the weigh-in before the Jock McAvoy (left) v. Eddie Peirce fight. When the two met at Belle Vue, Manchester. Jock won on a points decision.

seemed to lose their heads and shrieked advice to both fighters. McAvoy delivered a tremendous blow to the pit of Casey's stomach which saw the Sunderland iron-man wobble and suddenly look ashen-faced. The Lancashire fighter threw another similar punch and Casey, rising up on his toes, caught it low. There was no doubting that it was a foul blow, but it was accidental, and Cast-Iron Casey had most certainly contributed to the punch landing where it did because of the way he rose high on his toes, meeting the punch.

Naturally McAvoy was very distraught at the sudden ending to a fight he was winning by the proverbial mile; he was fuming and bitterly upset once back in his dressing room. Harry Fleming was trying to pacify him and keep him quiet, not wanting to incur the wrath of the Boxing Board officials who were scurrying around the vicinity. "Not for a second did I ever think I would lose to Casey," shouted Mac, to his manager and people in his dressing room. Then he added: "I also believed that I could be the first boxer to achieve what no other fighter had accomplished, by putting him on the canvas for the full ten seconds. I had got tired

All-action moment in the McAvoy-Peirce encounter. The South African sagging into the ropes following a terrific uppercut from the 'Rochdale Thunderbolt'.

of punching Jack on the chin round after round with punches that would have knocked any ordinary fighter cold, and with that I switched my punches to the solar - plexus region. As he went down for a nine count, it was only natural that I should concentrate on his mid - section."

It had been no secret that when the Northern Area Boxing Board of Control had first ordered McAvoy to defend his title against the North East fighting man, they had told the two respective managers to get together and thrash out terms and the venue. McAvoy suspected that the usual boxing politics would surface. As far as the two fighters were concerned, there need not have been any delay, but the people close to the boxing scene knew that protracted and heated arguments would occur over every conceivable point. Being champion, even the Northern Area Champion meant a great deal to McAvoy. He was a proud champion. He begged Harry Fleming and Jack Madden to get him a re-match against Casey. "I don't care if its in Casey's backyard," he told them. But the Sunderland fighter was now firmly in the driving seat, and McAvoy did not figure in his immediate plans. Though Mac told his friends that he didn't think his loss to Casey would make that much difference to his rating, he was wrong. The Board of Control completely ignored Mac, and matched Casey against Archie Sexton, the winner to oppose Len Harvey for the title. By any reasoning this left the Rochdale lad firmly on the outside looking in. He was fuming and called the Boxing Board every blasphemous name he could think of, and he knew plenty. There was nothing for it, he would have to start again and build up his record so that nobody could ignore his claims.

Jack Madden, promoted an August Bank Holiday open-air tournament on Blackpool's Football Ground at Bloomfield Road. The three Collyhurst stars, Jackie Brown, Johnny King and McAvoy were featured on the promotion. Blackpool in those days was the top British holiday resort. It was the equivalent to what Las Vegas is today. Such was the drawing power of these three wonderful fighters that over ten thousand spectators paid to watch them fight. McAvoy fought a tough Welshman, Tom Benjamin, who had been around the fight circuit for quite a while. Mac set about the Welshman from the start and decked him twice within seconds. Whenever he could, Benjamin hung on to McAvoy as if he was a drowning man. The fight lasted until round five, Tom being bashed from pillar to post and knocked down several times before his seconds threw the towel into the ring to save him from being annihilated. Both Brown and King also won their fights so Harry Fleming was overjoyed.

Four weeks later, McAvoy outpointed George Brown over 12 rounds. Incidentally, Brown had twice boxed the rising Welsh heavyweight star, Jack Petersen. Billy Roberts, another North East based fighter, from Bishop Auckland, claimed that he had never been knocked out, and he let it be known that McAvoy wouldn't be able to put him down either. This was a bold statement for Roberts to make though many felt he was foolish uttering remarks like this about a fighter like Mac. The N.S.B. Royton was packed to capacity on the Sunday afternoon that these two faced each other. Roberts must have regretted he boasted about his durability because for the three rounds their fight lasted, he hit the deck six times for counts totalling 43 seconds. After taking a real drubbing Roberts signalled to the referee that he had had enough. He protected his record of never been knocked out, but the shellacking he received was certainly no compensation.

In the meantime, Jack Casey knocked out Archie Sexton, and would now fight Len Harvey for the title. McAvoy was hoping to fight the winner of this bout. Harvey did eventually beat Casey, but only on points in a very closely fought contest. Harvey's successful defence against the 'Iron Man' did, though, clear the way for a title challenge from the McAvoy camp.

Bath is more famous for its Rugby than producing boxers, but Phil Green was a game fighter and carved out a career for himself in the 1930s. He accepted a 12 round contest against McAvoy and the bout was staged by promoter Harry Barlow at the Palace Theatre, Rawtenstall, in the Lancashire hills. With Mac's name on the blue and white posters, the place was heaving with many fans unable to gain entrance. The two fighters started quietly enough, Green showing he was nifty and nibble. After sampling one of Mac's right clips to the jaw, the Bath man became very aggressive, which the crowd loved. But as Green flayed away with both hands, he left himself open to Mac's devastating counters. These were delivered to the stomach, turning Phil green, (if you'll pardon the terrible pun!) and putting him down twice. When he came out for round two, he looked apprehensive. Jock walked forward, dipped slightly, bent his knees and came through with a right hand punch that landed with sickening effect and again put Green on the canvas. As he regained his footing, Mac hit him with a left hook that concluded the proceedings, the referee not even bothering to count. The crowd, though, were very indignant at the sudden ending of the fight and a chorus of yelling and hooting broke out, drowning out the Master of Ceremonies' announcement. Green, in the meantime, had been revived and walked over to the M.C. and held up his hand for silence. As the noise abated he said: "Listen to me please, I have fought a lot of good fighters, but Jock McAvoy is without a doubt the best I have ever fought, and only those who have boxed him could possibly know how good he is. He is a tremendous hitter, he beat me fair and square." Mac stood in his corner looking slightly embarrassed, then hurriedly went to his changing room. "I felt a bit bad about hitting him so hard," he told some friends. Then added: "It doesn't pay, though, to be sentimental in boxing."

Mind you, in his next contest he would certainly feel sorry and apprehensive, fighting Tommy Moore, a Royton lad, at the Morecambe Winter Gardens. There was a little bit of "needle" between the two fighters and they went at each other hell for leather, each landing with power-packed punches. McAvoy concentrated on the Royton boxer's mid-section, where he found him to be weakest. As the second round came to a close, Mac hit his opponent with a right to the heart followed by a left hook to the ribs, and even spectators at the very back of the hall could hear Moore's ribs crack. It looked all over as Moore's seconds rushed into the ring and physically dragged their man back to his corner. He was out! But to everyone's amazement including McAvoy's, the Royton man came out to contest the third round. Mac sized him up and could tell that Tommy should never have been allowed to come out for the third, yet showing no mercy, he immediately launched a lightning-fast right cross and sent Moore crashing to the canvas. The referee and his seconds rushed to the prostrate fighter. While getting changed, McAvoy was told the doctor had hurriedly gone into Moore's dressing room. Without bothering to continue dressing, Mac went to see his opponent, who looked ill. The doctor sent the stricken fighter to hospital. It seems that one of McAvoy's punches had damaged Moore's liver, and the doctor advised instant hospital treatment. McAvoy was punching mightily hard at this period of his career. He loved opponents who came directly at him for a toe-to-toe confrontation yet he always had problems with the men who boxed rather than relying on their punching power. He had a focused viciousness about him that one rarely finds in a boxer.

His next opponent was Londoner, Ted Covney, a couple of days after Bonfire Night. Mac made certain he let some bangers and rockets off in the Blackburn ring. He hammered the game Highbury fighter in four bristling rounds. A couple of weeks later McAvoy was featured at Belle Vue, against a beautifully sculptured specimen in Milhai Fubia, who was a Rumanian. When the contest started Mac found out that his opponent was a southpaw, and a rough, un-schooled type of fighter. After a mauling first round, Mac settled down and a terrific right hander had the awkward Rumanian taking a count of nine. When he was ordered to "box on" by the referee, he grabbed hold of the Rochdale lad and held on like a long lost brother. The third was fought in a similar fashion, but this time Fubia took two trips to the canvas. McAvoy was by this time furious with the Rumanian's clutching tactics, and he man-handled the foreigner by roughing him up, bringing a warning from the referee. By round four, McAvoy was determined to end the bout, and at the bell he moved into his opponent and sent a right and left under Mr Fubia's heart. Instantly he went down like a log and remained there distressed until he was counted out.

Mac's last fight of 1932 was just before Christmas, 7th December to be exact, and it was to be his second visit to London. He fought the number one challenger for the German middleweight title, Hans Seifried, in a contest staged at the Albert Hall. Mac travelled to London with Jackie Brown, his gym companion, who was on the same bill. Brown had won the world flyweight title in October, and was obviously a huge attraction. He was due to box Dick Corbett, the highly popular red-haired Cockney fighter in the top of the bill attraction, at catchweights. For some unknown reason the two Lancashire lads arrived late for the official weigh-in, and it appears Corbett didn't wait and jumped on the scales and weighed in at the stipulated poundage.

When Brown and Mac eventually arrived for the weigh-in they were with Dave Lumiansky, the manager of Panama Al Brown, the brilliant world bantamweight champion. They were told that Corbett and already been on the scales. Upon hearing this news Lumiansky was furious and insisted that Corbett should get back on the scales while he and Brown could check his given weight. All hell broke loose. Joe Morris, Corbett's manager, supported by the Boxing Board officials, refused point-blank. The promoters and the two managers tried for the rest of the day to reach an amicable settlement about the dispute, but both parties were stubborn and the fight was eventually cancelled. For the two boxers it meant losing out on a pay-day. Had it been left to Brown and Corbett, they would have willingly fought each other, but this was boxing politics. The outcome would end up in a courtroom with Lumiansky, losing the case and being suspended.

The McAvoy versus Seifried fight was now elevated to top of the bill status. The German proved a tough opponent and despite taking some shuddering whacks, and being decked several times, he managed to frustrate McAvoy and last the ten rounds, though Mac won with a great deal to spare. The reader should understand the standard of the opposition McAvoy was fighting. Though he was scoring eighty - five percent of his victories by the knockout or stoppage route, his opponents were nearly all of championship class. In the 1920s and 1930s, there were thousands of fighters throughout the whole of Europe. People were hungry, and if a person didn't work, he and his family went without food. There was no such thing as health services and social security, and the other such departments that are on hand today, in which help for the unemployed and destitute is readily available. In those days, you had to fend for yourself and your family. It bred hardness and the fighters fought anybody they were matched with. There were the Boxing Booths, the so called 'Blood Tubs' and various other establishments where boxing and boxers flourished.

British Middleweight Champion

1933 would prove to be McAvoy's most successful to date as far as his fistic ambitions were concerned. When the year started he fully intended in philosophical fashion to sweep aside all opposition who dared to block his way to championships and the money he so badly wanted. It was now becoming increasingly difficult for Harry Fleming to secure worthy opponents for the dynamite punching Northerner. January and February would find McAvoy in action four times. In January at Belle Vue, Glen Moody, brother of Frank, who was a former middle and cruiserweight champion of Great Britain, was matched with Jock in a 15 rounder. Mac was in whirlwind style and practically thrashed the game Welshman out of sight, dropping him frequently before the referee stopped the slaughter in round six with Moody staggering and in no condition to defend himself. At a later date, Moody would become one of McAvoy's sparring partners. At the N.S.B. in Royton, three weeks after the Moody fight Mac opposed Les Ward from Woking, and was again fighting like a typhoon, the result being that Ward was counted out in round six.

Red Pullen was a remarkable character. Born in Mountain Ash in South Wales in 1904, he had his first professional contest in 1924 stopping Dai Thornton in five rounds. From then up to 1946 when he had his last contest it was estimated by record compilers, that he had between 280 to 350 professional bouts. At one stage he was studying to become a doctor, but he never completed his studies. During his long career he fought every fighter of note and never turned a fight down. When he was asked if he fancied boxing McAvoy again in Blackburn, he jumped at the opportunity. He told his manager he had been waiting for the chance to prove his one round knockout defeat to Mac twelve months before happened because he took the fight at short notice. This time, he said, he was ready for McAvoy and fancied his chances to turn the tables on his conqueror. A week after demolishing Les Ward, Mac and Red Pullen faced each other again. This time Pullen lasted two rounds longer before being flattened again, this time, in the third round.

Belle Vue was the setting for his eight round battering of the tough Belgian fighter, Leonard Steyaert. This was a hard - fought thriller before Mac landed the knockout drops. On 10th April 1933, at the second attempt, Jock McAvoy became middleweight champion of Great Britain and the British Empire by winning a close but deserved points verdict over Len Harvey in a 15 rounder at Belle Vue. A detailed account of this key contest in McAvoy's career can be found in the special chapter dealing with the great Len Harvey. After beating Harvey and becoming British champion, McAvoy became instantly recognised and his picture was forever appearing in the newspapers. He was a big-name celebrity and everybody seemed to want to know him. He loved the adulation and basked in the glory. But just over four weeks after gaining the title he was back in action. He started off in London, fighting at the famous venue known simply as the Ring that was in Blackfriars. It was a Sunday afternoon tournament and Mac was featured in a 15 round non-title fight with Jack Hyams. After a rather boring affair McAvoy was declared the winner. He badly wanted to impress the crowd in his first contest since becoming champion but he seemed rather lethargic, though it must be said that Hyams was a cute, defensively minded scrapper.

His next outing was once again in London, this time Olympia, only a month after the Hyams bout. McAvoy's stablemate, Jackie Brown was defending his world flyweight crown against Valentine Angelelmann, of France, Brown winning a brilliant battle. Johnny King brought the British Empire bantamweight title back to Manchester when he clearly outpointed the Canadian, Bobby Leitham, over fifteen rounds. Also on this spectacular all star bill was Panama Al Brown, plus Len Harvey boxing Eddie Phillips for the vacant British cruiserweight championship, Harvey becoming the new champion. McAvoy fought a 10 rounder against Oddone Piazza, the Italian middleweight king. Piazza, was a tall, superb well-conditioned fighter. He took Mac the full ten rounds and had the satisfaction of actually decking the British champion for a brief count of three. McAvoy's greater variety and punch rate saw him a clear victor, but it had been a hard contest. This certainly wasn't championship form.

About this time, McAvoy's behaviour outside the ring was a credit to him. He would turn up at charity functions, fund raising events etc. He was on time, always immaculately dressed, and came across as a sort of unofficial ambassador for his sport. Also, unlike other periods in his life, there were not any adverse newspaper stories about him, and many people were wondering if McAvoy's fiery rage had quelled, or whether he'd ceased to burn on all cylinders. Was the violent moodiness in him extinct or merely dormant? Many sceptics wondered if his temperament had been not a blight on him as a private person and brilliant fighter, but in

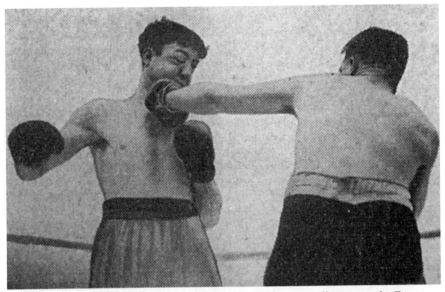

"My right eye closed up as tight as a drum and began to swell enormously. For a moment I thought I had been hit by a bar of iron..." A close-up of the Jock McAvoy–Teddy Phillips fight, when things looked bad for McAvoy (left).

reality a necessary fuelling of it. Had he turned over a new leaf? Was it possible for a leopard to change it's spots? Instead of his usual truculent self, he seemed calm and relaxed and at ease with people. Many put his attitude down to his status as a British champion. Well, it must be said that those close to him were sceptical about his current spate of saintliness. "I wouldn't bet a penny on his behaviour," said an old time fighter. "He's a very strange fellow, he always has been. I'm surprised he's kept out of trouble for so long. Maybe he's settled down to being a family man." If it all seemed a tad churlish it's worth remembering that Mac had not, in the past behaved with dignity. However, the serenity surrounding McAvoy was about to come to a stormy conclusion as we will see.

McAvoy's third outing since becoming champion was scheduled for Belle Vue Speedway Stadium, on a bumper open-air world championship tournament in which his pal and stablemate, Johnny King was fighting the near six foot Panama Al Brown. It was suggested that Clemente Meroni, who had recently beaten McAvoy's last victim, Oddone Piazza, taking the latter's Italian middleweight crown while doing so, should be his opponent. After a while, Mac's truculent

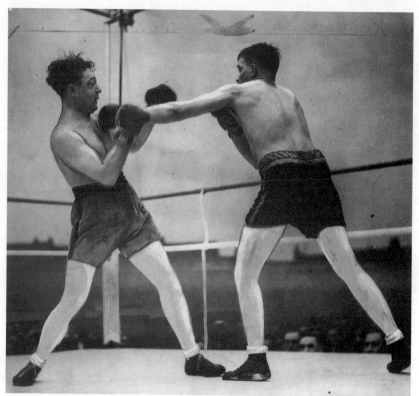

Look at McAvoy's right eye and bruised face as the big Canadian throws a long left jab,
McAvoy was almost blind.

behaviour surfaced once again. It appears that the newspapers had been misled
when they wrote that the British champion had withdrawn from his fight with the
new Italian middleweight champion, Meroni, supposedly because he was suffering from an outbreak of boils under his arm. Archie Sexton, his next designated
challenger for the title, took McAvoy's place on the Belle Vue bill.

The real reason for McAvoy's non-appearance was not because he was suffering
with any illness, but rather because he was not happy with the purse offered him.
It seems that Mac decided that he wasn't content with the money on offer and
withdrew less than twenty-four hours before the tournament took place. There was
a bit of friction between himself and Harry Fleming concerning the money and the
manner in which McAvoy pulled out of the fight at a late stage. Eventually things

must have been ironed out, and McAvoy was back in action four weeks later when he out boxed his old opponent, George Brown, the tough-as-teak East End fighter over the 12 round distance.

His three contests since defeating Len Harvey had proven something of a huge disappointment to the newspaper reporters and fans alike. Mac's forte was thunderous knockouts, not boringly fought full distance fights. It seems on the surface that becoming champion, being feted and treated like royalty had most certainly gone to his head. He would have to be back at his best form when defending his crown against the highly fancied Archie Sexton. Archie had good fighting credentials, and his father Jimmy, had been a tough bare-knuckle fighter. Later on Archie's son Dave became a famous football manager, and managed Manchester United for a spell.

Archie was a very good fighter in his own right, and he had built up a formidable record over the years. And though he had suffered a knockout defeat at the hands of the Sunderland Assassin, Jack Casey, the Londoner had strung together a very creditable record of victories and had, in fact, reversed his loss by beating Casey in a return. At this period, Sexton had fought in the region of 174 fights, losing only twelve times. Much more impressive, though, were the 84 knockouts he had registered. He was an exceptional boxer and was managed by Johnny Sharpe, a cunning and experienced pilot. Sharpe had waged a fierce battle with Boxing Board officials and the press to secure this title fight for his boxer. Sharpe had posters printed that said: "Why won't Jock McAvoy meet Archie Sexton?"

The fight was signed and set for Belle Vue, on 9th October 1933. McAvoy set up a training camp at the popular camping and holiday resort at Hollingworth Lake Country Park, which was just outside Rochdale on the Lancashire and Yorkshire border. It was situated in beautiful countryside up in the Pennines. It was the ideal location for training quarters, something similar to what the top American fighters were accustomed to having as a training base. In fact one would have thought they were in America as they drove carefully along the narrow paths that bordered Hollingworth Lake leading to the Lake Hotel. The manager and staff at the hotel looked after the fighters every need and whim, and everything was in fact excellent. His sparring partners, Paul Schaeffer, a Canadian middleweight, Fred Shipley, Glen Moody and Jack Lord, all lived together in the hotel at the lake. McAvoy knew in his heart that the adulation he had been receiving since becoming champion would soon cease if his performances were not of a higher standard than his recent previous three encounters. With this in mind he trained like a demented demon. He did his roadwork around the lake and up the hills, then down the country lanes. He punched the bags with extra venom, did his floor exercises and would then dive in the lake for a quick swim. Afterwards, Jack Bates would usually soothe out his aches and pains with a brisk massage.

When not training Mac went on the moors shooting duck, rabbit and snipe. He would often saddle a horse and go for a ride down the country roads. One day while out riding he was passing a little public house, when a big burly fellow who was working on the pub roof threw a spade to the ground which landed making a loud noise. Mac's horse, frightened, reared up on its hind legs and it took all of McAvoy's strength to control the animal and calm it down. Upon hearing the commotion the pub regulars dashed outside to see what was happening. Mac, red faced and angry, shouted abusive language at the workman calling him a stupid so and so. The workman answered him back, and within no time at all he had made his way from the roof to the ground, "Do you know who I am?" shouted McAvoy. "No I don't, and I don't effing care who you are either," replied the worker. After a further exchange of insults, McAvoy dismounted and within seconds the two men were going at each other like two fighting bantams. The landlord of the pub, with help from customers, stopped the two men from knocking seven bells out of each other. The workman wanted to continue the battle and had apparently given a good account of himself in the fracas. Mac himself was all for carrying on the fisticuffs, but he was calmed down by the landlord who pointed out the risk and bad publicity involved. This was another irresponsible act on the part of McAvoy, putting himself at the risk of injury and also jeopardising the Belle Vue show.

Hundreds of people visited the lake every day to watch McAvoy do his training. He would regularly row around the vast lake. The temporary gymnasium had been erected in the hotel's ballroom and cafe. There were newspaper reports that Mac was emulating Greta Garbo, with his distaste for the large crowds, but Harry Fleming chuckled when hearing this. The crowds were paying twopence admission to watch him train, and every session saw the place bursting to capacity. The hotel management was delighted. One day while training, Norman Hurst called to visit the McAvoy camp and while having some lunch he told McAvoy that he had been down to Shoeburyness in Kent, to watch Archie Sexton training. Mac wasn't in the least interested to know anything about Sexton's progress other than to know he would be there on the night of the fight. But Harry Fleming and Jack Bates were very interested in the journalist's observations regarding Sexton's con-

"The blow lifted Teddy off his feet and hurled him accross the bottom rope, where he lay like a dead man.." McAvoy has triumphed over a severe handicap. Phillips takes the count.

dition and form. "He looked fit and as sharp as a tack," Hurst told them. "I saw him sparring and he seemed to be working on speed more than anything else," Hurst concluded. McAvoy never uttered a word as he carried on eating.

Sexton had been receiving favourable reports from the southern press and they had tipped him strongly to beat the northern fighter. Archie did indeed look impressive in his gym workouts. Sam Carter, mine host of the Shoeburyness Hotel, where the Sexton party were staying and training, had sent word up to Manchester that he was coming up north a couple of days before the fight and was prepared to wager heavily on Sexton if anybody fancied having a bet. Archie was sparring with the clever Mile End welterweight, Moe Moss. Red Pullen one of Mac's former opponents was also getting him sharp, as was Laurie Raiteri. Raiteri was a light-heavyweight. "Make no mistake," Sexton had told Hurst on his visit. "I will beat McAvoy and bring the middleweight title back to London." This conclusion was also the view of Sexton's enthusiastic trainer, Whitey Buckingham.

Mac was in no mood for a long distance bout and intended to go for a knockout over Sexton as quickly as possible. As the days passed Mac became ever more irritable and nastier, and his moaning grew noticeably louder. Everyone in the camp kept a low profile when he was around. Most of his spare time was spent in his room listening to his collection of gramophone records. Larry Hoey, who was a personal friend of world champion, Jackie Brown, and who knew McAvoy quite well through Brown, happened to be convalescing at Hollingworth Lake. His doctor had advised him to get some bracing fresh air and go for long country walks, so Larry had booked into the hotel for a week. He struck up a friendship with Moody, Shaw and Lord. And when Jackie Brown drove up to visit him and watch McAvoy work out, they would all have a drink after the training session was completed. McAvoy, of course, didn't join in.

One morning at about eleven o' clock, Larry was sitting having a cup of tea with the three sparring partners when suddenly McAvoy appeared in the doorway of the dining room. He was unsmiling as always, and looking his usual glum self. He shouted over to the sparring partners that he would not be doing any sparring that day. Relief was etched on the faces of all three men. Moody liked his pint of ale and told Larry Hoey that he would now settle back and relax and have a drink or two with him. Later, when the bar opened, the four men downed quite a few jars. Just as they were having a laugh and enjoying their drink, Mac walked into the bar and announced that he had changed his mind and would be sparring after all, in an hour's time he added. With that he turned on his heels and strode back to his room to get his training togs on.

The men were upset at Mac's change of plans and the laughing turned into a chorus of complaints. Hoey told the fighters to go and talk to McAvoy and explain to him that though they certainly were not drunk, they had supped quite a few pints and would it be possible to leave the sparring for that day. Of course, they all realised that this wasn't worth the insults they would receive so they all left and went for a cold shower to freshen up before going into the gym. Larry felt a little guilty about the situation, having invited the fighters to share a drink with him. They obviously needed the money McAvoy was paying them otherwise they wouldn't have been there in the first place. Larry went in search of Harry Fleming or Jack Bates, but they had gone back to Manchester after Mac had announced he wasn't training that day. He ventured into the gym where McAvoy was doing some stretching. The surly looking champion looked at Hoey and without saying a word, went to his bag and pulled out a stopwatch which he handed Larry, telling him to stand on the ring apron and time the rounds. "Don't forget," said McAvoy in a menacing tone. "You start and stop after three minutes have been completed. Do you understand?" Larry had done time keeping many times in the Collyhurst gym so he knew what was required, but just nodded his head in agreement.

As the sparring commenced Moody was the first one to oppose Mac. He started very well and was catching the champion with stiff left jabs while evading Mac's swings. In the following round McAvoy seemed extra zealous and was soon throwing bombs at the Welshman. He seemed to be concentrating on body punches. It soon became clear why, and poor old Moody was soon feeling the effects, especially after the drinks he had consumed a little earlier. On seeing Moody was going to vomit, Hoey hurriedly called time. With that, McAvoy rushed across to where he was standing holding the stopwatch. "I want three fucking minutes," he screamed at Larry. "Don't you get bleeding cocky with me, or I'll fucking crack you." With this, Larry decided that he would not take any more insults and placed the watch on the canvas and walked out. McAvoy was raging and shouted obscenities after him.

"I was sickened by what he did to those poor fellows, especially Moody. He purposely hit them in the stomach. After the sparring Moody was violently sick and later he packed his clothes and left the hotel. McAvoy was a great, great fighter, the best, but he was also a nasty piece of work."

On the day of the fight Manchester was a hive of activity. Hundreds of London fans descended on the Cotton City in search of somewhere to lay bets on their man. Inside Belle Vue the weigh-in was attended by an unusually large crowd, including Jimmy Wilde, Johnny King and Jackie Brown. Mac looked superb. He was deeply tanned by his outdoor life at Hollingworth Lake. "I'm in wonderful fettle," he told his companions. Sexton looked edgy and apprehensive but admitted to a reporter from the Manchester Evening Chronicle, "I know I'm up against a tough proposition," but added: "I'm feeling fine, and I think I shall win the fight." However, he didn't make these statements with any conviction.

Dave Lumiansky arrived in Manchester for the fight and announced to one and all, that due to closer co-operation between himself and Jeff Dickson, the American promoter who was based in France, this had opened up new possibilities for British boxers. He added that McAvoy would soon be matched with Marcel Thil. He also said that if Mac performed well against Sexton, then there was every possibility that he could fight Lou Brouillard, who was recognised by the New York boxing authorities as middleweight champion of the world. When McAvoy was told what Lumiansky had said, he gave no hint of what he was thinking.

Belle Vue was a hub of expectancy on the night of the contest and both fighters were primed for action. The crowd in the King's Hall, though not a full house by any means, numbered about six thousand spectators. They were looking forward to seeing the rip-roaring Rochdale Thunderbolt blasting away from the sound of the first bell, and with Sexton also being a big hitter, they were justified in thinking they were in for a treat of dynamic fisticuffs. However, once the contest got going, instead of fireworks, the spectators saw both fighters hesitant and waiting to counter-punch each other. Instead of watching a battle of big punchers, the fans were watching a battle of wits.

The general consensus of opinion throughout boxing is that the challenger has to go and take the title from the champion. Sexton, for reasons known only to himself, did not seem prepared to do this. McAvoy decided that if he himself didn't do something, this fight was destined to go the full fifteen round distance. He attacked with both hands, but the Bethnal Green fighter tucked his chin down and frustrated the champion in his attempts to make this a slugging match. Sexton looked as if he was worried about the power of Mac's punches, and attempted to keep the fight at long range, and whenever the Rochdale fighter looked dangerous, Archie would wrap his arms around him in a clinch. There was murmurs of dissent among the throng of spectators who wanted action.

Each round saw McAvoy trying his hardest to prise open the Londoner's tight defence, all to no avail. It wasn't the champions fault that the fight was turning out to be boring. After all, he was the champion, surely it was down to Sexton to go after the championship he was fighting for. McAvoy, however, was out of range with most of his heavy artillery, though it has to be said that he was the only one who was trying to give the audience some excitement for their entrance fee. When Archie used his left jab he stung Mac, and these punches forced a cut to open over the champions right eye. Sexton's own left eye was swollen badly, yet still this didn't make the challenger throw caution to the wind and fire his own knockout wallops. The fans were feeling dejected as the ninth round opened and was similar to the rest of the rounds, with Sexton in his defensive shell and Mac wailing away but not being able to break through Sexton's armour.

In sport, especially boxing, and as sometimes in life, a boring event can be transcended by a moment so sweet, so unexpected that it seemed preordained. Such a moment came in the tenth round of this contest between the Rochdale Thunderbolt and his London rival. The tenth round saw Mac tear out of his corner annoyed, and he bobbed and weaved his way forward and attached his man with renewed fury. Archie rode the punches, and fired a missile of a right cross which smacked against McAvoy's chin with a rasp. The crowd stood, fully expecting the champion to tumble as it had been the best punch either fighter had connected with all night. Jock was hurt, and hurt badly, and had Sexton stepped in and threw another punch he could possibly have gone back to London with the middleweight crown, yet amazingly, he didn't. McAvoy shook his head and set up a blistering attack of his own. Sexton had a look of disbelief at McAvoy's aggression after taking that hefty right hander. Mac forced him against the ropes, this being where he wanted the challenger to be. He bit down on his gumshield and set about Sexton with a furious assault, and this was what the fans wanted, excitement. Terrific body punches doubled Archie in two, and in a split second, McAvoy threw his favourite punch, a right uppercut. All his weight was behind this punch and it hit Sexton flush on the chin. He was out the moment the punch landed, falling to his knees, and then hitting the floor face first where he lay motionless until the referee Mr C. B. Thomas, counted him out. He was hurt badly and was helped back to his corner where Dr Graham gave him medical attention.

The final moments of the fight would be remembered forever by those who were in the King's Hall. When McAvoy's punch ripped through Sexton's guard and the game cockney fell to the floor, Mac immediately went to a neutral corner. Sexton was by this time spreadeagled full length on the canvas with his arms straight out above his head, and Mr Thomas, in dinner suit and bow tie, was counting him out. If anyone had not have known what had happened they could have been forgiven for thinking the Londoner was demonstrating a diving position in the swimming baths. It was an amazing scene. All in all, it had been a very disappointing fight. Although McAvoy had in fact delivered the finish his fans wanted, and did it superbly. He also gained a second notch on the prestigious Lonsdale belt. He was pleased with the ending but knew he hadn't been seen at his best. Why on earth Sexton chose such tactics only he knew, but he certainly did not do himself justice by his ultra negative showing. He had the power to trouble the champion, the boxing skill to make openings, but he failed miserably to entertain.

"They will tell you that McAvoy won by a right uppercut. But he didn't, he won by a series of terrific body blows, culminating in an enormous punch that would have staggered a rhinoceros. The uppercut was just the finisher," wrote Normad in the Manchester Evening Chronicle.

*Top: "See the conquering hero comes" Jock McAvoy amongst the boys at Buckley Hall.
Below: McAvoy in a publicity photograph for a Baby Car in 1935.*

McAvoy sat drinking grapefruit juice in his dressing room when he was asked for his observations: "I wasn't troubled by one punch all through the fight. That punch (uppercut) was a good one, but not as good as some that landed before. Mr Thomas could have counted all night and Sexton would not have got up."

"It was never a fight. Sexton could not withstand the punishment, it was the most one sided championship fight I have ever seen. The Southern critics who voted almost solidly for a victory for Sexton before the fight, had no excuse to offer," added Nomad.

Some reporters talking to Jack Madden the matchmaker remarked that they had never seen McAvoy look so lively with his footwork and so accurate with his left jab. Madden told them that in his opinion the reason for this was because McAvoy left his Collyhurst gym and the usual routine and gone into a training camp. "Getting away from everything is the finest thing possible for a boxer," added Madden.

The Hollingworth Lake training centre played a big part in the future preparations of McAvoy, Jackie Brown, Johnny King and Johnny 'Nipper' Cusick. In that period the working class did not own cars, travel was by tram, train or charabanc. Hollingworth had its own station and when the Collyhurst team were training at the lake especially in the summer months whole families would pack a picnic and catch a train to the lake. The Collyhurst boxing fraternity liked the peace and solitude of the place. In the summer months, Hollingworth, was awash with holiday makers and there were plenty of the fairer sex paying visits. Jack Bates and Harry Fleming had to have eyes in the back of their heads when the girls were around. The fighters were treated like film stars and were constantly besieged by autograph hunters.

Four weeks after defending his title Mac was back at one of his favourite venues, Royton, facing Jack Forster who hailed from Norwich. The Royton fans were in their seats early by the time McAvoy and the good-looking East Anglian made their way into the ring. The Royton fans had seen Mac stop or knock out in the region of 24 opponents at this arena and were fully expecting Forster to become number 25. They couldn't have been more wrong. For twelve rounds the Norwich boxer defied McAvoy to flatten him, and try as hard as he could, Mac never looked like doing it inside the distance. Many have claimed that coming too soon after the title defence against Archie Sexton, and therefore McAvoy wasn't really 'up for it.' This is absolute nonsense. Mac always entered the ring in perfect fighting condition. Yes, it was true, he always expected to win and do it as quickly as possible if he could. But as he himself always said: "I never go into any fight looking for a knockout. I go in to win, if a knockout comes, all well and good. But my first priority is to win the fight."

The McAvoy-Forster bout turned out to be a humdinger from start to finish. It was McAvoy on the attack and the Norwich lad doing the neater boxing. Mac delivered tremendous sledge-hammer blows that caught Jack on the head and body. Lesser men had succumbed from such a bombardment, but Forster took everything the Rochdale man dished out and came back for more. The Royton fans, from thinking Forster was a 'cake walk' for Mac, now cheered the courageous boxer from East Anglia.

I digress once again. In the early 1950s, Jack Bates had a little gym at the side of Harry the Barber's shop in Collyhurst. McAvoy was a regular visitor. One day after training had ended, Mac, Bates, Tommy Fynan, and a few others sat having a cup of tea and the conversation got around to Mac's career. He was asked who his toughest opponent was? Bates smiled. He knew what Mac was going to say. Would it be Len Harvey, Cast Iron Casey, Joe Rostron, Marcel Thil, or some other well known name? Without a moments hesitation McAvoy blurted out: "A fellow named Jack Forster." A look of bewilderment came on the other people's faces. "Jack who?" They seemed to be saying to themselves. McAvoy sensing he had shocked them went on to explain what he meant. "You asked me who the toughest man I ever met in the ring and I'm telling you it was a fellow named Jack Forster, he was billed from Norwich but he came from Lowestoft, he was a man of iron. For twelve rounds I belted the life out of him without any visible effects. He was dead easy to hit, and by jove did I hit him, but he never gave any sign that he was hurt. As for sticking him on the boards or knocking him out that was well nigh impossible. I often wondered whether anyone ever achieved the feat. I know I couldn't. He was no fool when it came to skillful boxing too, and many of my attacks were broken up by his left jab. He knew how to use the centre of the ring and he was a master at clinching when I got close in."

Mac was asked by Andy Lambert, a young featherweight: "Did you give him plenty to the bread basket (the body)?" "I butchered him with continuous body assaults," answered Mac. "The punches I caught him with to the body would have finished off most men. In the fourth round I swore to myself that the fight was all over. I hit him with a hard right to the chin, it sent him reeling into the ropes, but to my surprise he bounced off them a stuck a long left jab into my face and boxed his way out of further danger. Christ, he was clever. At the finish I had won by a mile, but Forster received tremendous applause for his game showing and because he had stood up the best punches I could deliver without wilting. He must have had armour plated for his body. In terms of durability and physical condition Jack Forster took the biscuit and I take my hat off to him."

Mac went on to say that when he reached the top everybody seemed to expect him to fight like a superman all the time. If he won quickly the knockers said the other man must have been a 'mug' and if he only managed to win on points they used to tell everyone he was slipping. What the critics and fans didn't seem to appreciate he said was that when he was a champion and fought a non-title fight, his opponent instinctively tried that little bit harder and put on his best performance. They knew, said Mac of his opponents, that a lucky opening and the right brand of punch could make them a huge attraction overnight. "A lot of men I fought before I became a champion were fighters of an entirely different calibre when I opposed them after I became a title holder," he said. "You see, they had nothing to lose, and everything to gain."

"Ready to unleash a two handed attack". McAvoy punishing Burke on his way to keeping the Lonsdale Belt.

The Terror Of The Middleweights

McAvoy's first fight of his 1934 campaign was at Belle Vue against Eddie Peirce, a South African boxer. Peirce was a cagey type of fighter who had defeated Manchester's un-crowned champion, Len Johnson, who was barred from contesting a British title because of his colour. The South African set out to merely contain McAvoy and was warned on several occasions by a very lenient referee for holding and wrestling. Mac won quite clearly on points after twelve rounds, but it was a stinker of a fight.

McAvoy's next outing was about four weeks later in London. His opponent was Al Burke, real name Edward Pearce and born in Shepherds Bush, London, but had emigrated to Australia as a teenager. He had won the Australian welterweight title and decided to head back for London and pursue his career among the British middleweights. Burke had been quite successful since arriving back in England. On meeting Burke at the weigh-in, Mac couldn't fail to notice his opponent's prominent nose. "His nose rivalled that of Jimmy Durante's, and my knuckles itched to punch it then and there," said a smiling McAvoy.

The Burke versus McAvoy match was the featured top of the bill encounter for a charity tournament at the Royal Albert Hall. After a tame opening, it turned out to be a cracking good fight for the fans to watch. At the start of the contest, the transplanted "Aussie" had no intention of slugging it out with the Rochdale fighter and began boxing on the retreat, from the moment the gong sounded for the first round. Though disappointed at the tedious display of Burke, the Cockney fight followers were thrilled at the way McAvoy tore after his man, and they were striking up bets on how long it would take Mac to nail his elusive foe. Burke stood head and shoulders above the dangerous Rochdale man and he made his intentions quite clear as round followed round, and that was, that he was sticking to long-range boxing and moving in all directions away from Mac. For all this, it was an interesting contest.

By the time round five arrived Burke had gained a measure of confidence, due mainly because he had made McAvoy miss on a number of occasions, though it could be said that Mac had become a little weary of chasing after his man. Urged on by the vast crowd, the Aussie grew in confidence and foolishly decided to fight McAvoy instead of electing to stick to his boxing from long-range. The Collyhurst corner could see that this suited Mac, and within seconds he smashed a fearful, pole axing right cross into Burke's face. The Australian champion grabbed hold of McAvoy in a vice-like grip and it took the referee all his power to pull him off the Lancashire fighter, who was using his head, elbows, hands and anything else he could use in an effort to free himself. Mac knew he had hurt Burke and dazed him badly, and now he wanted to finish the job. When the two fighters finally broke free, Mac bobbed and weaved his way forward and, dipping down low, he brought a right uppercut through the middle of his opponent's guard which went like a torpedo and landed smack right on target, i.e. Burke's chin. What a punch! It lifted Burke off his feet and he landed with a resounding thud on his back. It was a chilling punch and amazingly, as the count reached nine, the valiant and courageous boxer was up and the referee ordered them to continue fighting.

The crowd were by now solidly behind this courageous Australian. Like McAvoy, they couldn't understand how on earth he had managed to beat the count after taking one of the best delivered and tremendously powerful punches they could ever remember being struck by any fighter. Mind you, as the two men met in the centre of the ring, you could have staked your house on the outcome. McAvoy was vicious, cold-eyed and like a shark which has tasted blood. There would certainly be no mercy from him and he tore after his opponent. Burke, though visibly distressed and tottering slightly, had the sense to keep his guard up high and his elbows close to his sides which made his defence hard to breach. Suddenly, like a flash, McAvoy delivered another bone jarring uppercut which once again went straight through the centre of Burke's tight defence, connecting right on target. The crowd gasped, and Burke hit the canvas like a sack of flour once more. What a game fighter he was, and he had everyone willing him to beat the count as he gamely attempted to get upright before the referee reached ten. As he got to his knees, however, he couldn't make it and fell face forward to be counted out.

"The first uppercut I hit Burke with was the most perfect punch I had ever delivered, of that variety. I brought it from my toes. As I waited in a neutral corner for the count to be given I said to myself: 'If he gets up after taking that punch, then he's a game 'un.' The second uppercut I hit him with, was also a perfect blow. He didn't know what hit him he went down as if poleaxed," said McAvoy.

In his dressing room later, Burke was still feeling light-headed, asked his seconds. "What hit me?"

After the devastating knockout of Al Burke, Mac had a few days off before going back into the gym for a contest at Belle Vue against another South African boxer, named Eddie McGuire. This South African though, was a true ring warrior, unlike his countryman, the reluctant, Eddie Peirce. Mac, delighted at his uppercutting in his last fight, worked in the gym with Jack Bates to perfect this awesome punch. He became an expert on this particular blow. In practice Bates, would put one of those big, heavy old sparring gloves on his hand, back to front. These were the days before more modern equipment like punch-pads were invented. Bates would throw a left jab and Jock would duck, roll, or bob and weave and come up throwing this uppercut. Poor old Jack Bates' palms would be tingling and his armpits would be sore for days after acting as shock absorbers for Mac's dynamic punches. Even while practising there were no such things as half measures with McAvoy. And if things were not working to his liking during his preparation he became unbearable. Other fighters and gym helpers kept well clear of him, as he was just as likely to lash out with a few back handers, and his tongue was every bit as nasty as his punches. He was very objectable at these times. Bates though, like Fleming, knew how to handle him when he was in these truculent moods.

The Manchester fans, who had come to love McAvoy's all-action brand of mayhem and dynamite punching power, were eager to see their favourite in action after his sensational victory in London. Right from the start of their fight, the brave South African took the initiative and went at Mac in determined fashion, throwing punches from every conceivable angle. This of course, suited the Rochdale banger and he engaged two-handed thunderous punches that would soon take effect. Some wag in the crowd said McGuire must have been "mad" for thinking he could stand and trade blow for blow with the Rochdale Thunderbolt, but that was precisely what he set out to do when he met McAvoy head on in the Belle Vue ring. It was quite clear that McGuire had no intention of being happy to merely survive the twelve round limit, he wanted to put a dent in McAvoy's record. He was shifty and clever, and though his punches carried power, he was rather foolish when he tried to match power with Jock. It soon became obvious that barring some unlikely event, this fight would not last too long.

The game South African cut Mac's left eye in the first round through a clash of heads. With blood seeping down his face, McAvoy was even fiercer than ever and he relished this toe to toe punch up. Just before the bell sounded to end the first round, Mac forced McGuire into a corner and, fighting like an infuriated bull, he let him have lefts and rights to the mid-section. These were vicious punches that found their target and brought a pained expression to Eddie's face. The crowd were yelling and banging their feet while thoroughly enjoying this slugfest of a contest and they had nothing but admiration for McGuire.

As the second round started, Mac was first off his stool, and in his element in a battle like this. The hall was a bedlam of noise. What a start to the round as the South African swung a body punch which caught Jock coming in square-on, and a following right cross opened the eye wound again and soon had the claret streaming down McAvoy's face. Mac was firing back two-handed and soon McGuire's ear came up like a pumpkin. Eddie was now hurt and his legs slowly turning to jelly, he staggered into a corner, precisely where Jock wanted him. And after both fighters threw caution to the wind once again and exchanged punches, a tremendous right cross dazed McGuire and he fell back into the ropes. As he did, Mac swept a right uppercut whizzing through his tattered defence and it landed with a sickening bang on the game South African's chin. From the moment this blow landed, the fight was over. McGuire seemed to be paralysed for a split second, then he pitched forward as if he had been shot by a rifle and landed on the canvas with a mighty thud. Everyone in Belle Vue was up on their feet, as this was indeed a most wonderfully and clinically executed finish to a fight seen for a very long time. Equally, the crowd had nothing but admiration for a fighter who gave everything he had to offer and fought as gallant a fight as they had seen for many a long day.

The plucky invader had to be helped back to his changing room, and he was still bemused and shaking as he made his way out of the ring. Sitting on the rubbing table in his tiny quarters, McGuire was fingering his chin, and in agony from those rib-bending body punches. This was McAvoy at his finest. He was brilliant and breathtaking with his exciting swashbuckling fighting. It was no wonder thousands readily paid the ticket price to watch him perform. He was everything any fight fan could wish to see, and he certainly gave the public full value for their money.

There was a great deal of speculation in the newspapers about world championship matches for the middleweight title involving McAvoy, and the Belle Vue officials were also trying to manoeuvre Mac into a light-heavyweight title match as well.

In those times a fighter was gratified to get the chance to fight for an area title, let alone a British, European or World championship. For a fighter such as McAvoy, Len Harvey, Jack Casey and their like, weight divisions did not matter that much. They readily took whatever opportunities happened to come their way, and they were grateful for the chance. Though a genuine middleweight, McAvoy fought cruisers and even heavyweights. This sort of matching would certainly not be tolerated today and rightly so, but in McAvoy's day things were tough and extremely hard and top class fighters took on everybody put in front of them.

After disposing of McGuire, Mac was matched with what seemed on paper like a formidable task. Eddie Simmons, born in Dublin but living in Birmingham, was a highly respected opponent for anybody in the British Isles. A fully-fledged light heavyweight, this fellow could dish it out and take it with the best of them. Mac conceded a full stone in weight, and was out-reached as well as being much smaller in height to the Brummie based Irishman. The Belle Vue spectators were expecting fireworks. Simmons had beaten future heavy weight champion Tommy Farr and held two victories over "Cast-Iron" Casey, so he was certainly no slouch. But for all his reputation and his physical advantages, the big raw-boned Simmons did not seem to fancy the fight after sampling a few rockets early in round one. From then on, until the 12th and final round, it was all McAvoy. The referee was kept busy parting the two fighters. Mac was ready and willing to give the fans a fight, but the Irishman appeared content to lose on points. It was however a good feather in Mac's cap to have beaten this fully-fledged highly touted cruiserweight.

After the Simmons fight Mac took a break for a couple of weeks before going back into training. Once back in the Collyhurst gym, he went through his paces with his usual zest. He was by this time a well-known celebrity and hero-worshiped, especially in Manchester and Rochdale. He loved the adulation, and though often looking surly and ready to fly off the handle at the least thing that upset him, he loved the celebrity status he was now receiving wherever he went. He loved visiting pubs, clubs and dance halls with his little stablemate, Jackie Brown, the world flyweight champion. These two were known around Lancashire as a pair of 'rum' rascals. They were characters and 'men's men!'

There are fights that live in the memory when hundreds of others are forgotten. Some stand out because of the brilliant boxing skill displayed by one or both contestants - like the memorable duel between those two master craftsmen, Nel Tarleton of Liverpool, and Panama Al Brown, the bantamweight champion of the world, when every move was sheer boxing artistry. There are other contests like the Zale versus Graziano, Ali-Frazier affairs that will be remembered for the ferocity of the fighting, the thrilling, pulse-stirring action and the never-ending roaring of the crowd feverish with excitement. McAvoy's next fight would live in the memory of those people lucky enough to have witnessed it. Yes, if anybody ever doubted Jock McAvoy's ability as a world class fighter or his status as England's greatest ever middleweight, his display against the big Canadian light-heavyweight, Teddy Phillips, would most surely have convinced them. It was a fight much similar to the Zale versus Graziano epic encounters, the Boon versus Danaher and the first Kane versus Lynch fights or Rocky Marciano's first fight against Ezzard Charles. Full of valour, excitement, ringcraft, punching power and determination.

Teddy Phillips, accompanied by his brother Jackie, had arrived in England from Canada with a big reputation. Jackie was a good fighter but it was Teddy who was the undoubted star of the Phillips family. The Canadian press, were proclaiming him as a future world champion. He was a big, raw-boned light-heavyweight. Teddy had run up a very impressive record since he moved to this country from his home in Canada. Jimmy Wilde, the former world flyweight champion, was managing him. Wilde was so certain that he was handling a future world champion that he had ensured his man had been given reams of publicity in the national press. One opponent McAvoy and Phillips had in common was a fighter named Jock Porter. Porter had defied Mac's bombs for fifteen rounds to lose on points. Phillips though, annihilated Porter, leaving him stretched on the canvas out cold in one sensational round. Though Jimmy Wilde was proclaiming his protege's achievements long and loud to all and sundry, Phillips himself was not slow in telling the newspapers what he intended doing to the Rochdale Thunderbolt. "This fight will not go the distance," he told the press. "I'm too big; much too strong; and I punch equally as hard as McAvoy, and I'm tougher than him."

Leading up to the fight the Collyhurst gym was a hive of activity. Not only was Mac on this open-air promotion which instead of being staged in the King's Hall, would be in the Belle Vue Speedway Stadium, Jackie Brown was topping the bill, defending his world flyweight crown against the classy French boxer, Valentine Angelmann. Also fighting from the Collyhurst camp were Johnny King and young Paddy McGrath. The gym was buzzing with all the fighters preparing diligently for their respective forthcoming important contests. Tommy Fynan, besides helping train his brother Tony, who was of course, Jackie Brown's chief sparring partner, also helped Harry Fleming's other fighters. Tommy, like Jack Bates, was good at giving the lads a massage. After McAvoy completed a training session he asked Tommy to give him a rub down. While on the massage table Tommy casually told Jock some of the unsavoury quotes Phillips had made about him in the newspapers, McAvoy, sniffed, looked at Fynan disdainfully and said in a chilling voice: "Is that so?, well we will fucking well find out what this big mouthed Canadian bastard can do when that first bell sounds." Tommy said that McAvoy couldn't wait to get Phillips into the ring. "I told neighbours to try and get a bet on Mac to chin this Canadian lad. Though, I must confess that when I went to the weigh-in and saw how big and fit he looked, I was a bit concerned for Joe (McAvoy). Jimmy Wilde didn't handle mugs either, so this big kid Phillips must have been good. But Mac was the best fighter we had in this country. He had the lot, believe me."

It was a sensational fight, and one that will live in the memory of those who witnessed it. It was an occasion for fight fans to savour and remember until the day they died. It was exciting non-stop action throughout the entire time the fight lasted. The bout was scheduled for ten rounds, but there wasn't one person who thought that this contest would go the full distance. These two fighters hit each other with everything but the kitchen sink. They also hit each other with their heads, elbows, shoulders and at times, their knees. In a fairly even first round, the Canadian had Mac's nose bleeding profusely. The second saw both men land with stunning punches to both head and body. Phillips, after being shaken rigid by one of McAvoy's attacks, rushed forward and caught the Rochdale fighter on his nose with a full-blooded head butt. It was an accident, but the damage had been done. Mac's right eye was swollen like a balloon and closed instantly. Later, McAvoy said he felt as if he had been hit with an iron bar. On seeing what damage he had inflicted, Teddy let fly with two-handed attacks. Most fighters would have retired then and there because of such an evident injury and been applauded by the crowd for acting sensibly. If it had happened today, the referee would have had no hesitation in calling a halt to the bout, but these were hard times, and McAvoy was allowed to continue fighting. "You wouldn't have given two bob for his chances," said Bert Daly who was sitting at ringside. "His face was like a pumpkin. The injury to his right eye was amazing, the upper lid was an abnormal size and was drawn down over the eye like a window blind. I've never seen a fighter before or since with such a frightening injury like Mac had on this occasion."

When McAvoy's hideous injury was spotted by the fans, there were loud cries for him to retire from the fight, and many spectators pleaded with the referee to stop it. Back in his corner, Jack Bates and Harry Fleming tried furiously to bring the swelling down but all to no avail. There was no let up in the melee: McAvoy was virtually blind, because his right eye was closed and his left eye was gradually becoming partially closed, and his face was swelling alarmingly yet he strived manfully to land a haymaker on the cocky Canadian. The spectators cringed and were sickened by the sight of their hero's features. Surely they thought, nothing was worth this, the fight must be stopped, every spectator around the ringside seemed to be saying. But the referee didn't seem too eager to call a halt so the Rochdale lad battled on, his fighting heart taking him above and beyond the call of duty. Phillips showed no mercy whatsoever and lashed out at every given opportunity. McAvoy's features were swelling with every passing second and his neck and chest were also swollen. How he managed to keep going under this extreme disadvantage only he himself knew. His fighting heart was most definitely put to the test in this bitterly fought out war of attrition he was waging with a fighter whose every advantage was highlighted even more clearly. McAvoy surged forward but was now having to leave himself more open to punishment because he had to turn his body more square in order to get some kind of view as to where Phillips was. The fans were by now almost hysterical and yelling their lungs out. Never before had any of this audience seen bravery to match what they were actually witnessing before their eyes.

As the rounds wore on the two fighters fought like tigers, never conceding an inch. Mac's face looked like he was wearing a mask from a horror movie so grotesque did he look. Between rounds Bates and Fleming pleaded with him to retire on his stool. The reply from the gallant but foolish fighter was unprintable. Tommy Fynan was situated in the McAvoy corner. "Every time Mac came back to the corner his eyes were put under what was obviously very painful first aid treatment. The crowd were yelling so loud and were so excited, I swear the ground was vibrating," he recalled. "I clearly heard Jack Bates tell Mac to call it a day. Bates was very concerned about the injury. But Mac muttered something that I couldn't quite hear, however, I clearly heard him say: 'If you stop it, I'll stop your fucking breath.' He didn't mean it of course, he was just hyped up and not wanting to lose a fight. Jack Bates shook his head. Whenever people tell me how great those Yanks were, I proudly tell them that they couldn't hold a candle to this fellow McAvoy."

"Mac was well ahead on points, but it looked as though he might eventually have to retire unless he could finish off his opponent with a knockout. As the rounds passed, Mac, fully realising the danger of his position, and showing wonderful pluck fought with a tigerish ferocity. I'll never forget how the crowd rose to their feet as Phillips under a battery of blows appeared to be on the verge of going down. However, the Canadian weathered the storm, frequently employing the old ruse of holding for a spell," said Norman Hurst.

So fiercely did the Rochdale lad fight that on quite a few occasions it looked as if the big Canadian would go down from the bombardment of blows being delivered by the half-blinded British champion. Ted Broadribb, known as "Young Snowball" in his fighting days, and who was then a very influential figure in the world of boxing beside acting as a manager and match-maker, ran round to McAvoy's corner during the interval for the sixth round. He pleaded with Bates and Fleming to concede defeat. Mac, came out with a mouthful of abuse and told Broadribb, who was a hard man himself on the cobbles, to mind his own business. "Don't be silly Jock, you could lose your bloody sight," As he walked back to his seat Broadribb was shaking his head but it was obvious that he had nothing but admiration for this man McAvoy!

During the rest period before the seventh round, Harry Fleming was ashen-faced and absolutely distraught, spectators were screaming abuse at him for not stopping the fight. He beseeched Mac to call it a day. The referee came to the corner, took a look, and amazingly walked back to his neutral corner to await the bell to start round seven. "I'll catch the bastard in this round, you'll see," shouted McAvoy. Fleming, beside himself with concern for his fighters welfare, was about to throw the towel into the ring when McAvoy rushed off his stool and tore into the surprised Phillips. The first few punches missed the Canadian and Mac knew in order to land the finisher he would have to get very close to his opponent. It's an old axiom of boxing that a puncher is never beaten until the final bell rings. Hopeless though his chance of victory might seem, he cannot be dismissed while he's still on his feet and has one punch left. Many times throughout the history of boxing a final punch had turned apparently certain defeat into a sensational victory. And this was one of those glorious occasions.

The two fighters exchanged fire in the centre of the ring. Like Samson in the temple, who had to get between the two stone pillars to cause damage, so McAvoy groped after his prey. Jimmy Wilde was shouting furiously for his boxer to get off the ropes and keep his left jab working. As Phillips bounced off the ropes, McAvoy unleashed a terrific right hand punch, which found its mark instantly, while following through with a sizzling left hook. This was the mark of all great fighters from Jack Dempsey to Mike Tyson, the will to follow through with their punches. Teddy was now utterly dazed and bemused, and he was being battered to a stand-still. The last punch thrown was Mac's speciality, the uppercut. The punch was so powerful that it lifted the big Canadian off his feet and hurled him across the bottom rope, where he lay like a dead man. A terrific roar hit the air and a mad scramble for a better view took place. This really was unbelievable, it really was. The whole place was a bedlam. The shouts and yelling could be heard for miles around. Everyone in the Stadium, including Boxing Board officials, now stood up.

McAvoy looked a ghastly sight, his face was hideous, resembling an over-sized melon with his eyes no more than mere slits, was standing in a neutral corner biting away at his thumbs just in case he needed to add more punches, but it was all over. As the referee indicated the contest was over, Phillips was still lying prone, his body lying over the bottom rope with his legs inside the ring but his head hanging outside the ring, apparently out to the wide world. What a punch! What an amazing fight! The excitement of Mac's victory had, inevitably, intensified as each round passed. This fight took the spectators through the whole gamut of big fight emotions, it left fans and boxing officials exhausted and exhilarated at the same time. The Canadian had proved a tough fighter and gave McAvoy much more punishment than it was usual for him to receive. However, it would have been a pity if Phillips had won the fight through Mac having to retire on account of his injuries.

The scenes that followed this truly remarkable victory were only matched by the occasion when Winston Churchill made his announcement that the war had ended. Jimmy Wilde could not believe what had happened to his fighter, but applauded the Rochdale man. He knew that Mac had beaten all the odds and pulled off a victory that only the great, great fighters were capable of achieving. In his dressing room, ice was applied to McAvoy's face and Doctor Graham worked hard to bring the swelling down. Though deliriously happy at the ending of such an unforgettable encounter, the Collyhurst team, nevertheless were concerned about Mac's injuries. Dr Graham ordered him to be taken to Manchester Royal Infirmary. "Good gracious me," said the doctor, while examining the grotesque looking McAvoy as he lay on the treatment table in the hospital. "If you're the winner, what does the other chap look like?" Later McAvoy was transferred to the Jewish Hospital in Cheetham Hill, Manchester, where he spent over a week receiving medical attention. It seemed that when he was butted on the nose he contracted emphysema. The doctor explained that emphysema means that when a bone in the nose is badly damaged, the breathing passage allows air into the nose, the face and neck regions become swollen.

Doctor Graham, talking later to reporters about Mac's injury, said: "The injury McAvoy sustained, was a very rare occurrence and after a few days everything will go back to normal." But he added: "In all my years as a doctor I have never seen a boxer continue to fight on with such a handicap, let alone go forward to knock out his opponent in the manner Jock McAvoy managed to accomplish over Teddy Phillips."

"This fight was fought under the tensest of excitement," remarked Paddy McGrath. "The end came with dramatic suddenness in that eighth round. Driving Phillips towards the ropes, Mac, landed with a powerful right to the jaw, followed by a left hook that in itself signalled the end. The Canadian was unconscious and had to be carried back to his corner and he was still in a very bad condition when he left the ring, over five minutes later. He was a tough opponent."

McAvoy's last fight of 1934 was on the 3rd December and it was another humdinger in every respect. Matched against the teak-tough and classy Cuban stylist, Kid Tunero, at the King's Hall, Belle Vue, Mac gave the huge sell-out audience another fight that they would talk about for years afterwards. It was a contest that had everything that makes boxing such a spectacular event: contrasting styles, nail-biting excitement, high drama, and a never-to-be-forgotten conclusion. Mac's popularity with the Lancashire fight fans was at its zenith. He came into this fight with Tunero by virtue of two cracking one round victories. More about this fight later.

After the Phillips encounter Jock had gone to Blackpool in order to recuperate. He loved walking along the beach breathing the fresh air and when he returned to the Collyhurst gym he was ready for action. Harry Fleming and Jack Bates had scoured the length and breadth of the British Isles to get him sparring partners. Jock's first fight back was against Mansfield's Battling Charlie Parkin, who considered himself the uncrowned middleweight champion of the North, and a fighter who really fancied his chances of upsetting the Rochdale man after Mac's war with Teddy Phillips. Parkin was one of those very underrated boxers whose record did not do them justice, though he had defeated Jack Hyams the crafty Cockney middleweight. Charlie did eventually become Northern Area champion at middleweight. He brought quite a lot of support to Manchester and both fighters were in the pink of condition. It was, however, less than eight weeks since the Phillips fight, and many observers were questioning why Mac was fighting so soon after suffering such terrible facial damage. Surely he should have been advised to rest for a longer period of time. But the name of the game was fighting and so Mac continued his march toward a world championship.

When Mac made his way toward the ring the crowd rose and applauded him with relish. They had not forgotten his fierce contest in his previous Belle Vue appearance a couple of months before. The crowd were anxious to see if the battle against Phillips had taken anything out of McAvoy. When the fight got underway the Mansfield fighter took the fight to his opponent, and this suited Mac perfectly. Using a snappy left jab Mac was sizing his man up, and suddenly when Charlie came in range, McAvoy pounced and sent a direct left hook to Parkin's unprotected jaw-this punch turning his toenails upwards. Mac then hit Parkin's chin with two bone-crunching right hands which toppled him immediately to the floor. These were short, powerful right smashes and brought gasps from the spectators.

As game as they come, Charlie was upright at nine, but he was soon in an horizontal position again after Mac feinted him then quickly dispatched a right cross which landed with a resounding thud just under Parkin's heart. The Mansfield man fell face downwards to the canvas and, although he tried to regain his senses, he lapsed into oblivion again with little chance of beating the count. It was indeed a dramatic finish and the crowd acclaimed McAvoy like a king. Unconcerned that the fight had not lasted three minutes, they had witnessed another ferocious knockout and were quite satisfied. Poor Charlie had to be helped to his corner.

Around this time McAvoy had become the landlord of a public house in the centre of Rochdale named the Brunswick Hotel. Being a pub landlord in those days was looked on as a prosperous and highly responsible occupation with a certain level of VIP status attached to it. Jock really fancied himself in this role of importance, and also as a businessman, and he appeared regularly behind the bar wearing his shirt and tie and garters around his arms. His family had moved into the pub with him. He had three children now, and besides his first child, Joe, he had John (known as Jackie) and a daughter named Leonora. A landlord needs to be a mixer in the social sense, having a laugh and joke with his customers while keeping order on the premises. But if ever a person was ill equipped for such a role it must surely have been McAvoy. He was completely devoid of any sense of humour. He was fond of barking out orders to the bar staff, who would screw up their faces at his sharp tongue, but they knew better than to answer him back. Now, of all the lines of business to be in, being a pub landlord would have to go down as the worst possible venture for the volatile-tempered fighter to have.

Word soon spread back in Manchester about Mac's new position. And it must be said that everybody from the Collyhurst area who knew him were slyly smirking to themselves, and the view was expressed by many that it wouldn't be too long before he would flatten somebody who fancied themselves after a few pints. Joe Burke, a regular 'watcher' in the Collyhurst gym and who knew McAvoy at first hand, smiled when talking about Mac's ill advised venture as a publican. "After he had been in the pub about three weeks, myself and a friend had a ride up to Rochdale and we called into the Brunswick Hotel. He was behind the bar when we entered the vault. Was he pleased to see us? Not really, but he hardly showed any emotion on any occasion. He was a miserable looking man at the best of times. My pal told me later that he expected Mac to pull our first drink gratis. He didn't know McAvoy like I did, he was a tight - fisted devil who wouldn't give a door a bang. There were a few rough diamonds in the vault and they respected him as the governor, but seemed very wary of him. He just didn't look right behind the bar. We were told that he had backhanded quite a number of undesirables and given them their ticket" (barred them from the premises).

One particular night Mac was not behind the bar, he was in fact upstairs listening to some new gramophone records he had acquired that day. Upon hearing loud noises coming from the bar downstairs and a great deal of bad language and listening to the bar staff trying desperately to evict a local well-known hard-case, Mac rushed downstairs and without questioning anyone he belted the fellow straight on the chin and put him spark out! Now this bloke was a huge fellow who had a reputation for violence, but this didn't bother McAvoy in the slightest. There were many other such instances during his tenure at the pub. Many times after hours, drunken fellows would shout up to his bedroom widow for Mac to come down and fight. They were never disappointed! Of all the business ventures he could have found for himself, being a pub landlord must rank as the worst possible occupation the volatile tempered fighter could have chosen.

While awaiting his next assignment, Mac challenged Len Harvey to a five-hundred-pound sidestake. Requesting that Harvey should put his light-heavyweight title up as the prize, Harvey expressed his interest but arguments over dates, venues and other matters saw this idea shelved. Meanwhile, Jack Madden, the Belle Vue matchmaker, was scouring the world for opposition to test the Rochdale

Thunderbolt. There was newspaper talk of matches against Len Harvey and even Jack Petersen, the British heavyweight champion. Even top American stars such as Mickey Walker, the former world middleweight champion were mentioned as possible opponents. Madden had even wired America and tried to get Teddy Yarosz who the Americans claimed was the new world middleweight champion after defeating Vince Dundee another American, for the NBA version of the world title. However, Marcel Thil was regarded as the real middleweight champion by most ruling authorities. Mac was ready and willing to fight anybody no matter how big or heavy. Madden though was in a quandary. He knew that in order to get the spectators flocking through the turnstiles they demanded to see McAvoy matched against genuine opposition otherwise they would probably not purchase a ticket from their hard-earned money. There was a great deal of speculation as to who the Rochdale man would fight. He was the punters' darling with his savage two-fisted attacking style of fighting.

After a lot of negotiating Madden settled for a return engagement for McAvoy with the Belgian light-heavyweight champion, Jack Etienne, who had gone the fifteen round distance with Jock two years previously. This Belgian was definitely no pushover, having beaten that great Manchester middleweight, Len Johnson. He had also held Marcel Thil to a draw and since his disputed points loss to McAvoy he had been undefeated. Word came from the Continent that Etienne was in superb condition and highly confident of reversing the decision against the British champion. If looks ever won a fight then the large Belgian was already a winner. He displayed a beautiful brown body and well muscled. Much taller and heavier than the Collyhurst based fighter, he was like an Adonis as he flexed his muscles in the corner of the Belle Vue ring. There were whispers going round the hall that Mac was in for a torrid time.

After the introductions were completed and the bell sounded, McAvoy flew at his foe and landed with a wicked left hook to the solar-plexus, then sustained a fierce two-handed combination of punches all to the Belgian champions body. After another right cross to the body saw Etienne wincing. Mac could be seen visibly balance off his toes, then leap up to smash home a left hook which landed with a crack on the side of his opponent's jaw. "I hit him that hard, I thought for a moment I must have broken his jaw," said McAvoy later. Down went Etienne in a heap. Somehow he managed to get to his feet, but stood with his both hands cupped towards his face expecting another blow to the chin. Mac went directly for the open spaces of his body and flayed away relentlessly. The brave Belgian straightened up and as he did, McAvoy was at him and sent a right hand straight into his unguarded stomach. This punch carried every ounce of Mac's body weight behind it and the big foreigner hit the deck wriggling in agony, his face contorted with pain. He was utterly incapable of beating the referee's count. The whole fight had lasted just seventy-one seconds. The crowd obviously spellbound by McAvoy's ferocious two-handed annihilation of this beautifully built Belgian, rose in acclaim. It was feared that Etienne had suffered broken ribs as he could hardly breathe, and Dr. Graham was attending to him. He was then rushed to hospital for x-rays to determine the extent of the damage. There could be no finer testimony to the immense power of McAvoy's punching than the execution of such a fine physical specimen as this Belgian boxer. McAvoy had proved his doubters wrong. Many were sceptical as to how he would perform after suffering such frightening injuries against Phillips. But this fellow was something else; he was completely different from normal fighters, he was one of the special ones.

Cuba's Kid v Rochdale's Thunderbolt

For the first time in many years the name of a British boxer was emblazoned across French newspapers. The boxer's name was Jock McAvoy. Critics in London and in Europe were a little fed up hearing the Lancashire newspapers calling McAvoy 'the uncrowned middleweight champion of the world'. They were saying that the Rochdale fighter should be matched with someone of real high class and see what would happen. But hadn't Jack Madden being trying desperately to get world class middleweights to cross gloves with him? However, when it became known that McAvoy was now actually matched with the classy, scientific Kid Tunero of Cuba, heads were being shaken. The general consensus of opinion was that this was one hurdle much too high for the Collyhurst trained fighter to surmount in his quest to become middleweight champion of the world. Kid Tunero, the Cuban middleweight, had a physique which every boxer dreams of owning. He was a beautiful physical specimen. The Cuban had done a lot of fighting in European rings and had in fact defeated world middleweight champion, Marcel Thil, in an over the weight 12-round contest. Later, Thil gave him a return with his world championship at stake. But over fifteen hard fought rounds the Frenchman was considered the winner on points, though there was really very little to choose between them.

Tunero was feted and treated like a hero when he arrived in Manchester and set up his training quarters at the Hulme Boxing Club. Hundreds of fans watched his workouts daily. Mancunians had never seen anything like this brilliant Cuban boxer with the ready smile. His amazing agility while sparring against Alf Smith, a London middleweight, Harry Evans of Salford and Harry Cheetham, a featherweight who he used for speed. The Cuban hardly took liberties though he had flattened a number of tough sparring partners when first arriving from Paris. He was a colourful character in more ways than one, the type who attracts good publicity, and who usually had something for the newspapers to print. After tremendous newspaper coverage and watching his training sessions in which Tunero was very impressive and looking awesome, the Lancashire fight followers were once again wondering if the Rochdale Thunderbolt could rise to the occasion and add Tunero's scalp to his belt. It seemed a mighty big task to undertake.

McAvoy, as always, was fully prepared for a tough fight. Tunero shrugged his square shoulders and a big grin lit up his dark face, when asked how he thought he would fare against McAvoy: "I have won 48 fights out of 52 and have never been knocked out. In fact, I have never taken a count. I will destroy McAvoy."

A few days before the contest, Belle Vue announced in the press that every ticket had been sold. It was a sell-out. Norman Hurst was rubbing his hands in anticipation of a battle royal. He told friends that he was impressed with Tunero's calm disposition. "This fellow is a subtle as a Greek lawyer," he remarked. "He has the speed of a featherweight, and is as cunning as a fox. This is going to be one heck of a fight."

Mac was in the best physical condition of his life. He had been sparring with two full sized heavyweights and a middleweight. People who had watched Kid Tunero train told McAvoy in an alarmed tone: "This fellow is electric." Mac gave them an icy stare and blurted out: "That's fine because he's due to receive some shock waves." Talking to Jack Bates after the weigh-in, Mac said: "I have fought some fine physical specimens of manhood in my time, but this fellow is tops in my opinion. The crowd are in for a terrific fight tonight."

When Kid Tunero, the chocolate coloured Cuban middleweight champion, slipped off his dressing gown in the Belle Vue ring, the sight of his wonderful physical development brought gasps of admiration from spectators. Tunero's body definition was like a bronze marble statue. It was inch perfect. And when he stood under the arc lights in the King's Hall ring for the introductions, he gave the stone-faced British fighter a big smile, showing a mouthful of gleaming white teeth. The seven thousand spectators who crowded into the venue all sensed that this was going to be a fight they would remember for a long, long time. The air was electric from the first moment these two faced each other, as the introductions were being made. The moment that the bell clanged to start the fight, the flashy Cuban boxer was up on his toes moving like a featherweight. He delivered three rapid-fire left jabs to McAvoy's face, but the blows were a fraction short of their target. The Britisher was too eager to return fire and lunged in throwing a wild left hook that was way off the mark. Tunero was using a brisk left lead and Mac decided that he would need to get underneath this punch and flay away at his opponent's wasp - like body. A booming left and right to the stomach saw the Cuban holding on. A few seconds later he repeated this delivery and this time the Kid was badly shaken but hung on like a limpet, and the referee, Percy Moss, had to part them. The referee issued two

BELLE VUE BOXING GAZETTE

SECOND CONTEST.

Twelve Three-Minute Rounds Contest.

JOCK McAVOY v. KID TUNERO

Weigh' in at 11 st. 8 lbs.

JOCK McAVOY.
(Rochdale). Middleweight Champion of Great Britain and Lonsdale Belt Holder.

KID TUNERO
(Cuba). Conqueror of Marcel Thil (World's present Middleweight champion).

McAvoy v. Tunero from the Belle Vue Boxing Gazette, December 1934.

stern warnings to the invader for clutching. It was quite obvious that McAvoy's body bombardment was taking effect.

This Cuban was a classy performer though, and soon used the ring to his advantage. Stabbing out his left hand and mixing up his punches with lightning fast combinations. He connected with a few solid right hands but seemed alarmed when these did not even make Jock blink. Instead, he countered with his own rights that were stunning. It was a memorable contest with plenty of full-blooded excitement that had the fans on the edge of their seats throughout.

During the interval at the end of the fourth round, Ted Broadribb who was acting as a second for the Cuban, was frantically demonstrating to Tunero how to cover his chin from Mac's punches. In the fifth and sixth rounds Tunero moved round the ring like a skater and picked up points. McAvoy looked a bit puzzled. In the seventh Mac bit down on his gloved thumbs and stalked after his foe. Bang! He landed with a jarring left hook that sent the Cuban's head back on his sturdy shoulders with a mighty jolt. He was visibly hurt and clinched, but Mac flung him off, screamed out some foul language, then sent a pile driven left uppercut which caught his man under the chin. The Kid was on the deck looking up at the arc lights, and the record crowd of 7,500 rose to their feet as one man and went almost delirious with excitement. Even the newspaper reporters were up on their feet in hysterics. Mac danced with glee in a neutral corner, as the din became more uproarious. Belle Vue had never seen such a scene. How the Cuban got to his feet at the count of eight was amazing. He was glassy-eyed and his legs were trembling as if he had received an electric shock. Meanwhile the crowd remained standing and shouting themselves hoarse. Further hurried punches from the Rochdale man saw the brave Cuban on the floor once again. It looked all over and thinking it was, McAvoy headed back to his corner and sat down. But Tunero was a courageous man and he bravely beat the count. Staggering upright and clutching the top rope, there was tremendous excitement amongst the fans, who were once again up on their feet rooting and yelling their lungs out.

Ted Broadribb, realising that his man was a sitting target and knowing that Mac showed no mercy to anyone and would pulverise his boxer, threw the towel of surrender into the ring. However, as luck would have it, the towel sailed right through the ropes and landed outside the ring, so this act of surrender was ignored. The referee ordered McAvoy out of his corner and signalled the fighters to "box on." It was a shameful decision and certainly would not have occurred in modern day boxing. The Cuban was hurt badly and in no way in position to continue. However, the fight had to be fought and Jock dashed across the ring and butchered his willing but now totally well beaten opponent. The power of Mac's punches deposited Tunero through the ropes. The fight was over. Kid Tunero was well and truly out to the world. One of McAvoy's punches was delivered so hard that it made the Cuban's crinkled hair stand up straight!

Tunero, the Cuban middleweight, meets Jock McAvoy at the weigh-in before that nights important fight at Belle Vue. Jack Bates is standing at the back and Jack Madden in the centre.

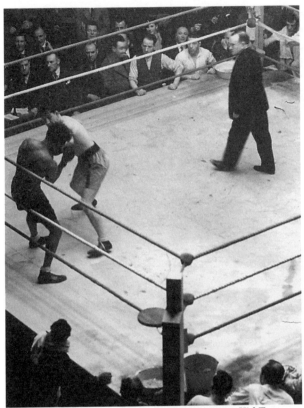

McAvoy gets set to deliver a right uppercut at Kid Tunero.
In the right hand corner, Harry Fleming and Jack Bates
look on apprehensively.

Later in his dressing room, Tunero speaking through an interpreter, was full of praise for McAvoy. "He surprised me," he said. "I was told McAvoy was just a puncher. Take my word for it, he can also box far better than anyone gives him credit for." Mac knocked on Tunero's dressing room door and walked over to the Cuban and shook his hand. Tunero smiled, felt his jaw and told McAvoy that throughout his entire career he had never been hit so hard. "You punch twice as hard as Marcel Thil," he said, which was encouraging news for McAvoy. Later that night when Mac returned home to Rochdale there was a personal congratulations message from Gracie Fields. Many years later, Kid Tunero would re-visit England with a boxer he eventually groomed into a world champion...the featherweight Jose Legra!

Norman Hurst writing in the Sporting Chronicle, said: "The world's greatest middleweight! That's what the crowd were saying after McAvoy's electrifying win over Kid Tunero. Faced by one of the cleverest boxers and ring tactitions in the world, he proved that he could box as good as the best and fight, too. He achieved what had been deemed impossible - the knocking out of the splendidly built

Kid Tunero flat out. Look at his hair – standing straight. McAvoy is shouting something at Harry Fleming, who is banging his hand on the canvas.

Cuban, who held a victory over Marcel Thil, the world champion. Never has there been a middleweight contest fought at such continued speed. Never have I seen a huge audience so uproarious and then fall so quiet. That seventh round was startling. McAvoy slipped a punch, and then with every ounce of his strength sent a right hand that skimmed Tunero's body and landed under the Cuban's chin. The latter's head jerked back, his hair stood on end as if he was electrified, and his body was lifted a full foot in the air to finally crash on the canvas. Then pandemonium broke loose. The crowd let itself go in one wild yell. Tunero's seconds hammered the canvas and yelled at him, the Cuban's head jerked like a marionette when the count reached eight, and, strictly speaking, he was 'out' there and then, for at ten he was still in an unstrikable position. But in the excitement he reeled to his feet and nobody noticed the towel that had been badly thrown from his corner and went out of the side of the ring again. McAvoy, like an unleashed tiger, was after his man and, backing him to the ropes, placed wicked, merciless punches at will, slowly the game spirit of Tunero was punched into unconsciousness and he sank

The Cuban takes the full count. McAvoy looks down on his opponent, admiring his handywork.

to the floor. Percy Moss, the referee, declared it over, even as the seconds were entering the ring. Tunero is still a great fighter, but I doubt if there is a middleweight in the world who can live with this lad from Lancashire."

The year of 1934 came to a close and McAvoy had strung together eight victories. In these eight contests, six of his wins were accomplished by a series of sensational knockouts. And I do mean knockouts. His true greatness was displayed in these eight fights. Another factor was that all his eight opponents were bigger, heavier, and in most cases, far more experienced than the Rochdale fighter. It is a fact - and student's mull over it - that a man doesn't always relate to contemporary history. Imagine if Hannibal had possessed jet bombers instead of elephants...If Napoleon could have moved supplies over paved roads instead of the mud of Russia...If Socrates could have had a television audience to lecture to instead of the boys in front of the Forum. If Jock McAvoy was fighting today he would be a world champion!

New York, New York

1935 was a year of high drama for McAvoy - The Fighting Machine. It started off with a flight to Paris by aeroplane, something that was in its infancy in those days. Later, McAvoy would say that the journey by aeroplane was the only good part of the trip. He travelled to Paris with Harry Fleming and Jack Bates, Jeff Dickson the promoter, and Dave Lumiansky. McAvoy was matched with the teak-tough, balding, hairy-chested Frenchman, Marcel Thil, who was the National Boxing Association world middleweight champion. Jeff Dickson the promoter, had announced the signing of the Thil versus McAvoy contest at a lunch he laid on for reporters in the Savoy Hotel, in London. He revealed that Mac and the French hero would box fifteen rounds for the light-heavyweight championship of Europe. Instead of praise for his matchmaking, Dickson received a storm of abuse from the press and public for not making the match for Thil's version of the world middleweight crown. The press pointed out that the other title didn't mean a thing, and they asked why was the Briton being side tracked?

McAvoy was bitterly disappointed and disgusted with the situation. He believed this contest should have been for Thil's version of the world middleweight title. Jeff Dickson told the press that he had been trying for two years to get Thil's manager to agree to a championship match with the Rochdale man at the middleweight limit, but he had steadfastly refused. In fact, added Dickson, it took a great deal of persuasion before he agreed to his champion meeting McAvoy at the heavier poundage, and knew that if Jock licked the Frenchman, the latter would be forced to give McAvoy a return with his world title as the prize.

This Frenchman was one very tough and rugged fighter. He wasn't particularly good at any one thing, but he utilised his enormous strength to its full capacity. The conditions which the Rochdale fighter was forced to comply with were that the bout was to be held in Paris, for obvious reasons, and they had to fight under an American originated ruling which at that time was termed "The No Foul Rule." Thil, who looked older than his years due to his early balding, had had his first professional fight in 1925. There was nothing stylish about him but his strong points were his ruggedness and his aggressive body punching, and he was an extremely hard man to hurt. During his 97 professional fight career he won the European middle and light-heavyweight championships. The Frenchman was one hell of a proposition for any fighter to meet. He was a fighter who had improved greatly with maturity, and was into his thirties when facing McAvoy. His credentials were indeed impressive. In 1932 he beat Gorilla Jones for the NBA World middleweight title, defended it on no less four occasions, outpointing the masterful Len Harvey, Mac's victim - the Cuban Kid Tunero, a Spaniard, Ignacio Ara and the Belgian, Gustave Roth, and was then held to a draw with Carmelo Candal. (His overall NBA world middleweight championship record was ten fights; won nine, drew one.)

The Collyhurst party arrived in Paris eight days before the contest. At once Mac complained about the different food and the surroundings. He just couldn't get used to them, and nothing upsets a boxer more than this kind of situation. This was actually his first contest away from home, and he was already at a disadvantage. The Lancashire boxer's second setback occurred three days before he was due in the ring to face Thil. An ugly, painful carbuncle appeared on his forearm, and this worried him mentally as well as physically. Doctor Graham who looked after the Collyhurst team in north Manchester was hastily put on a train bound for London where he caught an aeroplane for Paris. Unfortunately he didn't arrive in Paris until lunchtime on the day of the contest. He did what he could for McAvoy, which under the circumstances wasn't very much, he had to lance the wound. McAvoy was in terrible pain and uncomfortable. Jeff Dickson was concerned and suggested postponing the fight, but McAvoy was fed up with Paris and wanted to get it over with and wouldn't hear of a postponement. "I won't let you down, Jeff," he told the promoter. "I know a postponement might ruin the gate for you."

Jack Bates recalled the preparations for this contest: "Jock hated the food in France. He found the fancy, oily food didn't agree with him and he moaned continuously. In fact, after a while, the only food he ate were oranges, French rolls with butter and he drank coffee the whole time we were in Paris. Because of his painful carbuncle he wasn't his normal self when he went into the ring."

Mac was certainly up against it, there was no doubt about that. Though not in top form due to the boil which had to be lanced just a few hours before entering the ring against Thil and being upset with the food, nonetheless, Mac put up a courageous performance in front of a crowd of fifteen thousand who paid 524,050 francs. Another extraordinary aspect of the affair, and to Dickson's astonishment, was the presence of some 'away' supporters. Over a hundred had travelled from Manchester and Rochdale to cheer their idol. Together with their tickets for the fight plus the fare to France it had cost them £15 each.

Jock McAvoy arrives in Paris for the fight with Marcel Thil, promoter Jeff Dickson
shakes his hand

The Palais des Sports arena was buzzing with expectation of a great contest. From the first bell it was very much a fight to the finish. Thil came at the British boxer, hitting to the body from a crouch, his short, powerful arms going like pistons, and the arc lights gleaming of his bald head. Mac was snorting like a bull, dashing in and throwing his poleaxing right hook, and biting the thumbs of his gloves in a fury of concentration. They were like express trains colliding. It was a perfect match for the promoter, first one would force ahead, then the other. The place was in uproar, and the odds fluctuated with each punch. They both could dish it out and take it, and in their anxiety to gain the upper hand, they took plenty from each other. Every round was a thriller. The two fighters stood toe to toe, with very few clinches. The fourth was Mac's best round, he came surging out of his corner and cracked Marcel with a right hook on the chin, the Frenchman shivering from head to toe. The following left hook missed by a whisker, and if that punch had connected the clash would have ended then and there. Thil staggered and was in trouble. Any other fighter would have gone down, but the Frenchman must have been cast in an iron foundry because he took fearsome punishment as McAvoy battered him into the ropes, yet he clung on and weathered the attack.

Thil eventually won the bout, there was no question about that, but the Englishman's gallant stand had won the admiration of all. In fact, he put up one of the best performances ever seen in a French ring, though taking two counts. He was out-hustled, out-manoeuvred and out-fouled by the grim world champion. This defeat was considered the worst setback McAvoy ever suffered during his peak period, though it has to be said that he took his walloping without complaint and his two fists were still giving him plenty of concern. Dr Graham who was a front row spectator said: "McAvoy put up a wonderful showing. There is no doubt whatsoever that the boil contributed in no small way to his defeat at the hands of a very tough opponent".

The next day before leaving Paris, Jeff Dickson handed Jock a cheque for 106,642 francs, the largest purse he had received. When he arrived back in Manchester, McAvoy never denied Marcel Thil beat him, though he expressed the view that the odds were stacked against him and, given the opportunity, he firmly believed he could turn the tables on the durable Frenchman. However, a re-match never happened. McAvoy never uttered any complaints in public about Thil's blatant fouling, though he was confident that he had the ability to knock Thil out with his heavier punching. At this point in his career he had scored 82 knockouts while winning 19 by points decisions. He stated that if Thil would grant him a return he would fight him anywhere, except in France. "I would love the opportunity to fight abroad every week if only to destroy the American illusion that there are no good scrappers at the middleweight poundage in the British Isles."

Dave Lumiansky had plenty to say about the Paris fiasco. He told the press that the Frenchman was guilty of landing several low blows in the early rounds and this had weakened Mac, and he was unable to come on strong in the later rounds. "How the Lancashire man withstood this treatment was a credit to his physical condition and his toughness," screeched Lumiansky. "Never once did Jock complain, despite taking crunching punches well below the belt."

McAvoy begged Harry Fleming and the Belle Vue officials to get him a return against Marcel Thil in Manchester, but the Frenchman showed not the slightest inclination of accepting their offer. It was April before Mac entered the ring again when he won on points over twelve rounds against a Spaniard, Garcia Lluch. Then in June he defended his British middleweight title while outscoring Al Burke over fifteen rounds. Mac's damaged fists were giving him more problems and he received treatment from a top London bone specialist. It was October before he was back in action again.

Jeff Dickson the promoter, was a character in his own right. McAvoy earlier in his career had quarrelled with him and threatened to sue the promoter regarding a fight that eventually didn't take place when Dickson was promoting in London. However, they had respect for each other. Apart from his activities as a boxing promoter Jeff Dickson was a character! An American he moved to Europe and joined the American Eagle Squadron to fly with the French Air Force before America entered the First World War. The members of the Eagle Squadron were later disowned by the Americans when they flew against the Riffs in North Africa on behalf of France, in which country Jeff afterwards made his home. He died gallantly, fighting in the air for the Free French during the Second World War.

McAvoy's contract with Harry Fleming was coming to an end and, like his stablemate Jackie Brown, Mac had agreed to be managed by Dave Lumiansky. In the meantime, Lumiansky had been making plans to take McAvoy over to America with the intention of forcing the New York recognised world middleweight champion, Eddie "Babe" Risko, to defend his laurels against the Rochdale man. Lumiansky reasoned that if Jock was actually in New York, and performed well in the gym sessions he was organising for the British champion, and Mac was successful in the fights he was arranging for him, then Risko and his connections were hardly likely to ignore his challenge.

During the summer Mac received a citation from his hometown for a wonderful and courageous act of bravery when he brought a runaway horse which was pulling a milkfloat under control and helped avert a serious accident. Apparently, he showed amazing athleticism when jumping straight at the bolting horse and brought it to a halt. He never gave a thought for his own safety and was later commended by town hall officials and the police for his bravery. Furthermore, Mac insisted that a financial reward he was offered be given instead to a local orphanage. Later in the summer months McAvoy became infatuated with a stunning 23 year old lady named Joan Alice Lye, who used the same horse stables as Mac. Miss Lye came from a very wealthy family. Her father James, along with his older brother Frederick, were directors and major shareholders in John Bright and Brothers, a huge textile business. Mac and the young lady went out riding regularly. Joan came from a completely different background than the one Mac had grown up in. He was flattered with Joan's attentions and was on his best behaviour while in her company. Over the following two years he would carry on meeting

Marcel Thil beating McAvoy in Paris. During the fight, Thil placed two low blows which caused McAvoy some pain.

Miss Lye, and in December 1937 she became the second Mrs Bamford.

When Belle Vue gave Mac a date for his next contest which was against a high ranking French boxer named Marcel Lauriot, the light-heavyweight champion of his country, they had certainly done him no favours. Five months before the Frenchman had taken Len Harvey the full ten round distance while losing on points. Today, a champion having his first bout back after any kind of injury would most probably insist on an 'easy' opponent. McAvoy decided to train at Hollingworth Lake for this bout. Sparring partners were hired and the camp set up. Fred Shaw, the Shipley fighter who had taken Mac 15 rounds in 1931 before losing on points, was contacted to help. Fred willingly agreed. The first three days saw the Yorkshire boxer more than holding his own with the Rochdale man. During their leisure periods, Shaw joked with Mac and the other people in the camp that he had never been put on the floor by any one. He was quite rightly proud of this achievement. On the fifth day, after a torrid and hectic session with McAvoy in which Mac did his upmost to deck his man and couldn't, he flew into one of his rages. Jack Bates calmed him down and gave him a massage. "You know your problem Joe?" said the trainer. Mac never answered. 'You're trying too hard to flatten Fred. Relax, let your punches go fast, don't try to hammer him and you will find it much easier." While having their evening meal Shaw boasted again about never been put on the canvas by anyone. McAvoy had heard more than enough and decided that he would be the first to grant the big Shipley fighter his wish.

The following day Mac and Fred put the big pillows on their fists and commenced sparring. Bates could see that McAvoy was determined that this was going to be the day he would sort out Shaw once and for all. Jock set about his man in earnest, a power-packed left hook catching Fred on the point of his jaw. This time, he was hurt - and badly. In these situations the fighter hurt would be allowed time to recover, but this was a McAvoy sparring session and he immediately smashed home another block busting left hook to the identical spot on Shaw's chin, and down he went with a thud. Bates and Harry Fleming jumped into the ring and helped Fred onto a chair they had quickly put into the ring. Fred looked ashen faced and as if he was going to be sick. Mac shadow boxed waiting for Shaw to be given treatment then continue. This sort of thing had happened before, not with Shaw, but with other McAvoy sparring partners and after dousing them with cold water and massaging their necks, the sparring partner would be expected to carry on. However, Fred was in no condition to hold his hands up let alone spar and he was helped to his room. "Those two left hooks Mac hit poor old Fred with would have knocked an elephant off its feet," said Jack Bates.

After appearing to have shaken off the effects of the punches, Fred expressed the opinion that Mac had taken a liberty. It was quite obvious to everyone that his pride was hurt badly. He took a bath, got dressed and told everyone he was going for a walk for some fresh air despite it pouring down with rain and not wearing a hat or coat. "You'll get soaked Fred, wait till the rain stops," Mac told him. But Fred insisted he was going out no matter what, and off he went. A couple of hours later, a telegram arrived at the camp addressed to Fred. It was decided to open it in case it was important. "Fred, come home at once, wife ill," it read. It was decided that everyone would go out and locate Shaw. Mac looked at the postmark on the telegram and it wasn't from Shipley at all, it was in fact sent from a post office about three miles from Hollingworth Lake. The post office was located and a car sent there. Poor Fred was sitting down on a chair looking sorry for himself and soaked the skin. He was taken back to the hotel and dried out before going back home. There was no more talk about his record of never having been put on the floor. Despite twice dropping Marcel Lauriot, at Belle Vue, Mac damaged his right hand again and had to be content by convincingly winning a twelve round points victory. Afterwards, Mac was dejected at his injury and despite Dave Lumiansky telling him of his plans for New York, he expressed concern about his damaged hands. But the persuasive Mr Dave told him that everything would be fine and not to worry himself unduly. The suave American assured him that he would get the best bone specialist in the world to take care of the damaged mitts. "Besides," said Lumiansky, "you won't be fighting straight away." This pleased Mac a great deal. Ever since he decided to make fighting his chosen career, McAvoy had dreamed of fighting in America. He had read all the boxing magazines that stated America was the place to be for all potentially great boxers. He was thus anxious not to miss out on this trip of a lifetime. And how else could a fellow from his background ever have afforded to visit the States if it wasn't through boxing? His badly damaged right fist, though, put doubts that he would not be able to give off his best against America's finest middle and light-heavyweights. 1935 was also the first time since he turned professional that he hadn't scored a knockout or stoppage victory. Though pleased with the prospect of a trip to the States, deep down he was worried, very worried indeed. With hindsight Mac should have got proper medical attention on both hands straight away, even if it meant undergoing an operation and putting the American adventure on the shelf until such time as his fists were healed satisfactorily.

As suggested earlier in this book, Jock McAvoy's fighting activities were by no means entirely confined to the boxing ring, and many tales abound of McAvoy's 'extra-curricular' fistic encounters. McAvoy was the kind of fellow who, because of his mercurial temperament, could make enemies more easily than most people. Walter Howard, a well known publican who was acquainted socially with Mac in the pre-war years, recalls an incident back in 1935, when the reigning British middleweight champion was attacked by some men while out for the evening in the Ritz Ballroom in the centre of Manchester. One of the men apparently had a grudge against McAvoy for some reason and, enlisting the help of several of his friends, attempted to settle the score once and for all. The band of would be avengers followed Mac into the toilets inside the Ritz with the intention of teaching him a mob handed lesson. Little did the vengeful posse realise what a foolhardy course of action their plan was! McAvoy took on the whole group all at once, and quickly smashed them all up, delivering a severe physical chastisement to each and every one of the half dozen would be attackers. By the time Mac had finished, the walls of the toilets were literally covered in blood in an incident

Look at the look of utter contempt McAvoy is giving the world class light-heavyweight, Al McCoy.

which showed just what a formidable fighting force, in or out of the ring, the middleweight champion was at that time in his life.

There was also the problem of the beautiful Joan Lye. Despite their backgrounds being poles apart, she was absolutely besotted with the husky, brooding fighter. Of course, he was quite famous and a huge personality in Lancashire. Miss Lye's parents, however, were far from happy with the situation and told McAvoy in no uncertain terms. They requested that he cease meeting their daughter. He took no notice of their objections and carried on his relationship as if nothing had happened. Did Mac's dutiful wife Eliza know of the affair? Well, most probably, because it was well known that her husband was a womaniser.

Jack Bates, who was well liked and respected by both Lumiansky and Mac, was asked to travel to the States with them. The manager no doubt believed that Bates would be the ideal person to calm McAvoy down if he should go into one of his blinding rages while away from home. But, regretfully, Jack had to decline their offer because of family commitments, though he looked after Jock's bull mastiff dog while he was away. McAvoy loved this dog which he named "Major of the Mount," and it was a prize winning show dog which the fighter often entered in shows at Belle Vue. It was a big, fat roundish brute of a beast, weighing about 12 stone. Bates' wife Sarah wouldn't have it in the house under any circumstances because it was so huge. Jack and McAvoy built a shed to house the animal. It was eight foot long, seven foot wide and over six feet high. The Bates children used to ride on the back of the dog. At times Mac seemed to care more about this dog than he did about anything else.

Arriving in New York in the early part of November 1935, the Rochdale man was amazed and a little taken aback looking at the vast canyons of skyscrapers when he walked down Broadway, and seeing all the hustle and bustle. He could not stop himself from looking upwards at every opportunity. "It made Manchester and even London seem like country towns in comparison," he said later. And obviously there was nothing like these huge buildings in his hometown, Rochdale.

Many sceptics were divided about the value of Dave Lumiansky. Some journalists in the south claimed he was a damn good manager who had steered Panama Al Brown to a world title while others, especially those in the north of England, per-ceived him as nothing more than a silver-tongued manipulator, a chancer and a businessman first and foremost, concerned only with making money, and as quick-ly as possible. The question must be asked though, why he took fights for McAvoy - a genuine middleweight - with world class light-heavyweights. It was all very well for people to claim as they did later, that McAvoy was not concerned whom he fought or how big and how heavy his opponents were. They also point out that Mac was such an argumentative person who would suddenly turn violent and was liable to lash out with his fists and ask questions later, that perhaps Lumiansky, like Joe Tolley before him, could do no other than let him have his own way. Managers were known as pilots in those times, and surely 'Mr Dave' should have navigated a better route for his fighter to take than the one he eventually charted for him.

On his first training session in the Pioneer Gym which was situated on West 44th Street, the little known McAvoy was looked on by the other fighters and trainers very cynically. The Americans' continual boasting and glib talk cut no ice with Mac and he kept his own counsel. The Yanks laughed at his broad Lancashire accent. The gym was bursting at the seams, a real hive of activity. There were four rings and each one was busy with fighters waiting their turn to spar. Joe Olucci, who was to act as one of McAvoy's sparring partners over the coming weeks, extended his hand in friendship, but the rest of the people in the gym looked very threatening and imposing, and there were dozens of white and black fighters all doing their routines. McAvoy, of course, was not the type to be easily intimidated and this cool treatment did not overly concern Mac in the least. Back home in his Collyhurst gym, he was well known for his mean moods while training, so the American hostile atmosphere suited him down to the ground, though he was not used to training with so many other fighters.

The first day Mac ducked through the ropes to box he was surprised to see so many celebrities, famous champions of the past, a posse of well-known managers and promoters and several of New York's sternest newspaper critics, were crowded round the training ring. Jock, for once, was nervous and it showed. Nonetheless, he resolved that he would let them see that he was not yet another British failure. His sparring partners wore the customary headguards and gumshields, and Lumiansky insisted that Mac wear these also. Though he did not relish these things he put a headguard on his head though declining to also put a gumshield in his mouth. The Yanks were amazed at the Englishman's reluctance to not box without a gumshield. Red Finnegan, a tough local scrapper, was the first fellow to cross gloves with him. At the shout of "time" a deathly hush fell over the gym and the two men walloped each other in non-stop fashion. Suspicious eyes glanced at the ring and Finnegan left himself open and crack, a short jolting left hook from the Lancashire lad put him on the floor in a sitting position. The ringsiders nudged each other in agreement that at least the Limey could bang, but they were still very sceptical, thinking it was more luck than anything that had decked Finnegan. After this, Dan Lyons was brought in to box with Mac and they had a real old dust up. Mac was warmed up by now and feeling ready to stuff any insults about British fighters' frailty down the Americans' throats once and for all. Now this should have been enough sparring for the day, but one of the Americans suggested they let McAvoy spar some more and finally a fellow named Gordon Donaghue was hastily gloved up and told in no uncertain manner to "test him."

Donaghue was a full blown light-heavyweight, and much taller than Mac and this fellow could punch solidly and crisply, as he soon showed by knocking the Rochdale lad back on his heels in the first seconds of their sparring session. This brought a knowing wink from the ringside wags. "Is this another typical Limey?" they were asking each other. Mac was raging, he tore off the headguard that had been a hindrance to him and threw it out of the ring onto the gym floor. He was now in a foul temper. Snorting violently he then proceeded to knock seven kind of bells out of the much bigger and huskier man, and it was to his eternal credit that Donaghue prevented himself from being flattened into the resin dust on the canvas. There was an unbelievable look of sheer astonishment on the reporters' faces. Mac had won them over with his own special brand of mayhem. Jimmy Johnston, known to all and sundry as the 'Boy Bandit' and wearing a white felt hat, nearly swallowed his cigar he was so excited at what he had just seen McAvoy do to Donaghue.

Later in the dressing room, Johnston walked over to where McAvoy was taking off his boxing shoes and said: "Son, you've heard a lot about British fighters and what we in New York think of them. Forget it. Any bad opinions about your countrymen have been the fault of the fighters themselves with their wishy-washy displays in the ring. I'm English myself, I come from Liverpool, but I know the game through and through. If you can't take it, and you curl up under punishment, we have no use for you over here. But if you can fight, I'll back you up, and get you all the breaks you need."

McAvoy decks McCoy – look at McCoy's right leg.

Johnston, like the other doubters, was fascinated and extremely intrigued by what he had seen McAvoy do to the three hired helpers who had been told to knock the Lancashire lad out if possible. The reason for the cynicism was quite simple. The American fight fraternity had no respect whatsoever for most British fighters. Of course they had applauded the likes of Jim Driscoll, Owen Moran, Ted Kid Lewis, and Jack Kid Berg, but the Yanks reasoned they were the exception and not the rule and pointed out Len Harvey as an example. In 1930, Len Harvey, who was revered in England as the Prince of Boxers, had toured America for a series of fights, but he was certainly not the success the experts at home thought he would be when boxing in the States. In fact Len left America without winning a single contest. Going home after his self-proclaimed disastrous adventure on American soil, when he was on the liner, the Leviathan he was openly delighted to be leaving America. As the ship passed the Statue of Liberty, Harvey turned to his wife, Florence, and remarked: "This is the best part of the trip for me - going home."

Just to digress for a moment. Back in Manchester, after the American trip, McAvoy went to Jack Bates' house to collect his dog. While having a cup of tea with his trainer and discussing the trip to the States. McAvoy, who never suffered with an inferiority complex at any time, told Bates. "The Yanks tried to 'do' me before I even fought. I soon found out that the sparring-partners they chose for me were out to make a reputation for themselves at my expense if they could."

The trainer gave a knowing smile as Mac continued. "Every time I sparred they tried to flatten me."

"And did they manage to achieve it?" asked Bates fully expecting the reply which came with a look of utter disdain.

"Neigh, Jack, neigh, I knocked the – out of them."

McAvoy then told his trainer about a little incident in New York that obviously riled him and made him extremely angry. It seems that on the afternoon of his fight with Babe Risko, Mac was resting in his hotel room when a loud knock on his door disturbed him. Getting up and going the door, he was met by the hotel bellboy holding a large bouquet of flowers, a bunch of blue forget-me-knots. By this time Mac was absolutely livid about being disturbed, and even more so when learning that Risko had the audacity to send the flowers with the message. "Smell these, because you won't feel like smelling much after I finish with you tonight." Being a man of short temper and no sense of humour, he let out a torrent of abuse and four letter words that would have embarrassed a docker. He threw the flowers down the hotel landing, and the bellboy, frightened for his life, quickly turned and headed for the elevator. Jack Bates smiled upon seeing McAvoy's obvious annoyance while relating this incident.

"What did you do Joe?" enquired the trainer.

"What did I do?" said Mac in a loud, gruff voice, still clearly annoyed about what happened in New York. "What did I do, I'll tell you what I did. I decided then and there that – Mister Babe Risko would receive a lesson that he would never forget. That's what I did, and a lesson is what Risko received." McAvoy also told Bates that he knew he would beat 'Babe' Risko before they even met in Madison Square Garden. Bates

Note the alarmed expression on McCoy's face as Mac stands over him admiring his handywork.

asked him how he knew. "Well the Americans were still very sceptical about me, even after I licked Al McCoy," replied Mac, who went on to say that they thought his first victory on American soil might have been a fluke. McAvoy might well have had a point in his reasoning, because so confident was 'Babe' Risko and his manager, that they had booked a fight in Philadelphia against a stiff-punching Canadian fighter named Frank Battaglia on the 9th of December, just twenty days before facing McAvoy? That was either super confidence or downright stupidity. "When Risko fought in Philadelphia, I was sat at ringside. He used a solid left lead, but he was decked by a right hand. I smiled to myself, I knew I could flatten him and he'd wish he'd stayed in the Navy!"

Jimmy Johnston was fascinated with Mac, though he couldn't fathom out the Rochdale fighters lack of fear once the sparring session got started. A few hours after the training session, the dapper little matchmaker took Mac and Lumiansky along to Jack Dempsey's restaurant on Broadway. They were hardly seated when the great man himself came over to their table. McAvoy was excited and like a school kid meeting his hero, the very same man whose book on training to be a boxer Mac had studied so religiously. This was the man whose career he had read and re-read lots of times, the great Manassa Mauler himself in the flesh. This was certainly a red-letter day for McAvoy. "Jack, this is Jock McAvoy, the middleweight champion of England, and he can fight," said Lumiansky.

"I know," replied Dempsey to Jock's great surprise. "I've been watching you and if you can fight in the ring as good as you showed today in the gym, there's a lot of money to be made over here for you. Good luck and I'm looking forward to seeing you in your first fight." Later that night, Dempsey turned to Johnson and said: "Are you sure this guy comes from England and not Brooklyn?" The 'Boy Bandit' laughed loudly. He knew what Dempsey meant - McAvoy's broad, Lancashire accent was hard for the Americans to understand. He told the former heavyweight king "Next time you speak to him Jack, I'll get an interpreter."

Lumiansky had certainly not looked for an easy opponent for the Rochdale man's first contest on American soil. Every promising American light-heavyweight was ducking Al McCoy, basically because he was too good. In fact, McAvoy himself remarked later when back home in Manchester: "For my first opponent they picked me a good 'un' in Al McCoy, a Canadian with a reputation of being both a boxer and a puncher. They told me he was in line for a title-fight with John Henry Lewis, but this didn't impress me. Though I had travelled to the States to fight their

Jock McAvoy (right) pounds McCoy.
'Making his American ring debut, Jock McAvoy, the British middle and light-heavy-
weight champion, scored a clean cut ten-round victory over Al McCoy, the Boston
French Canadian, in Madison Square Garden here tonight (Nov.29 1935) – The New
York Times.'

middleweights and I was after the world middleweight champion, what did I want to be getting myself tangled up with light-heavies for?"

After days of discussions between Lumiansky, Jimmy Johnston and McCoy's managers, Bill Brennan and Barney Fox, the details of which McAvoy said he knew nothing about. The powers that be finally made the match with McCoy. McCoy, despite his name, was a French-Canadian but based in Boston and was already regarded by the Canadian Boxing Commission as the world light-heavy-weight champion, though John Henry Lewis was otherwise recognised as the legit-imate world title claimant. McCoy, however, was certainly one of the best light-

A few of the 'Fistic' heroes of McAvoy's era. He gets a mention (bottom left).

heavyweights in the world and his fighting record was a formidable one. He had lost only one professional contest, and that was to former world middleweight champion, Vince Dundee. McCoy's real name was Florian le Brasseur. Jimmy Johnston, the Madison Square Garden matchmaker, stated that the winner of the McCoy v McAvoy contest would definitely box John Henry Lewis for the world light-heavyweight crown early in 1936. Back in their hotel in New York, Lumiansky was living it up and Room Service were kept busy with 'Mr Dave's' regular orders. There were always a few ladies in his company and he entertained these and his other guests lavishly. Who was paying for all this expensive service? Sadly, and much to his regret, McAvoy would find out the answer to this question a few months later, though it must be said that he himself had been carrying on his affair with Joan Lye by letter and expensive long distance telephone calls. Transatlantic calls in those days cost something in the region of £4 for three minutes and Mac made several to Miss Lye.

Lumiansky was also forever making calls to Norman Hurst in England, so one can imagine the phone bill alone must have been enormous. A few days before the fight with McCoy, Eliza McAvoy (Bamford) suddenly arrived in New York. It was said that Lumiansky sent for her because Jock was becoming a little too fond of the ladies that he himself was entertaining. Whatever the reason for Eliza's arrival, Jock made a big fuss when his wife arrived. Her presence curtailed his activity on the telephone and his amorous ways with Lumiansky's wenches. Mr Dave, using all his undoubted charm, was overjoyed to see her, and welcomed her regally.

Just prior to his fight with Al McCoy, Mac was feeling quite confident although very concerned about his dodgy right hand. Despite all his golden promises, Mr Dave had not taken him to see any bone specialist or for that matter, any doctors about getting treatment for both his problematic fists. Even while training Mac had depended entirely on his left hand, saving the right. In his dressing room in Madison Square Garden, as Mac was limbering up, a strange fellow walked in and announced that he was a doctor. Laying his bag of medical equipment out on the rubbing table he ordered McAvoy to place his right hand, palm downwards on the table. Pulling out a hypodermic syringe from his bag he jabbed the needle into the back of Mac's knuckles and injected the fluid which was Novocain. With this, Jock let out a piercing yell and flaked out on the floor. Pandemonium ensued as everyone picked up the unconscious fighter and walked him round the room until he regained consciousness. It appeared that this so-called 'doctor' had accidentally pierced a vital spot. When McAvoy came to he felt dizzy and ill, virtually a disas-

McAvoy's homecoming from a successful tour in the States meets the crowd at Manchester Station. He is holding his son.

ter for his opening fight on American soil. He was due in the ring within minutes. Mac shook his fuzzy head and did some light shadow boxing and within seconds he was back to normal, though his hand felt like a rock. This situation was shocking to say the least, and what a way to get ready to fight one of the best light heavyweight contenders in the world!

When the referee, Arthur Donovan, called the two fighters for their instructions Mac couldn't wait to get started. He tore straight after his man with no feeling his man out or posing, going on to the attack using his left jab and hooking briskly off it and shaking the Canadian down to his toes. It was not until the sixth round that the effects of the numbness to his right hand began to wear off and the English fighter had to revert to the use of his left. But he certainly made good use of this weapon, marking the rated light - heavyweight and cutting his eye besides having him on the deck twice. The crowd loved his all-action style, his ducking and weaving a la Jack Dempsey. McAvoy had really made a big impression on everyone in the arena and at the finish the crowd stood yelling and cheering him to the echo. He was awarded a unanimous decision from the referee and both judges. Winning a points decision was not the way Mac wanted his first victory on American soil, he would have preferred to have flattened McCoy and left him in the resin dust on the Madison Square Garden ring. However, despite his pessimism there was not the slightest hint of criticism, in fact he received nothing but praise from the media and everyone associated with the event. Eliza McAvoy commented: "I don't regret coming to America. Joe's a changed man."

Such was the interest in Lancashire that, in the early hours of Saturday morning, many short wave wireless sets were tuned in to try and pick up the ringside broadcast of the fight. McAvoy had sent a message back home saying: "I will fight in Madison Square Garden as if I was at home fighting in the King's Hall, Belle Vue. Don't worry about me."

To be dubbed a "small Jack Dempsey" by the hard boiled American sports writers was the very highest praise that those cynical critics could bestow on any fighter, especially if the fighter happened to be a "Limey." But this was exactly how they described McAvoy. Some reporters had also christened him the "Rochdale Rocket." Just prior to the fight Mac announced "I don't think I have ever felt so confident over any fight as I am feeling over this one. This is not bravado, I have never been one for boasting but I'm really ready for this one and the folk back in Lancashire will be certain I won't let them down." He asked Norman Hurst to give the following message to everyone: "To all the folks in the North we send our heartiest Christmas greetings. It will certainly be our happiest Christmas if I can win tonight. Not just for my own or my wife's sake, but for the sake of British boxing and Lancashire I shall go all out to win. I know that all my pals at Belle Vue wish me the very best. I shall not let them down. If I can do anything to raise the prestige of British boxing in America, I shall be a very proud man. There has been too much talk of 'Horizontal' champions on this side of the water. I am determined that the cynics shall not have a chance to say that about me."

Though McAvoy's clear-cut victory over the world's number one light-heavyweight contender, Al McCoy, had been convincing enough, the American fight fraternity thought that it could possibly have been some sort of fluke. After all, some reporters stated that, McCoy did have to lose weight on the day of the fight and was not feeling right. All sorts of excuses were doled out about why McCoy lost to the Englishman. Eddie 'Babe' Risko, though, was something else again, the sceptics reasoned. Jimmy Wilde the former world flyweight champion was delighted with McAvoy's American debut and said: "McAvoy is the type of fighter the Americans appreciate. Not for him is the fancy stuff, he is an all action fighter with a punch that hurts."

"Through the gate and almost home". McAvoy escaping after victory.

Ed Risko was one of the biggest American fistic discoveries of 1935. He started boxing while in the American navy under his real name Henry Pylkowski, born in Syracuse of Polish-Lithuanian parents. While in the United States Navy and as a sailor he won several service titles between 1931 to 1933, and had gained vast experience by boxing in navy bases throughout the world. When he was discharged he fought on bootleg tournaments and picked up valuable experience. When he started to box for money he took the name of Risko from the popular Cleveland heavyweight, Johnny Risko. He could box and punch and had created a minor sensation a year previously when in an over-weight match he thrashed the daylights out of the reigning world middleweight champion, Teddy Yarosz before knocking him out. After this victory, 'Babe' Risko was chasing the rainbow. In their return match with the world championship at stake, Risko convincingly out-pointed the champion thus taking the crown.

The short lived McAvoy - Risko bout was featured in detail in the opening chapter of this book, but after the fight with the world champion, Mac his wife, Lumiansky and his, company went to a night-club to celebrate the Rochdale man's victory. Seated at another table was Risko and his handlers, and they did not seem at all pleased at seeing the Englishman. In fact the atmosphere was less than cordial. Lumiansky, still bubbling after Mac's dramatic and sensational victory, excused himself from his own company and went over and sat with the Risko party no doubt to try and arrange a championship match. From the obvious looks and glances toward him and angry voices being raised, McAvoy detected that relationships were not too friendly. Gabe Genovese, from the Risko camp, was pointing his finger almost in Lumiansky's face. Hoping that Mr Dave would stop his chattering and come back to their table, Mac and his wife proceeded to enjoy the night. When Lumiansky eventually made his way back to Mac's table he was smiling like a Cheshire cat. "They want a return," he told Jock. "But they will not put the title up. They claim that you could never make 160 pounds so there was no point in discussing a championship bout. He merely wants a return in order to get revenge over you," concluded the manager.

This seemed to be either Risko or his connections' bravado coming out. After taking such a walloping why would Risko think a return fight would end up any differently? It would seem with hindsight that somebody in the Risko camp had made fatal mistakes in their preparation for the fight against McAvoy. Firstly, over-confidence and secondly in allowing the champion to enter the ring weighing so light. But, if as they claimed, Mac could never make the middleweight poundage why not give him a championship chance in the knowledge that the Britisher would be absolutely drained and weak at the weight thus giving Risko an easier task? The truth was that they never had any intention of putting Risko back into a boxing ring with McAvoy, it was talk and nothing more when telling Lumiansky and the press that they wanted a return. The fact was that the two fighters never fought again and McAvoy proved right up to the conclusion of his career that he could and did make the middleweight poundage quite easily.

Just to conclude about Risko as a boxer and a world champion: after the shellacking he received at the hands of McAvoy, the American was never the same fighter again. And after defending his crown by winning a 15 round points decision against Tony Fisher in February 1936, he lost the title to Freddie Steele a few months later and his career was then all downhill.

It was stated in several newspapers that McAvoy had been driven out of America by threats from gangster elements. Some writers over the years have claimed that this was no more than rumour and small talk with no substance whatsoever. However, if that is the case, one has only to look at the career of poor Primo Carnera, world heavyweight champion in 1932/33 whose career in the USA

Out! Jimmy Smith of Philadelphia takes the count face down against McAvoy at the St. Nicolas Arena, New York.

became very largely stage managed by gangsters, before claiming it was absurd that this sort of intimidation could never happen to a fighter. They should also remember the bitter experience the great Len Harvey suffered while touring America. There was not the slightest doubts in the mind of his companions that Harvey had been well and truly taken for a ride by what they described as the gangster elements that seemed to have New York boxing in its grip at that time. Gilbert Odd wrote in his book Len Harvey, Prince of Boxers: "After his second rebuff (Harvey lost to Vince Dundee on points. It was claimed that the gamblers cleaned up that night) it was forced on Len to realise that he was a mere pawn in the hands of gangsters, racketeers, bootleggers and the like over whom the State Athletic Commission was practically powerless."

Well known gangsters had always been around the fight business, ruthless villains such has Owney "The Killer" Madden, regarded at one time as America's public enemy number one, was one notorious villain. He was born in England but had emigrated to the States while only a schoolboy, and incidentally, was related to Jack Madden, the Belle Vue matchmaker. Al Capone, Legs Diamond and Lucky Luciano were other notorious racketeers connected in one way or another with American boxing. Indeed, Gus Greenlee the manager of world light-heavyweight champion John Henry Lewis, McAvoy's future opponent, was known to be a

Pittsburgh 'numbers' racketeer.

Furthermore, on Tuesday, 24 December, 1935, Norman Hurst writing in the Sporting Chronicle, said: "I have received a cable from a close friend telling me that threats have been issued to Dave Lumiansky, because he refused to fall into line with certain people. This sounds rather blood and thundery, but strange things have happened and will happen again in little old New York."

So do not dismiss the accusations about McAvoy being forced out of America as just baloney. Vic Richardson, a relation of the Belle Vue matchmaker, Jack Madden, was told in confidence that Owney Madden himself had a hand in helping to secure the 'Babe' Risko fight for McAvoy. Apparently, the Risko connections met Mac and Lumiansky in a New York bar to discuss terms and the Americans were laying the law down about certain things. Mac was getting fed up with their demands and threats and was about to either say something to them or get to his feet to wallop one of them when Madden gently kicked him in the shins, gave him a knowing look and Jock sat back while the negotiations continued.

Another story concerning the gangster element of McAvoy's trip to the States was told to me by Larry Hoey, a close friend of Jackie Brown, and who was often in the company of Brown and McAvoy. Larry distinctly remembers one night not long after McAvoy returned from America when he and the two fighters were playing billiards in the Railway Club on Rochdale Road in Collyhurst, and Mac mentioned an incident which took place in a night club in New York. Mac told them that he and Dave Lumiansky were in this club for a meeting with 'Babe' Risko and his manager about a rematch with Risko's title at stake. It seems that Lumiansky was his usual loud-mouthed self, and he was demanding a championship fight. The conversation seemed to be getting out of hand, when all of a sudden Mr Dave felt something hard touching his leg. It was a gun. "Lumiansky's face changed colours, and he shut up straight away. And I knew something was wrong," said McAvoy. "I looked down under the table and right enough one of Risko's people had a gun near his knee. Lumiansky shit himself and so did I." A world middleweight title fight was never, ever mentioned again, Mac told them.

The following appeared in Boxing in December 1935. "The brightest spots on the British boxing scene of 1935 were the two pleasing victories in New York Jock McAvoy. The news of Mac's prowess in the States bursts through the December gloom like real rays of sunshine. It gave British boxing fans something to be pleased about. It was not so long ago, or so it seemed since one of our champions did nothing but present himself as a butt for the sardonic wit of the American sporting journalists, with the effect that McAvoy's recent successes were all the more refreshing. In view of the high place he has won in the esteem of most in the world of sport in New York, it was a pity that our champion had to return home. In the past it has been rare indeed for an English boxer to have the good fortune to get the right limelight within a few weeks of arriving in the United States. McAvoy had earned the right to fight for the world title, and what was more to the point, his right was acknowledged in America. One might even say that he had proven himself entitled to fight for the middleweight title and the light-heavyweight title."

On New Year's Day 1936, smartly attired and wearing a nifty trilby, McAvoy was waiting to disembark from the giant French Liner, "Ile de France." Sitting in the liner's palatial gymnasium, the Rochdale fighter explained to the inquisitive horde of pressmen why he had come back from America in such a great hurry when he was on the verge of earning fame and fortune which would have lasted him a lifetime. "I came home because I'm aching to see Joe, Jack and Leonora, my three kiddies," he said. "I was not frightened out of America by gangster threats, you can deny that story. People may think I am throwing away a chance of a lifetime," he added.

"I thoroughly enjoyed my seven weeks in the States, and you can take it from me that I haven't come back home because somebody didn't like the idea of an Englishman knocking out American fighters. I didn't know that such a story had got back to Manchester, and I am sure that nobody will believe it. The fact is that I am as keen as mustard to get back over there again. There are two fighters in the world that I want to have a crack at more than any others. One is John Henry Lewis, the world champion, and the other is my old opponent, Marcel Thil, who beat me a year ago. I intend to go back to America and get a fight with Lewis, but at the moment I have absolutely nothing fixed up either at home or abroad. My wife and I have never been separated before from our three kiddies, and we want to get back to them, especially at this time of the year."

His wife smiled, and said that the most pleasant sound she had heard for weeks was the Lancashire accent of Harry Fleming who had travelled to Plymouth to meet the couple. They had presents for the children including a miniature pair of boxing gloves. On the journey back to Manchester Mac told Fleming all about life in America, emphasising that he preferred fighting in the States than anywhere on the Continent. "The people and the food, especially the food, suit me better than that foreign food," he said. "But New York at Christmas is the coldest place I have ever been in. The moors round Rochdale are nothing compared to it. Walking up Broadway the first time I kept dodging in doorways to keep out of the fierce, biting wind."

Speaking further he told his former manager that he had formed a friendship with the great Jack Dempsey and the current world heavyweight champion, Jimmy Braddock. Fleming was intrigued to learn more about two of his favourite boxers, and Mac relayed his conversations with the two champions, adding: "Braddock told me his parents came from Manchester," He admitted that some of the American fight customs rather unsettled him. "I was sparring in the gym one day, preparing for the Risko fight" he said. "When to my astonishment I saw Risko himself walk straight over to the ring and watch me. As you are well aware Harry, we never do that in England. Of course, I immediately eased up on my sparring partner so as not to give away any helpful tips about what I intended to do to him."

Eddie 'Babe' Risko.

He then outlined how American boxing was full of stories and rumours that certain boxers were "got at" by gangsters. There was also a rumour that Joe Louis, who was tipped to become the next heavyweight champion, had either died, been killed in an accident, or been "bumped off" by hoodlums. "But all these stories didn't bother me he in the least," he concluded.

When the McAvoy party arrived at London Road station in Manchester, (now known as Piccadilly Station,) Mac was greeted by his mother, and sister Rose, giving them a big hug and a kiss. He then put his arms around the children who had been hoisted on some skips to avoid being crushed. He was so pleased to see them that he smothered them with affection. There were hordes of people on the platform, press photographers, reporters, and fans even other passengers waiting for their trains, and railway staff joined in with the rest clapping and cheering him and patting him on his back as he made his way to a waiting car which was ready to whisk him the 12 miles or so back to Rochdale. He now realised what it felt like to be a conquering hero.

If he thought the reception he received on his arrival was magnificent, it was nothing compared to the fever pitch of emotion awaiting him in Rochdale. There were bands, and people swarming all over the town hoping for a glimpse of their hometown hero. His grey-coloured saloon car when spotted entering the outskirts of the town was besieged and waylaid by folk wanting to shake his hand or ask for his autograph or just congratulate him on his phenomenal achievement in America. The police had to escort the car to his home, and once inside the throngs would still not go until Mac went outside and standing on a wall, thanked everyone for the wonderful reception and support before they would disperse and go home.

Back To The States - 1936

In late January 1936, just before McAvoy left England to return to America, 14 year old Joe Wrigley and his pal, Andy Sheeran, who both came from Ardwick decided to play truant from school and go to Belle Vue in the hope that they might see their idol, Jock McAvoy. They heard he was doing some training in the Belle Vue gym. It was a perishing cold day as the two star struck youngsters sneaked through the turnstiles and walked around the showground. After being told that McAvoy was not training the youngsters decided to see the Zoo's large collection of exotic animals. At about 2pm the lads were standing outside the Lion House, which was situated near the luxurious Palm Court restaurant. After a short time a car pulled up outside the Palm Court and out stepped Jackie Brown, smartly attired in a grey suit and matching trilby. The lads couldn't believe their luck. Two beautiful ladies also emerged from the car wearing smart long dresses. Then to cap it all, the driver got out and it was McAvoy himself.

Young Wrigley and his friend were delighted. "I couldn't believe my luck," said Mr Wrigley as he related this story over sixty years later. "Jock McAvoy and Joe Louis were my idols, McAvoy more than Louis because he was British. To be honest, Mac was my inspiration. The car was a two-tone, four seater Riley sportscar, I can never forget it. It was brown on top and a cream or white colour on the bottom. And it had chrome wheeled hubcaps. Mac looked the picture of health, bronzed and marvellous with his thick head of hair parted in the middle. He was wearing a Harris Tweed jacket and grey slacks and his shoes were Plus 4s, brown and white like his car. I rushed over to McAvoy and pushed the two pictures I had of him and asked him if he would autograph them. Brown wanted to get into the Palm Court and sort of brushed us aside. But Mac told Jackie and the two women to go ahead telling them he wouldn't be long. He then asked me where I got one of the pictures from. I told him out of a Senior Service packet of cigarettes. He said he hoped I didn't smoke and signed it. He then asked why we weren't in school? We said we were on holiday. It was obvious he didn't believe us. He then asked if we were hungry. Then to our surprise and great delight he told us to follow him into the Palm Court. Now, you must understand that only rich and famous people went into this place, so for two scruffy snotty nosed kids to go in with our idol, well it was more than we could have ever imagined.

"Jackie and the two women were already seated at a table. Mac asked one of the

waitresses to bring two more chairs. And when we sat down the waiters were giving us quizzical looks. Jock told us to eat whatever we wanted but we felt uncomfortable. And we had fish and chips. It's funny when I think about it now. But that
really was the only food we could think of asking for. He showed two young kids
an act of kindness that I shall always treasure until the day I die. As I grew older,
I heard all the stories about his tantrums but I used to tell folk about that freezing
cold January morning in 1936."

In February 1936 Mac found himself back in America and ready for the challenge
ahead. New York was still in the grip of winter, but Mac would be out first thing
in the morning doing his roadwork. Bobby Dawson, a London based boxing figure had been hired to help train Mac while in the States. The explanation for this
could have been because Harry Fleming had a full-time job as a cooper and might
not have been able to take the amount of time off required for this American
adventure. Jack Bates was having domestic trouble and though Lumiansky and
Mac himself wanted Bates out in America with them, the little trainer again regretfully declined their offer.

Lumiansky had mapped out a programme, which would be condemned by boxing
managers today as sheer lunacy. There was absolutely no doubt whatsoever that
money was the manager's ulterior motive. For his first fight Mac found himself
matched against Jimmy Smith, a really tough and durable campaigner from the
equally tough city of Philadelphia. Smith had defeated Lou Brouillard, a former
world champion at welter and middleweight, and Ken Overlin, who would win the
world middleweight title four years later, so he was certainly no mug. This fight
was staged at the St. Nicholas' Arena, a well-known boxing hall which was used
as a nursery by managers for the bigger events which were held at Madison Square
Garden.

There were five thousand spectators seated when Mac ducked through the ropes to
face the aggressive Philadelphian. The Rochdale Thunderbolt looked mean with
his close cropped hair-style, and the crowd waited to see if what they had heard
and read about the Britisher was true. From the first bell the two fighters settled
down and traded blow for blow. The three minutes flew by and the fans in 'St
Nick's' stamped their feet and clapped their hands and raised their voices in
approval of what they had seen. The second was the final round as far as Smith
was concerned. Mac elected to change tactics, and instead of charging forward and
meeting the American in another toe-to-toe confrontation, he used his boxing skill

Historic picture taken as McAvoy and Lewis sign to fight. To the back of McAvoy is Dave Lumiansky.

and was soon stinging his man with jarring blows, one a short, crisp left hook hurt Smith. But tough as they come, Jimmy fought back with desperation and forced Mac against the ropes where he flayed away. McAvoy threw caution to the wind and, after ducking and rolling under Smith's avalanche of punches, he fired back with two handed punches of his own to Smith's mid-section. He then he followed through with a beautifully timed left hook which hit Smith on the side of his jaw which deposited him on the floor for a count of nine. The crowd were hysterical with excitement as the American tottered on unsteady legs. Mac, knawing away at his thumbed gloves, immediately tore after his opponent and rained blows in a non-stop fashion until another power -packed left hook hit the target and Smith hit the deck with a resounding thud, taking the count of ten.

Lumiansky was ecstatic at his fighters thrilling victory and was in the ring with a big grin on his face. "That was a world class performance," he shouted to Jack "Kid" Berg, Phil Scott and Nel Tarleton, three British fighters sitting at the ring-side along with John Henry Lewis and Lou Brouillard. This was what he wanted and needed, and he could safely claim he had been proven right about McAvoy's fighting qualities.

Jimmy Johnston, also at ringside, was absolutely gob smacked and delighted. "Jeez, this guy can flatten 'em with both hands," exclaimed Johnston to boxing officials seated close to him. Lumiansky and the Boy Bandit visualised making thousands of dollars by matching Jock with all the American stars from middleweight up to heavyweight. Johnston had plans for Mac to fight Jimmy Braddock, the heavyweight champion of the world, Joe Louis, the murderous punching heir to the heavyweight crown and the giant, Primo Carnera. Now if anyone needed convincing that these two were thinking about McAvoy's welfare, then here indeed was the proof!

Back in their hotel, Mr Dave explained to Mac that news had reached him from London that the match with Jack Petersen, the classy, cultured Welshman, was signed and sealed and it was for the British and Empire heavyweight titles which, at that time, were held by Petersen. Mac was thus in the somewhat unusual position of fighting for two championships in two different countries, and at two different weights to his own accepted weight, both to take place within the space of six weeks.

The next destination was Philadelphia for a contest against Anson Green, a tough black middleweight from that city. Mac's hands were still both very tender and painful. They had been frozen as usual for the Green fight but, instead of freezing them just prior to him entering the ring, this time the promoters decided to put another bout on before the McAvoy versus Green encounter. By the time Jock climbed through the ropes the effects of the injection had worn off and he was forced to fight virtually one-handed. He out boxed and even outclassed his opponent to win clearly by a points decision. However, it was a boring contest and the crowd of 9,000 who had swelled the arena expecting to watch the Brit with a hammer in both hands demolish his opponent were very disappointed with this messy affair, and they booed and jeered him. A further bout scheduled for New Jersey, against Eddie 'Kid' Whalen, of New York, due to take place ten days prior to his challenge for Lewis's title was hastily cancelled due to the state of Mac's damaged hands.

Four fights in the States and four victories. This was a wonderful foundation from which to build, while also giving British boxing a massive boost. However, Mac's hands were in a terrible state, and the damage was permanent by this time - with long term career consequences for the Rochdale man. It was indeed a miracle what he had achieved so far with such badly mauled fists, and also what he would even-

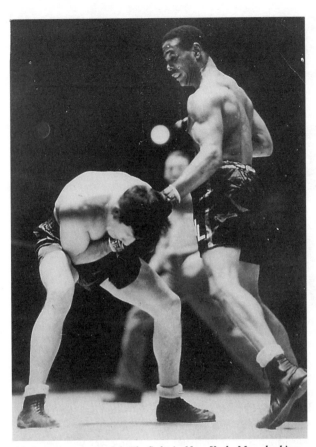

McAvoys unsuccessful title fight in New York. Mac ducking one of John Henry Lewis's best punches, a stiff left jab, during their fight at Madison Square Garden, in which Lewis successfully defended his world light-heavyweight crown after a hard 15-round battle.

tually continue to do in his boxing career. It was plainly obvious that McAvoy was just a commodity to the likes of Lumiansky and the American fight moguls, whose idea was to make as much money as possible as quickly has they could. They never took into account weights, size, experience or whatever. They were hard-nosed businessmen, especially 'Mr Dave.' For his part, McAvoy, like his friend and stablemate, Jackie Brown, the former world flyweight champion, at that time thought Dave Lumiansky was the greatest creation since the aeroplane, and he had convinced both of them that the world was their oyster. His silver tongue and his smoothness, charm and personality had them hooked.

Both boxers thought he would make them rich beyond their wildest dreams, and sadly, both would live to regret their trust and faith in this person.

The build up for the world light-heavyweight title showdown was underway. As the fight approached, McAvoy received more publicity and attention from the American newspapers than he could have ever imagined he would be accorded by

Lewis and McAvoy exchange punches in their historic world light-heavyweight clash.

these hard-to-please cynical scribes. One day while training in the old Pioneer Gym, Mac received a visit from Paul Berlenbach who had been the world light-heavyweight champion in 1925. Berlenbach, known in America as the 'The Astoria Assassin' and 'Punching Paul' had, like McAvoy, been renowned as a tremendous puncher. After watching the Lancashire lad go through a hectic workout, the former title holder walked over to where the Britisher was sitting wet with perspiration, and placing his hands·on Mac's shoulders he said: "Mac, I regarded myself as a good fighter. I fought and beat some good fighters. I'm not boasting, because my record speaks for itself. I am telling you right now, and in front of these people, that you are the best looking fighter I have seen since the days when I was fighting, and Mickey Walker, Harry Greb and Jack Delaney were names fight fans talked about." Mac thanked the former champion and made his way to the changing room. As he was going through the door Berlenbach shouted. "One piece of advice I offer you Mac," and looking straight at Dave Lumiansky he added, "you are going to make a lot of money, and when you do make sure you hold on to it." Poetic words indeed as Mac would later find out to his cost.

Though he had fought four times on American soil and was getting ready for a world championship match, McAvoy had not received a single penny from Lumiansky at this point. Mr Dave must have used all his cunning and charm, and sweet-talked the fiery-tempered Rochdale man in order to keep Jock satisfied with his explanations of why his purse money had not been paid. Mr Dave promised Mac, that after the Lewis fight he would receive his just rewards, his purse monies in full. Lumiansky, though, was extremely worried about the outcome if confronted by Mac again regarding his purse money, and a couple of days later Norman Hurst unexpectedly arrived in America. It can safely be assumed that Lumiansky had contracted Hurst and pleaded with him to get to New York immediately before the situation got out of hand.

Mac was out on his own watching a basketball game in Madison Square Garden when Hurst tracked him down. "Hello, Joe" said the journalist throwing his arms around Mac. "How are you?" After the usual small talk and getting all the Manchester news, Hurst told him that the negotiations for the forthcoming fight against Petersen had been finalised. Knowing how greedy Mac was for anything concerning money, Norman, appearing officious and serious, looked straight into the fighters eyes and smiling said: "Joe, you're getting the biggest purse you have ever had in your entire career." Letting this news sink in, Hurst continued. "Four-thousand pounds, Joe. Yes, four-thousand quid," he said very slowly letting the words four thousand really sink in. "How does that grab you?" It only took a moment or two for this news to sink in, then a big smile came across McAvoy's face. He jumped to his feet, grabbed Hurst by the arm and said. "Come on, let's get out of here and go somewhere where its quiet, and I want you to tell me all this again."

Out in the long corridors of Madison Square Garden they walked in comparative peacefulness. Hurst charmed Mac with tales of how the whole British nation was behind him one-hundred percent for his clash with Lewis. "But they are even more enthusiastic about your fight against Petersen," said Hurst. "Remember Joe, when me and Lumiansky told you that you would reach the top if you tried hard enough. You thought we were kidding. Yet, here you are in America, fighting for a world's title and matched to meet the British and Empire heavyweight champion when you get back to England." Mac looked at the newspaperman and chuckled. "I can't believe my good luck, Norman."

A look of sheer relief and satisfaction appeared on Hurst's face. He was, and had looked, petrified ever since he had first arrived in New York and the prospect of coming face to face with Mac had given him sleepless nights. Now his worst fears were over. The relief was etched on his large, round face. Now Hurst focused his attention on the upcoming fight with John Henry Lewis. The world light-heavy-weight king was only 21 and was born and raised in Phoenix, Arizona. John Henry,was a good looking fellow standing just over six feet tall and was built like Charles Atlas. Mac asked the journalist to let the folk back home know he was going out to win from the first bell. Hurst smiled and assured him he would win, telling him: "Of course you can do it Joe, because you've got the strength and fighting heart." Letting his words sink in, he added: "Remember Sam Langford was no bigger than you, and he scared the pants off those big heavyweights. Even Jack Johnson wouldn't fight him for the title after he'd sampled his punches."

What was the reality about McAvoy's opponent, John Henry Lewis? The folk back in England did not know a great deal about the coloured champion and were being fed all kinds of stories. Larry Grill, the sports editor for the Phoenix Gazette, described Lewis as a wide-eyed, kinky-haired little tyke of four years when he was first introduced to the fight fans of his home town, Phoenix. John Henry's father, John E. Lewis, was a veteran of the prize ring as well as being a widely-known trainer of athletes. The truth was that John Henry Lewis was an outstanding boxer whose accomplishments made him a formidable opponent for anyone at or around his weight, McAvoy included.

To stand any chance of winning against Lewis, Mac knew he would have to do it in the early part of the fight. It stood to reason that the longer the fight went, this superb champion, with his greater physical advantages in height, reach and weight would be favoured to win on points. There was also the problem of Mac's right fist. He would have to have it injected again, otherwise he was virtually a one-handed fighter. It was a ludicrous situation when you think about it, and would never be allowed today.

On the eve of the fight the photographers insisted on Mac shaking hands with Lewis. He agreed and it was very noticeable how much smaller the British fight-er was compared to the tall, well-muscled world champion. It was another David and Goliath job for the Lancashire man. The only advantage he held over the beau-tifully sculptured title-holder was his chest expansion. Mac's was 43 inches while Lewis' was 42. In addition, the British challenger was eight years older. Whichever way one looked at it, he was under a considerable handicap. It was true McAvoy was not bothered by the size difference, he never had in the past, and

Jock McAvoy returning from the states, on board the liner 'Berengaia'. Note he is unmarked.

wouldn't be in the future.

When Mac climbed into the Madison Square Garden ring to attempt to wrest the light-heavyweight crown from the head of that majestic champion, John Henry Lewis, the dice were well and truly loaded against him. As usual he was knawing away on his gloved thumbs waiting for the opening bell. He started in typical fashion, moving forward trying to connect with his powerful punches. Lewis fleet-footed, backed away and carefully picked him off with a stiff left jab. Every time the English lad jumped in to attack, the American would cleverly pull back and glide away. This fight was being fought to his dictates. On the occasions McAvoy landed with brisk left hooks, Lewis would tie him in a tight clinch. He was clever at smothering Jock's attacks. The champion was using right hand feints a great deal but Mac bobbed and weaved out of danger. The smaller man was putting up a tremendous battle, though John Henry was a very accomplished boxer indeed.

In the fourth Mac launched a two-handed salvo and cut Lewis over the left eye. The champion lost his cool composure and fought savagely. He was in a class of his own with his long-range boxing. Mac had fought bigger opponents before, but this fellow was the best by far. From the sixth McAvoy's dodgy right hand was

Out! Jock McAvoy hears the referee toll the 10-second count over Bill Wainwright in round three of their Belle Vue encounter.

absolutely useless again. He had banged it up on the champions elbow. In similar circumstances most other fighters would have been forced to call the referee over and withdraw from the contest and with every good reason, but Mac laboured on against all the odds. Jock saw openings for a right cross, but couldn't risk it and was forced to back away, which was against the grain, but he had no other choice. To make matters worse his left hand was swollen and causing him pain. Spectators couldn't help but admire McAvoy's fierce determination and his will to win.

The thirteen thousand spectators cheered the British lad's brave attempt to nail the classy champion with a left hook. In round eleven Jock hit Lewis with a swinging left hook which rocked him back on his heels, the crowd cheered enthusiastically. The American was stunned! His hands dropped down to his sides, he was badly hurt. There was a glorious opportunity to nail him with a right cross. Mac threw it instinctively but immediately pulled the punch and tried another left hook. It was obvious he was in too much pain in his right hand to chance landing with it. There is no doubt that if Mac could have connected with the right, the fight would undoubtedly have been over. But it wasn't to be! They fought toe to toe in the 15th and final round and Mac tried hard, but the champion did just enough to win. Joe Humphries, the famed Master of Ceremonies roared into his microphone in his piercing American drawl. "The winnah and still champion - John Henry Lewis." McAvoy was heartbroken. He tried, oh how he had tried, but he had little chance of beating a champion of the American's class with both fists damaged.

Back in his dressing room Dr Walker, from the New York State Athletic Commission examined Mac's damaged right hand, which by now was twice its normal size. The doctor shook his head and told the beaten fighter he must rest both hands for several months. "There is contusion of the tissues caused through old dislocations of the joints. My advice to you is go and see a top bone specialist when you get back to England, and don't fight until your hands are healed properly. Both your hands are in a shocking state," added the doctor. The fact that he was able to go fifteen fast, hard fought rounds while suffering agonies with two badly damaged hands against a champion of John Henry Lewis's calibre was striking testimony to the Lancastrian's spirit and toughness.

A few weeks later, a film of the fight with Lewis was shown in picture houses all over the British Isles. Though the cinemas advertised the complete film of the fight was to be shown this was not the case. A fifteen round contest of three minutes each round takes exactly fifty nine minutes, when the minute rests have been added, but the film in the cinemas lasted precisely twenty minutes. However, hordes of fans queued to watch it and said they had enjoyed it tremendously. Jack Bates saw the film and mentioned that Dave Lumiansky was very photogenic. Knowing that he was being filmed, Mr Dave was at his most egotistical, shouting and posing as the camera panned him on him. Thankfully his voice was dubbed out.

The contest against Jack Peterson is best forgotten for many reasons. It was a foolish match to say the least. At this period, Peterson was regarded as a superb British heavyweight champion. This fight must be ranked as McAvoy's poorest display of all his 147 recorded professional contests. Prior to the contest, the newspapers and boxing magazines gave it a tremendous amount of publicity. This obviously whetted the fans' appetites for this bout and within hours of the tickets going on sale, they were completely sold out. Jack Peterson was born in Cardiff in 1911. He won an A.B.A. light-heavyweight championship before turning professional in 1931. He was a tall upright boxer, cultured and classy. He had terrific power in his right hand and he was considered one of Britain's best heavyweight champions ever. In three fights with Len Harvey, he lost the first, stopped Harvey in 12 rounds in the return and, just for good measure, outpointed Harvey in their third encounter. He had also stopped Larry Gains, the highly respected heavyweight from Canada.

McAvoy disembarked off the liner "Berengaia" on 25th March 1936, and had little over four weeks until his 23rd April date with the heavyweight champion of Britain and the British Empire. This was absolutely ridiculous in every respect. Despite being told by a doctor to rest his hands that were still swollen, sensitive and painful, this contest was staged for one purpose and one purpose only - money. Yet here was Mac getting ready to fight a huge colossus of a man. He should never have been allowed to fight Peterson. He gave away over 20 lbs in weight, height, and reach.

The fight turned out to be a dismal flop. Petersen won on points, but was severely criticised for not being able to put the much smaller Lancashire boxer away inside the distance. McAvoy was criticised for not being able to bring off a spectacular knockout victory; the referee was blamed for not calling the two fighters together and insisting they put more action into their work, and the promoter received flak for making the match in the first place. Mac said: "You get fights like this sometimes, they don't live up to expectations. I did not have any inferiority complex seeing how big Petersen was compared to myself. In fact, he looked and was a size bigger than me. He decked me for eight in the fifteenth round but I wasn't badly hurt. Of course I'm disappointed but I'll be back."

Jack Bates always maintained that McAvoy put on an amazing performance against Petersen. "Despite all the negative publicity after this fight, Mac showed his greatness," remarked the trainer. "He was at every disadvantage. Petersen was the most colourful heavyweight in years, his right hand wallop was a decider for many of his opponents. Mac was cautious, and he changed from a hitherto murderous knockout merchant, and turned into a defensive boxer for fourteen of the fifteen rounds! He made the bigger man miss with his punches time after time. I understand how the crowd and reporters felt, because this was a strange and unreal McAvoy. There was none of the old tearing-in, two-handed attacking stuff. Petersen was a clear points winner but I only wish they could have fought on equal terms regarding height, reach, and weight!"

Bert Ikin was a well-known heavyweight, from Stoke-on Trent. He stood 6ft 2ins and weighed over 14 stone. He made his living as a sparring partner and had helped such notable fighters as Jack Petersen, Ben Foord, the German heavyweight, Walter Neusel. George Cook, Tommy Farr and as a 16 year old, he sparred with the Man Mountain himself, Primo Carnera. When McAvoy was preparing to box Jack Petersen, Big Bert had been helping the Welshman, but quite suddenly he was told his services were no longer required. Petersen told him he needed a smaller fighter, like McAvoy. Straight away Mac contacted Bert and hired him. "I found a big difference in McAvoy's style and that of Petersen's," he told the press. "Jock came at me wild-eyed, in a crouch, bobbing and weaving, hooking with both hands. Petersen attacked by standing straight up and fired out straight lefts and right crosses. I soon found out that McAvoy could dish out punishment like a kicking mule. He was one of the strongest two-handed hookers I've ever faced." Ikin said that boxing with Petersen had improved him as a boxer.

After a break of three months Mac entered the ring again for a contest arranged by Harry Fleming with the venue being Broomfield Road, Blackpool's football ground. It was another Bank Holiday Monday tournament that ensured a bumper crowd. McAvoy was now ready to fight again. He had been stung by the criticism after the fiasco with Jack Peterson, so he intended giving his opponent Bob Simpkins, from Bridlington in the North East, a real walloping. The crowd were hollering and yelling for both fighters before the fight even started. There were a number of Geordies in Blackpool on holiday and they were right behind their man. Bobbing and weaving, Mac went after his man from the opening bell. It was obvious to Fleming that Mac's timing was out. He was missing with punches and falling short as he attacked. Simpkins was giving a good account of himself boxing from a side on position and countering briskly whenever Mac missed, which was quite often.

The crowd were thrilled and excited by the action and the Lancashire fans whistled and screeched for McAvoy, while the North East fans gave a rendering of the Blaydon Races. With each passing round, Mac's ferocious body attack was taking affect and Simpkins was slowing. In the seventh Bob reverted to his side on boxing, keeping Jock at long range. Within a split second Mac unleashed a tremendous two-handed attack which hit the Geardie like machine gun bullets. Mac was remorseless and bludgeoned his man to the floor. It was bedlam, and the referee, Toe Tolley, McAvoy's former manager, was screaming out the count. Simpkins regained his feet as Tolley screamed "out." With that, all hell broke loose. The fans started booing as Simpkins pleaded with the referee to be allowed to carry on fighting. He was undoubtedly a very brave man. McAvoy told Tolley to let the fight continue, but the official refused and said his decision was final. Mac was thus declared the winner by stoppage in round seven.

Just prior to McAvoy's next contest at Belle Vue in September, he asked the trade paper Boxing to correct their previous week's statement that his real name was Joe Bamber, and that he was of Jewish origin. "No disrespect to the Jewish fraternity, but I can trace my forbears and they are of Irish - Lancashire stock," he said. Mac asked for this correction, not because of any anti - Semitic feeling, for he had many Jewish friends, but for the same feeling of clearing the air that any of his Jewish friends would have if it were announced that they were Gentiles.

The newspapers reported more conflict involving the middleweight champion that had nothing to do with boxing. McAvoy appeared at Stockport Magistrates court. He could well have done without this kind of bad publicity. The incident concerned himself and a Gorton resident, Billy Dixon. Mr Dixon had cycled into Cheadle and was browsing outside a shop looking at some gardening equipment. He was stationary and half mounted on his cycle which was into the kerb when he was bumped from behind by McAvoy's car. Mr Dixon dismounted from his bike and checked the rear of his bike to see if any damage had been done. By this time Mac got out of his car and walked over to Mr Dixon. "What are you looking for?" He asked the cyclist. Mr Dixon asked Mac for his credentials. With that, claimed Mr Dixon, McAvoy pushed him with one hand while he hit him with the other. "That's my name," he said. In court Mac said Mr Dixon was wrong when he claimed he was punched. He also said that it was the bicycle that bumped into his car and, he said, Mr Dixon was just being awkward when he produced a notebook. There was no damage done so there was no problem, said Mac. There were no witnesses but McAvoy was found guilty of assault and required to pay eleven shillings cost. Why he got involved like this was a complete mystery to the ordinary citizen.

There was a large turnout at Belle Vue's King's Hall, when the top-liner was a 12

Standing over a beaten Bob Simpkins, waiting for the bell to confirm yet another K.O.
This time it's the seventh round.

rounds match at 12st 2lb between McAvoy and Albert Barjolin, the cruiserweight champion of France. Both fighters looked in excellent condition with the Frenchman the taller of the two and with a fine physique. He marched into the ring wearing his championship belt, and he certainly looked the part with his tanned complexion. Fistic fireworks were anticipated. At the first bell Jock was forcing the proceedings effectively, scoring with straight lefts and hooking to the head. Barjolin was completely on the defensive while going backwards around the ring. Mac tried several rights, but he aimed them at his opponent's body. In the second round, however, Mac used his right hand punch with powerful effect and had his man rolling round the ring like a drunken sailor. The crowd were on their feet as Jock tore after the unhappy - looking French champion. A terrific right cross hit Barjolin flush on the whiskers and he dropped to one knee and took a short count. When he got up, Mac walloped him again with a more powerful right which knocked his opponent over the top rope. On regaining his feet he was holding his jaw and looked badly hurt. Jock beckoned him into the ring to continue the fight, but the Frenchman signalled his retirement, and the referee declared Mac the winner. There was a great deal of gesticulating from Barjolin's cornermen, and when going over to enquire the referee indicated that the foreigner had a possible fractured jaw. It was a disappointing finish to a keenly anticipated bout. It was later revealed that one of Mac's tremendous punches had dislodged a few of Barjolin's teeth, which had been embedded in his jaw.

In October Mac was signed to box Welsh light-heavyweight Charlie Bundy at Belle Vue, however, a few days before the contest, Bundy had to withdraw because an ailment and his place was taken by the Swandlincote heavyweight, Bill Wainwright. To make matters more appealing, Wainwright told the press that he had lodged a certain amount of his purse with boxing officials, stating that McAvoy would not knock him out, if he did then Mac would receive the money. That was confidence for you! The difference in size was quite evident as the two fighters stood in the centre of the ring listening to the referee's instructions. The Swadlincote boxer towered over McAvoy, he looked like a giant. When the bell sounded the two boxers circled each other and seemed to have a great respect for each other. This was not what the paying public had paid to see and pretty soon the

Left: Cheo Morejon, the tough Cuban light-heavyweight, staggers backwards from the impact of McAvoy's power.
Right:Morejon writhes in agony on the canvas after taking a body punch from McAvoy.

fans started shouting out for action. Soon afterwards McAvoy caught the big fellow right on the belly button with an awesome right hand, down he fell and his facial expression showed he was in agony. He gamely got to his feet before the referee reached 'ten'. Within seconds of the resumption, he was on the canvas again from another power-laden right hand to the body, the bell came to his rescue.

The second saw Wainwright catch the Rochdale fighter with a few stinging two-handed blows before he was dispatched to the floor once again. On getting to his feet, Mac was firing punches from all angles and the heavyweight was once more down on the canvas. He was as game as they come and trying to fight back when he was wobbled and in deep trouble when the bell sounded. In the third, Mac slipped inside Wainwright's leads and placing a perfect right hand he hit the Swadlincote man smack on the target and there was no way he could beat the count. It was revealed after the fight that McAvoy was so impressed by the Swadlincote heavyweight's game showing that he had declined to take any money from Wainwright's purse.

On the 1st of December, Mac travelled to Sheffield to face Dutch light-heavyweight kingpin, Rienus de Boer, in a ten round contest. Though Mac won easily on points it wasn't a good contest and the crowd gave vent to their feelings by booing lustily. The Rochdale man received a bad press, however it wasn't as bad as the news that appeared in the newspapers that Mac had assaulted two railway workers on Preston Railway Station. Richard Bennett and Arthur Aymes, two ticket collectors, told the police that they had been assaulted by McAvoy. Mr Bennett claimed he had his hat and glasses knocked to the ground, and Mr Aymes said he was punched to the ground. "This was a stupid thing McAvoy did," said Sammy Butt, and old time Collyhurst fighter. "It all started over Mac interfering with railway workers who were putting some of his horses on a train. He ended up in court and fined. There was no need for what he did. It brought him bad publicity and accusations that he was nothing but a bully, which in reality he wasn't. He never seemed to learn from his mistakes." When he appeared in court, Mac and was fined ten shillings on each charge.

The Wembley Roar

In January 1937 McAvoy was due to fight the classy Cuban light-heavyweight champion Cheo Morejon, at Leicester, but he had to withdraw because he had suffered another injury to his damaged right hand. That was not his only problem. On the domestic front his wife had been granted a divorce from him and given custody of their three children. It was reported that McAvoy had ill treated his wife besides having affairs with other women. He didn't seem in the least concerned or upset by the divorce proceedings, in fact, he had already set up home in Stockport with Joan Lye, a woman he had been having an affair with for some time.

Mac did eventually box his postponed contest against Cheo Morejon at Belle Vue, winning handily on points over the splendidly built black boxer. This was a good contest to start the year and the good news was that after 12 busy rounds his dodgy right hand had not troubled him unduly. At this time, Len Harvey, his arch rival, was acting as the matchmaker for promoter, Arthur Elvin who was staging a bumper attraction of a bill at the beautiful Empire Pool, Wembley in April 1937. The handsome Irishman Jack Doyle was opposing the top-class American, King Levinsky, in a potentially sizzling match-up, while popular Londoner Pat Palmer of Battersea faced Filipino, Small Montana. Thrown in for good measure was a contest between the lightweight champion of Britain, Jimmy Walsh and George Oldwell of Camden Town. But though these pairings were excellent matches, it was the top of the bill contest that was the most eagerly awaited fight of them all. It was a 15 rounder for the British light-heavyweight championship between the champion, that great Cockney favourite, Eddie Phillips of Bow and his challenger, Jock McAvoy. Mac had been suffering from a bad dose of bronchial influenza that had called for an earlier postponement. However, he had now recovered and was back to his best form and feeling on top of the world. He was feeling on top of the world because three days before the Phillips contest he became a father again when Joan Lye presented him with a baby son whom they named Michael.

Eddie Phillips was a big, good-looking fellow, and a solid champion who had travelled a hard road to get to the position of British champion. He could punch with the best of them and, at the start of his career, he had ran up 23 undefeated fights with 15 of them ending inside the distance. He had acted as Len Harvey's chief sparring partner on several occasions. Indeed, he had fought Len four times, drawing their first contest and losing the other three by very close decisions. He had won the title when Harvey, his close friend, had relinquished it and Eddie had out-pointed the durable Tommy Farr at Mountain Ash in South Wales, in 1935. This was a remarkable feat considering the heights Farr later reached. Eddie stood over six feet and possessed a very imposing physique.

The promoters had originally intended putting the Phillips-Mac fight as the last contest of the night. But the spectators complained that this would mean they would miss the contest because they would miss their train and tube connections. The fans were supported in this grievance by several newspaper reporters, the reporters claimed they would miss their deadlines for the following morning's papers. The promoters relented and it was 9-20 at night when Phillips and McAvoy entered the Wembley ring.

Jock McAvoy with his wife, Joan Lye.

It was not often that two boxers were seen in the ring with their nervous systems so highly strung as these two displayed. Almost every muscle in Phillips' lean body was quivering, while McAvoy bit so often at the thumbs of his gloves that it was surprising the tops of them did not drop off. Jack Bates said the reason for Mac's tension was that, though he had fought in London on quite a few occasions, McAvoy himself felt that he had rarely impressed and wanted this fight to be one the southern crowd would remember for a long time. Mac looked the stockier, but by comparison, Phillips looked liked Charles Atlas. As lean as a

"I jumped in again, only to be met by a well timed right cross that caught me smack on the chin and made me drop on my knees..." First round drama in the McAvoy v. Phillips fight at Wembley. Jock was up almost immediately and began his great task of beating Eddie and winning the title.

greyhound, he had the advantage of a few inches in height. He was also heavier. As usual when Mac was fighting, the crowd were tense and waiting patiently for the proceedings to start. Always there was the expectancy of fireworks straight from the first bell whenever he fought. He rarely disappointed the spectators. On this occasion there was a special kind of atmosphere around the ringside, and Tommy Farr sat with former world heavyweight champion Max Baer, waiting with baited breath for the first bell to ring. Another interested spectator was Egypt's King Farouk.

At the first bell Jock was out fast bobbing and weaving in his usual fashion and throwing rock - solid combinations in an effort to unsettle the slow starting title - holder. Mac had said before the fight "I know Phillips does not shape up too well against an aggressive fighter like myself, and I therefore have made up my mind to set up a strong attack and keep it going for the full fifteen rounds." And that's precisely how he started the fight. He was landing good, solid shots from his crouching style. Quite a few of Mac's punches got home and hurt the champion. But just as the Lancashire man jumped into the attack, Phillips calmly stood his ground and directed a corking right hand punch that hit the challenger flush on his jaw, dropping the middleweight champion to his knees. It was a stunning blow and would have written 'finish' to many other fighters on the receiving end, but this fellow McAvoy was a tough and durable man who most certainly didn't fold when the pressure was on him.

"It wasn't until my knees touched the canvas that I realised I had been caught good and proper by Phillips' punch," Mac later recalled. "But even so I was on my feet before the referee could start a count."

McAvoy made sure he kept his wits about him in case a further bombshell like that right cross came his way. He was determined that Eddie would pay a price for decking him and he flew into the attack.

In the second round Mac caught a glimpse of the title-holder's chin. Bang-a right cross landed with a resounding crack on Eddie's jaw and he went staggering into the ropes, badly hurt. Mac showed no mercy as he stormed after the cruiserweight king and dumped him on the floor with another crunching right hand blow. The game Cockney was in trouble and stayed on the deck for a count of nine. As he got up, Mac roared after him and soon had his opponent bleeding from the mouth.

The following round saw the Rochdale dynamiter surging forward. He was now in his element, this was what he loved and a further volley of two-handed blows saw the champion falling into the ropes and taking a short count. But Phillips wasn't British champion for nothing. He had an abundance of ring 'savvy' and class and was as brave as anything. On reaching his feat he glanced side ways and saw McAvoy flying toward him. Setting himself again the man from Bow delivered a terrific, power - packed right cross on his assailant's jaw, and this punch visibly shook Jock down to his toe nails. "I felt that punch, I can only thank my superb condition for the fact that I didn't go down and take the full count," Mac recalled later.

McAvoy had pasted Phillips with body punches since the opening bell, and it was no surprise to find Eddie holding on like a limpet. The referee reprimanded him in the fourth for clutching. The heavier champion was staging a counter - punching contest and despite Mac's invitation to have a punch - up, he refrained and bided his time. It was all pressure from the Rochdale fighter, who was like a tidal wave coming at Phillips all the time. Eddie's nose was bleeding badly again, he was having trouble breathing, and he was taking some heavy punishment. The crowd was getting more than their money's worth and were yelling like banshees as Mac grunted his way inside and flayed away with two - handed punches to the champions body. In the ninth round Eddie had been told he was falling behind and tried to stem the tide, but this fellow McAvoy was something else, refusing to be subdued or contained and his punches were damaging and landing like claps of thunder. He staggered the title-holder several times and it was the right hand that was inflicting the most damage time and time again. Yet Phillips fought back gamely and tried long-range boxing. His trusty right connected on Mac's chin once again and Jock was driven on his back foot. Round eleven was the champions best round. "He hit me with a powerful body punch in this round, it almost finished me, but somehow I contrived to keep upright and smothered his follow up attack," Mac recalled later.

Another good round for the champion was the 12th, and his uppercut brought blood pouring from Jock's mouth. McAvoy was as strong as a bull though, and just as combative. His sheer power finally wore his rival down. In the 13th the crowd were almost hoarse from cheering and shouting. Mac caught his man with a terrific barrage of leather that had Phillips gasping and doubled over in pain. The Londoners were silent as Mac meted out a whirlwind attack of non-stop punches. It was all McAvoy now and the Lancashire fighter was remorseless in this mood.

The challenger was off his stool quickly for the 14th round. Jock was swarming all over Phillips, stabbing five unanswered left jabs into the title-holder's face. The gutsy cruiserweight king tried desperately to fight back but he had shot his bolt, the body punches having taken a heavy toll and drained him of his strength. Back came the challenger, bobbing and weaving and his grunting and snorting had a terrifying sound to it. He dug a savage hook to the pit of Philips' stomach followed by a crunching right cross which ripped a gash over the champions left eye and dumping him on the boards as if hit by a thunderbolt. Half on, his side legs up in the air, head hanging over the bottom rope, though still trying to get up. It was no good he was out, he could not beat the count.

Eddie's seconds administered over their man as he lay prone on the canvas, and it was some considerable time before he was allowed to leave the ring and go to his dressing room where a doctor gave him assistance.

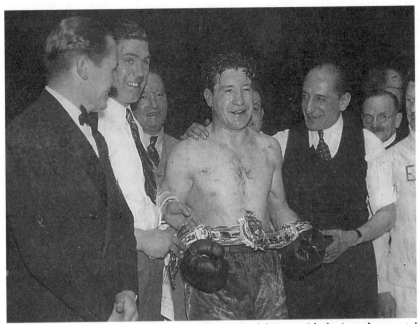

After the fight with Eddie Phillips, Jock McAvoy celebrates with the 'usual suspects'.

The winner and new light-heavyweight king was the rugged Lancashire lad, Jock McAvoy. He was now the middle and light - heavyweight champion of Great Britain, a truly memorable feat and a wonderful achievement. There was a further honour in store for Mac, and something that pleased him enormously, when he received a "Certificate of Merit" from the editor of Boxing, a weekly boxing newspaper. One thing was certain, he would never forget this night at Wembley for as long as he lived. Neither would the 11,500 lucky spectators who had paid £15,200 for the privilege. What a fight!

"Wembley's night of pugilism was the most notable for several years," wrote Trevor Wignall in the Daily Express the following morning. "The fights aroused terrific applause, what more could be desired? McAvoy was so tremendous that I would hate the prospect of having to face him in the ring. The pity is that he has no hope of putting on an extra couple of stone which would make him a real heavyweight."

Though he had been celebrating his excellent victory over Phillips and becoming light-heavyweight champion, McAvoy was back in action only a week after winning the title. Dai Jones, a Welshman was his opponent and the bout was at the Colston Hall in Bristol. With hindsight this was absolutely stupid to say the least, how on earth could any fighter be expected to give off his best less than a week after winning a prestigious national championship contest, and being in a fight already being regarded as a classic? Yet, rather than pull out and let the fans down, Mac went through with the bout. He tried hard to end the contest quickly, but Jones, the Welsh middleweight champion, was fired up for the contest and thwarted the champions every attempt to land the knockout blow. In fact, Jones himself nearly pulled off a shock when in round eight, the Welsh fighter caught McAvoy with a sledge hammer of a punch. Mac's knees briefly touched the canvas, but he was up without a count and knocked Jones all around the ring in retaliation. In the tenth and final round McAvoy had the courageous Welshman holding and clinching for all he was worth as he battered him unmercifully to gain a points victory. Needless to say, Jones was cheered all the way back to his dressing room for putting up such a gritty showing. McAvoy, though, was obviously stale. Take into consideration also, that Dai Jones was no mug. He had fought all the best in the country and, had lost an eliminator with Mac's next challenger, Jack Hyams, for McAvoy's middleweight title and that shows his pedigree.

The familiar and infamous McAvoy "Red Mist" surfaced again in an incident that had nothing to do with his boxing exploits and resulted in another court appearance, making McAvoy the talk of the pubs and clubs around Lancashire for weeks. Today, this type of incident would be called "Road Rage." While driving down Oxford Road in Manchester, McAvoy's car was involved in a slight collision with a delivery van, it was nothing serious, but a minor argument followed. Harry Fleming was sitting in the front of the car with Mac. It's not certain whether the van driver knew who McAvoy was or not, nonetheless, obscenities and heated words were exchanged between the two men. Fleming, knowing only too well Mac's explosive temper begged him to forget the whole thing and for them to continue on their journey. But Mac, being the hot-headed type of fellow he was, wouldn't let the matter drop. In the meantime the van driver accelerated away, and there the matter should have ended.

As the van driver called into a petrol station he was visibly shocked to find that McAvoy had followed him. Leaning out of his car window, Mac shouted to the van driver that he had a good mind to report him for his behaviour and bad driving. With a few people on the forecourt looking on, the van driver looked at Mac and,

"Phillips went reeling to the floor...gamely he struggled on to beat the count, but could n't make it.." An historic picture taken at Wembley as McAvoy became light-heavyweight champion.

smirkingly, shouted something derogatory, to which the fighter replied: "You're a cheeky little so and so, I've a good mind to report you to your company." Further insults were exchanged between the two men and the van driver pointed to the side of his van indicating the name and address of his employer. "Go on, report me", he shouted, then adding: "Do you fancy yourself?", or words to that effect. This was like waving a red cape at a bull, and McAvoy, by this time raging, jumped out of his car and went over to the man and allegedly whacked him in the stomach. Harry Fleming was beside himself with worry in case they were recognised and the newspapers found out. There were two witnesses, one was an ex-policeman who said that the van driver made no attempt to defend himself, the other witness was a lady who told the court that McAvoy's punch seemed to have a great deal of force behind it. Giving evidence in court, Mac denied he punched anyone, claiming that he merely pushed the van driver. Mac was found guilty and fined five pounds. Incidents of this kind dogged McAvoy throughout much of his life, giving him lots of publicity of the wrong kind.

McAvoy was due to have a few more non-title fights before defending his British middleweight crown against Jack Hyams in July. These contests were cancelled and Mac decided to have a break from the rigours of training and fighting. What was to follow, though, was certainly not what McAvoy had planned or visualised would happen. He would often ride his horses at Woodhall's Farms in Cheadle Hulme near Stockport. One day while out riding his thoroughbred steeplechaser, Mac went over a high jump. While in mid-air, the saddle girth snapped, and Jock was thrown to the ground head first, with a terrible thump. Other horse riders gathered round to help, but McAvoy was in a bad state. He was cut and his head hurt badly, and due to a massive swelling it looked as if he had broken his neck. Without delay, he was rushed to Stockport Infirmary.

It was at first feared that McAvoy's boxing career would now be ended because of the seriousness of his injury. The doctors attending him explained that fortunately nothing was broken, though his neck muscles were severely damaged and told him it was only his marvellous physical condition that had saved him from much more serious and lasting damage. After more medical tests, his neck was set in a plaster cast, and he had to sit rigid for twenty-four hours, drinking only liquids. On reflection, he was indeed a very lucky person to escape with the damage he had, though perhaps this injury might well have resulted in his permanent disability a few years later. Jock must have been the worst patient the hospital had ever encountered, forever moaning and groaning, not, I hasten to add, because of the extreme pain he must obviously have been suffering, but because he was immobilised and incapacitated. It must be said that he was a remarkable human being. It's not certain whether the hospital had had enough of his complaining or McAvoy himself asked to go home, but after only a few days, home is where he went. Of course, all his planned fights were shelved.

At home Mac became impossible to live with. What upset him more than anything was that he couldn't go out gallivanting. Wearing the plaster cast must have obviously caused discomfort, because he couldn't lie down, and consequently he got very little rest. He found that he had to turn right round in order to see anything that wasn't in front of him. His skin underneath the plaster became itchy and this made him even more irritable. Taking everything into consideration, he had done exceptionally well not to explode a lot sooner. One night he got out of bed and went into the kitchen and took a sharp knife from the drawer, he then proceeded to cut away at the plaster. It was madness, as he would soon find out to his cost. When the last bit of plaster was removed, his head fell to one side and he was in agony from the resulting pain from his neck. The result of this foolishness was that he was rushed back to the hospital. After the doctor examined him and a brand new

Famed for the intensity of his sparring, Jock McAvoy looks fearsome in this action shot of a gymnasium work-out.

plaster casting applied he was told in no uncertain terms that if it didn't stay on until the doctor saw fit to remove it, then the injury would take a lot longer to heal. McAvoy showed patience this time and paid a few visits to London where Dr Marlin treated him. In fact, Mac openly stated that this specialist was responsible for him being able to resume his boxing career when everyone else said it would be a physical impossibility. The reader will have gained an impression of what a hard man McAvoy was in and out of the ring. The injury he had suffered was very serious indeed, and similar accidents have resulted in other injured persons being crippled for life. He had made a miraculous recovery.

After being inactive for over six months, Mac was itching to start training and doing his road work again. Harry Fleming, though no longer McAvoy's manager, was still acting as his trainer and cornerman and was very concerned when Belle Vue announced the date of 25th October for his long delayed middleweight championship defence against the London boxer, Jack Hyams. Harry told McAvoy that in his opinion, because of the seriousness of his neck injury and the length of time he had been out of action, Mac needed more time to prepare. Characteristically,

McAvoy over-ruled him and agreed to fight on the date set. In training Mac had the usual variety of sparring partners: the Canadian Carl Rooney, Jimmy McKenzie from Scotland, Jack McKnight, a Leicester fighter, Fred Shaw, the Shipley fighter who had beaten Marcel Thil; and Billy Kelly, a young Manchester lad. These fellows were good but they were told to be extremely careful and avoid hitting Mac in the neck region. This must be the only time throughout his career that McAvoy's sparring partners had it easy.

For hours before the championship contest started, Jack Bates massaged McAvoy's neck. Bates was worried that the damage Mac had suffered in the horse riding accident might not stand up to the strain of a long fifteen round battle.

However, when fight time came, McAvoy was fully prepared for Hyams. Belle Vue was packed to capacity as the contest started. The Stepney taxi-driver poked out a useful left jab and moved around the ring like the craftsman he was. McAvoy looked sluggish, and this of course, was only to be expected after his injury and lay off from action. As the rounds progressed the challenger was producing the smarter boxing while the champion was his usual aggressive self. In the fifth, Hyams stunned Mac with a left hook-right cross combination. Instead of following up his advantage, Hyams back peddled. In the sixth, a cut was opened under Jack's left eye and the blood was flowing freely. Jock poured on the pressure sending punches toward the target area, causing more trouble for the Cockney, and a huge swelling closed the left eye completely. Sensing that his time was limited, Hyams fought ferociously and caught the champion with solid blows. The crowd were enjoying the battle and both fighters gave everything they had. The left side of the challenger's face was bruised and swollen, and it was now just a matter of time before the end came. In the eleventh round, McAvoy increased the tempo and threw every punch in the book. Hyams was tottering, but his fighting heart kept him upright. When the bell sounded to end the round, Jack wobbled back to his corner and his seconds retired him, which was the sensible and humane thing to do.

McAvoy, having won the Lonsdale championship belt out-right, was now presented with his second. The man who made the presentation was none other than Doctor Marlin, the doctor who had treated the fighter for his neck injury. Mac also had a third belt after he beat Eddie Phillips. "I was as jumpy as a jack-in-the-box during the fight," said Jack Bates. "Hyams concentrated on getting inside, and many of his punches landed with a thud on the back of Mac's head. Each round

McAvoy leaving hospital in Altrincham, Manchester, March 1939.

was a shock to Mac's spinal system. But he never flinched, and what a finish. He was like a hurricane in that eleventh round. We were relieved though that Jock came out without further damage to his neck."

Immediately after the Hyams fight negotiations commenced for a return contest against the American, John Henry Lewis, for his world light-heavyweight crown, and also with Tommy Farr, for the British and Empire heavyweight titles. Circumstances would, however, see to it that these plans were soon scuppered. Farr, the gallant Welshman, had won the hearts of everybody by his heroic stand against the great Joe Louis when he took the Brown Bomber the full fifteen rounds before losing on points and had decided to remain in America for further fights. Lewis and his connections demanded far too much money plus expenses, so that contest never came to fruition.

Eager to keep active, Mac fought a month after beating Jack Hyams, when at the Victoria Hall, Hanley, he was matched with a light-heavyweight named Alban Mulrooney, who hailed from Macclesfield in Cheshire. Mulrooney had been one

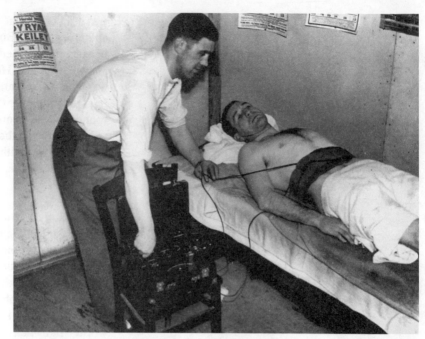

McAvoy being tested by Tom Hurst for his physical condition, prior to the fight with Jack Hyams, in London, 1937. Mac won after stopping Hyams in round 11.

of Jock's sparring partners several times in the past, so should have known what to expect. He certainly received no favours from his former employer. Mac was in a spiteful mood and set about the Cheshire boxer from the start of the contest, bombarding him with two-fisted body shots. In round three it was all over. Alban took three counts and was hurt badly but extremely relieved when the referee called enough.

Vasile Serbanesco, the Rumanian cruiser and heavyweight champion was McAvoy's last opponent of 1937. The Belle Vue crowd wanted to see their idol in action once more before the year ended. The Rumanian was a huge man, and obviously very strong. Their contest turned out to be a lot harder than anyone anticipated and, in fact, Serbanesco proved to be an extremely powerful and a very useful right hand puncher. McAvoy certainly got more than he bargained for during the four rounds the fight lasted. It was give and take with plenty of full-blooded action with each fighter scoring with heavy, stinging punches. In the fourth round, the two fighters swapped blows and the crowd were by now expecting the fight would last perhaps the distance. Then the two fighters went into a clinch, there was a great deal of rough stuff taking place with Mac guilty of butting and being over-zealous and the Rumanian boxer came away with blood streaming down his face from an ugly-looking gash over his left eye. He was infuriated and knowing that he was badly cut, Serbanesco met McAvoy in the centre of the ring and both fighters flayed away at each other much to the fans' obvious delight. But the eye damage was much too severe for the big Rumanian to continue and his seconds were forced to concede defeat to Mac. Nonetheless, he had given the British champion a stern test. McAvoy, who was now 30 years old, had had a splendid year, apart from his near disastrous accident. He had had six contests, winning them all in style scoring four stoppages while taking Eddie Phillips' light-heavyweight title in a classic contest.

McAvoy rounded of the year by getting married to Joan Lyle on 20th December at Stockport Register Office. His new wife was 25. Sadly, the marriage was doomed from the start and less than a year later the couple would be split up.

Losing the Light Heavyweight Crown

Billy Hardy was a young promising cruiserweight prospect from Leicester who had ambitions of going to the top of the boxing ladder. Taking advice from his friends, he challenged McAvoy to a twelve round contest at the Granby Halls, Leicester in January 1938. Johnny Best, the astute Liverpool matchmaker and promoter was staging the contest. Mac, of course, readily agreed after terms had been settled. Hardy, was managed by George Biddles, the well-known manager of that time who later would pilot the late Hogan "Kid" Bassey to the world featherweight championship in the 1950s. Biddles was touting Hardy, who came from Barlestone, which was just outside Leicester as a certainty to capture boxing's highest honours. Hardy was already the Midlands Area light-heavyweight title-holder. The publicity the Midlands press gave to the fight created a big demand for tickets. There was nothing like a puncher to gain the publics' attention, especially if he was matched against an up and coming young prospect.

Over 7,000 fans packed into the Granby Halls for the contest. McAvoy knew that he couldn't afford to take any chances and trained in his usual diligent manner at the Belle Vue gym. He hammered his sparring partners, Tommy Henderson, the Scottish boxer, Kid Scott, the clever Sheffield light-heavyweight and Carl Rooney the big Canadian. Word came back to Manchester that Billy Hardy was looking sensational in his gym work-outs and had spent more money on hiring extra sparring partners than he had received in purse money for a number of his contests. McAvoy, though, was typically unconcerned with this information. When the fight started, Mac was fully expecting the local favourite to come out of his corner and start bombing, but it soon became obvious that Billy had no such plan, instead he was content to last the distance and try and pick up enough points to win by decision. The fans rallied round and cheered their man to the echo. Whenever McAvoy got close, Hardy would wrap his long arms around him like an octopus. In the sixth the referee pulled the two fighters apart and ordered both men to put on a better performance and give the crowd some excitement. This, of course, suited the Northerner, and he soon cut loose with a flurry of two-handed blows to the head and body. With the crowd now roaring both fighters forward, McAvoy drove rib-bending punches into the Leicester prospect, driving him against the ropes.

Fighting a heavyweight in Jack Strongbow, McAvoy comes in with his guard well up and is about to counter with the left.

Suddenly, Mac whipped a left hook to the body that had a devastating effect and hurt Hardy, this blow being followed by a short right hand to the jaw. It was a lethal punch. Hardy dropped like a log and, though he vainly tried to lift his hands, the referee completed the "ten" and out while Hardy groped aimlessly on the canvas.

The next contest on 28th February, was a warm up before McAvoy's challenge to Len Harvey. Jack Madden fixed him up for a bout with the champion of Switzerland, Walter Von Buren. For some reason or other Herr Von Buren, upon hearing about McAvoy's phenomenal knockout record, decided it would be safer to go skiing in the Alps rather than cross gloves with Mac at Belle Vue. Jack Strongbow, from West Hartlepool, replaced the Swiss boxer at short notice. Strongbow was over two stones heavier than Mac, and stood more than a foot taller and, obviously, as he was a fully-fledged heavyweight, he also had a reach advantage into the bargain. Nevertheless, Mac battered this big fellow from pillar to post. The big-hearted north east boxer had a heart as big as his frame, but took an eight count in the second and third rounds. McAvoy was ducking underneath Strongbow's hefty swings and digging his own punches into the heavyweight's body with a fearful thud. Just before the conclusion of round five Mac decked his opponent with a vicious right cross. It looked all over, but the bell came to Strongbow's rescue, or did it? After dousing him with cold water, his seconds sent him out to face the rampaging Rochdale man in round six. McAvoy flew at his man and connected with a fearsome left hook that nearly took the big fellow's head off his shoulders. Jack was down, but he was as game as they come and got to his feet ready to fight on. It should have been stopped because he was obviously badly hurt, yet without waiting Mac sprung at him and delivered another cracking left hook which hit the button and flattened the giant for the full count.

McAvoy's next assignment was to defend his British light-heavyweight title against the number one contender, Len Harvey, on 7th April at London's Harringay Arena. This contest, staged at London's Harringay Arena saw Mac lose this championship to the clever Harvey in a fifteen rounder, details of which are given in the chapter which deals with the McAvoy-Harvey encounters. Although he was bitterly upset at losing his light-heavyweight crown to Len Harvey, McAvoy knew he had to get on with his career. Of course, he hoped to win the light-heavyweight title back again. Harvey, with his own career aspiration in mind, had his sights set on winning the British heavyweight championship, and in this eventuality Mac needed to be ready to fight for his old title. Within four weeks of his contest with Harvey, Jock was back in action. He was booked to fight the French cruiserweight champion, Marcel Lauriot, a fighter he had previously outpointed a couple of years before. The venue was the Theatre Royal in Dublin. Though McAvoy already had beaten the Frenchman, it was thought that Lauriot would give him a much sterner test because of his own improved form since they had last fought. Nonetheless, Mac had every intention of rendering the champion of France unconscious and flat out on the canvas.

Jock arrived in Ireland a few days before his contest and thoroughly enjoyed himself. Appearing at the Theatre Royal that week were famous music-hall artistes such as Charlie Kunz, the well known, brilliant pianist, and comedians Sid Field and Norman Evans. Evans was a keen boxing fan who had followed Jock's career from his early days at Royton. He and Mac would play endless hours of snooker together. McAvoy trained at the Trinity Gym, and the stars came to watch him work out. In the gymnasium one particular afternoon was an Irish boxing official who was to be the timekeeper for the forthcoming tournament. When he saw that Mac had nobody to time him while shadow boxing the official offered his services, and with his stopwatch in hand he climbed onto the apron of the ring. As we know, when McAvoy trained, he trained as hard as he fought. Unfortunately, the man got a bit too close to the ropes and whoosh, Mac let fly with some imaginary punch-

McAvoy's wife, Joan Lye, with her horses.

es, hit the poor fellow's hand knocking his hand back and nearly tearing it out of its socket with the stopwatch smashed in little pieces on the floor.

The fights were scheduled to start at midnight and McAvoy entered the ring at the unearthly hour of two o' clock in the morning. Having heard of Mac's fearsome punching reputation, the Irish fans had patiently waited for his contest, though many of the four thousand or so spectators were yawning by the time the introductions were made. McAvoy didn't intend keeping the fans up any longer than necessary and as the bout commenced the tall Frenchman poked out several left leads to the British fighters head, all which were nonchalantly slipped. McAvoy, cold-eyed like a hungry tiger waiting to pounce, bided his time. As the second round got going the two fighters had a spell of ferocious body punching but, after sampling Mac's body bombardment he soon broke off proceedings. Straight away the Rochdale 'banger' delivered a left jab which forced Lauriot's head up high. That was the opening McAvoy was hoping for. Wham, he instantly let a right cross go, and smack, it hit poor Marcel flush on the chin. The sheer ferocity of the whole movement and punch brought the spectators out of their seats and on their feet hooting and hollering. The power of the punch sent the Frenchman flat on his back. He was completely unconscious. In little more than five minutes, McAvoy's fearsome punches had completely destroyed the good-looking French champion. By this time the crowd were fully awake and cheering wildly. It had been a long time since they had witnessed such devastating power. Lauriot though, still lay prone on the floor as his seconds and the doctor worked feverishly over him. It was quite some time before he could be moved from the ring and as he was being helped back to the dressing room, he cried unashamedly.

This was the first time in his entire career that he had been counted out. This, though, was McAvoy at his most devastating.

After his impressive victory in Dublin, McAvoy felt in peak physical condition and a programme of fights was duly planned to keep him sharp and ready for any championship challenges. Unfortunately, further tragedy was waiting for him. Despite the horrific riding accident he had suffered twelve months earlier, his love for horse riding and his buccaneer approach to danger had not deserted him. Most folk having sustained such a terrible injury while riding would have been very reluctant indeed to venture on to a horse ever again. But, if anything, Mac was just as reckless while in the saddle, throwing caution or safety to the wind. While out riding one day his horse, a bad-tempered animal, suddenly, for no apparent reason, rose up on its hind legs and fell over on its side, trapping McAvoy underneath it. The outcome was that he had broken his left leg badly. When help arrived he was taken to Stockport Infirmary. His leg was set in plaster and he was told that this cast would remain on his leg for the next three months. Of course, Mac's future plans had to be shelved and re-arranged and fights cancelled. Injuries are the bane of every fighters life, because they prevent him earning money. McAvoy was in a foul mood for the full duration that the plaster was on his leg.

To make matters worse, a few weeks previously he had appeared in court at Bolton on a charge of speeding and driving without insurance. The magistrate fined him a fiver, but worse was in store, he lost his driving license when he was given a five-year ban. This was a severe shock to Mac and would cause him no end of hassle.

There were even more problems for Mac, for in the summer he appeared in court at Stockport. He was ordered to pay his wife Joan a maintenance order for eleven shilling a week. It was also revealed in court that McAvoy had admitted persistent cruelty to his wife. He had always been a cavalier type of fellow, but was also a

This picture was taken when McAvoy was famous and trained in the county's finest gymnasiums. It was not always like that.

selfish person, as I have mentioned earlier in the book. Not domesticated by any means and not a man to sit at home with a book and slippers, he had an urge to be constantly on the move. He would not be tied down by anybody, especially a woman.

Once the plaster cast had been removed, McAvoy was back in training, jogging and working out in the gym. "I can tell you one thing," said Jack Bates. "He was bursting to start sparring, he wanted to hit somebody. Many boxers might have thrown in the sponge after the serious accidents Mac had suffered. But the fellow was an amazing character." Harry Levene, his manager, wasted little time in fixing Mac up with a schedule of four fights all against cruiserweights, within seven weeks.

Birmingham was his first stop. On promoter Ted Salmon's show at the Tower Ballroom, big Jack Strongbow was his opponent for a re-match. One would have thought that Jack might have learned his lesson after the shellacking he had taken

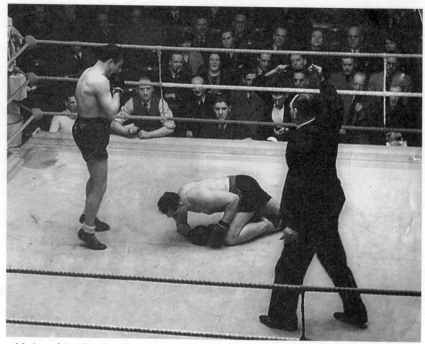

McAvoy bites his thumb as Jack Strongbow fails to beat the count, Harry Fleming looks on.

from Mac only a few months earlier, but he insisted that he had taken that fight despite adequate preparation, as a substitute. Norman Hurst sent word back to McAvoy that he had been to watch Strongbow training and was impressed by what he saw. "Strongbow showed terrific form in his workouts, and promises to spring a surprise on you," Hurst told Mac, adding that the West Hartlepool fighter asked Hurst to pass on a message to Jock. "I am going to use my weight this time!" "Don't take him lightly," added the reporter. Jock came to the scales at 12 stone while the Leicester heavyweight was 14 stone, so in reality Mac was fighting a genuine heavyweight-again.

The crowd waited with baited breath for the bell to start the first round. The North easterner was soon on the deck for an eight count. Considering the six months he had been out of action, Mac looked razor sharp and powerful. Strongbow was down again in the third for eight, and in round four Mac dropped his giant sized opponent twice more for counts of seven. It was all one way traffic-straight to

Strongbow's chin and body. Round five saw McAvoy increase the tempo and after flooring Jack once more referee Jack Curphey mercifully put an end to the massacre as Strongbow, bleeding profusely, staggered around the ring on on-steady legs.

Arthur Ashworh was a teenager in 1938. His father was a friend of McAvoy's from their schoolboy days, and the two of them had been in many scrapes together. Arthur recalled on occasion when around about this time Mac was teaching his wife Joan, to drive. "I was sat in the back of Mac's car along with my dad," said Arthur. "It was bloody murder. Joan was making a lot of mistakes and Mac was shouting and bawling at her. The poor woman's nerves must have been in shreds. It ended when she crashed the car into a gas lamp." When I asked Arthur what happened next he was hesitant, then said: "He whacked her in the face!" A few days later, Arthur saw Joan and her eye was bruised and swollen. "It was a real shiner," added Arthur.

There was another incident which occurred about this time. Arthur and his dad were sitting in the back of a car driven by Harry Fleming. They were dropping Joan off at the Empire Picture House in Rochdale. There was a large queue and Mac jumped out of the car and dashed up to the pay desk. Just as he was asking for a ticket a chap named Warburton, who was waiting to purchase a ticket, told McAvoy to queue up like everybody else. With that Mac shouted at him: "Do you know who I am? I'm Jock McAvoy, the famous boxer." With that Mr Warburton, who according to Arthur Ashworth was a local bricklayer and a handy fellow with his fists, said: "I don't give a – who you are, queue up like the rest of us." And he belted McAvoy, knocking him down the steps. Harry Fleming jumped out of the car and finally persuaded Mac to leave it and get back into the car.

Len Harvey was singing the praises of the Irish light-heavyweight champion Joe Quigley who came from Sligo. Harvey had taken the young Irish fighter under his wing and tipped him as a future champion. Joe was a happy go lucky character and did a great deal of crooning in pubs and clubs. When promoter John Woodhouse offered him a contest against McAvoy both he and Harvey accepted immediately. In the fight itself, Quigley made not the slightest attempt to beat McAvoy in their ten round contest at the King's Hall, in Derby. After winning every round Mac was a clear winner though the crowd were disappointed in the Sligo fighters negative showing. This was a fight Mac declared was best forgotten. It was estimated by reporters at ringside that Quigley didn't throw more than half a dozen punches

"It was a non-stop thriller." McAvoy sinks Frank Hough at Belle Vue, Manchester.

throughout the entire ten rounds so intent was he on survival. The ebullient Quigley, however, was later taken into the McAvoy training camp and soon became one of Mac's favourite sparring partners due to his ability to keep the Rochdale man amused with his Irish wit and engaging conversation.

Walter Metcalfe, the manager of Tommy Reddington who was billed as "the Salford heavyweight prospect", but was in fact born and bred in north Manchester, issued a challenge in the newspapers for his man to tackle any boxer in the country up to 13 stone. Walter also stated he would add a £100 side-stake to any takers. McAvoy immediately accepted the challenge. Manchester fight fans were rubbing their hands in glee at the prospect of another rip roaring all-Lancashire confrontation. Tommy had a good pedigree and was indeed regarded as a possible future British champion. He was also known as the best gym fighter in the British Isles. Later in his career go on to beat Freddie Mills and fight Bruce Woodcock beside many more of the country's top heavyweights.

Harry Fleming, acting as McAvoy's spokesman, contracted the newspapers saying that Mac had accepted the challenge and let it be known that he would also cover the £100 side stake. However, Fleming made one condition, and that was in the event of Reddington and McAvoy fighting each other the winner was to receive 75 percent of the purse and the loser 25 percent. The prospect of these two fighting each other created interest in all the newspapers and their meeting was written about for a couple of weeks. However, Walter Metcalfe said he wasn't happy at what Fleming had suggested and stated that if and when his man met McAvoy he would do so for the highest purse offered to him and not under the conditions laid down by Fleming. Mac wanted this fight, he was supremely confident that he could demolish the young up and coming Reddington. He told Fleming to arrange the fight as quickly as possible.

The arguments raged long and loud. Jack Smith the promoter and British Boxing Board of Control steward got involved in the argument and Norman Hurst also got into the act until there was a real slanging match between Metcalfe, Fleming, Hurst and Smith. Despite all the publicity, no promoter made even a token offer to stage this contest. When all arguments came to a stand still, McAvoy was fuming. Norman Hurst then suggested that McAvoy and Reddington to settle the argument should fight each other in a big gymnasium and charge a select 150 or so sportsmen two guineas each to watch the match, let the winner have the £100 side stake and give the rest of the money to charity. Needless to say the fight never took place.

Frank Hough, known as "The Fighting Hussar," to British fans, was McAvoy's next opponent. And Jock knew that he would have a much tougher scrap on his hands with Hough than Quigley had given him. Hough's slogan was: "Pay me the money and I don't care who the opponent is, I guarantee to make it interesting for him." The amazing thing was that Mac was fighting Hough only a week after going the ten rounds against Quigley. However, this didn't bother him, not in the least. Hough, from Battersea, was a bull-terrier of a fighter, had been matched with the Rochdale fighter previously, but when Jock nearly broke his neck obviously their fight had to be cancelled. Several attempts had since been made to pair these two tear-away scrappers, but it never seemed to materialise through one thing or other. Frank seemed to get the wrong impression that McAvoy was not keen to take him on. Nothing could have been further than the truth, and the fight was set for Belle Vue on 21st November. Both fighters trained diligently. Mac sparred with the Anglo-Italian light-heavyweight Tony Arpino who was matched against Carl Rooney on the same bill. Arpino was tremendously tough and created a record of sorts because he stayed as McAvoy's sparring partner for ten days (usually his hired help left after a couple of days!)

Frank Hough had sparred with Mac when he was preparing to fight Eddie Phillips and also for one of the Len Harvey fights, and insisted he had the punch with which to beat the Rochdale fighter. He referred to his left uppercut, a punch he had exploited with telling effect on some of the best light-heavyweights in the business. Hough had also defeated Tommy Reddington, which added more spice to the fight against McAvoy. The Battersea fighter was certainly full of himself and he was telling everyone who visited him at his Shrewburyness training quarters what he was going to do to Mac. One of his sparring partners was big Larry Gains, and according to reports, he was giving Gains a torrid time. Of course this chatter was relayed to the Lancashire man causing more 'needle' to enter into it.

A couple of days before the fight Jack Madden, the matchmaker, was told to pay Hough only one third of his purse from his fight with McAvoy, and forward the remainder to people with whom Hough had some form of agreement. "It places me in a bit of a quandary," said Madden, who said he knew that Hough had an arrangement with the National Sporting Club whereby the greater part of his earnings are banked for him with the idea of making provision for his future. However, what actual percentage governed the arrangement, Madden didn't know.

This was a contest that fans throughout Great Britain had been clamouring for, two big hitters with only one thing on their minds, and that was to knock the other fellow into oblivion. The ex-Hussar was both experienced and in a hurry, having over a hundred fights in just over four years. He had fought all the top names in the middle and light-heavyweight divisions. By fight time there wasn't a single seat left, it was another sell-out. This was another of those eventful nights in the lives of everyone present on this night in the King's Hall. It was a non-stop thriller from first bell to the sudden ending of hostilities. Hough was one of the best counter punchers in the game, and boy could he punch. First one fighter would force the other backwards then they would reverse roles, all the time swapping punch for thudding punch, with the audience in raptures at the sheer excitement of the occasion. It was a battle worthy of any championship and the Londoner was giving as good as he received.

The ending came in the sixth round, the fighting Hussar rushed at McAvoy winging punches toward the Lancashire fighters body area, although using these suicide tactics meant that he was leaving his chin exposed. Mac, slipped inside these punches and hit Hough in the pit of his stomach, then like lightning took full advantage and sent a pulverising right smash, which hit Hough solidly on the jaw knocking him cork-legged and stretched out on his back. Game as ever, Frank tried to beat the count but was unable. This was a tremendous victory for Mac, and the sell-out crowd rose to acclaim both fighters. McAvoy certainly knew he had been in a fight as he was aching all over afterwards. "One second I was fighting strongly, then McAvoy slipped inside my guard and drove home the two blows that registered victory for him," said the courageous Londoner.

Jackie Brown fought on the undercard of the McAvoy-Hough bill, stopping the out-classed Ginger Murphy in four one sided rounds. Later, the two former stable mates went for a meal before visiting a night club. There was a collection in the King's Hall for Bernard White, a Bolton boxer who had lost a leg in a motor accident. £61.5 shillings and 4 pence was collected for the unfortunate lad.

After his sensational victory over Hough, McAvoy was pleased to hear the news that negotiations were underway with Hymie Caplan, the manager of Solly Krieger, New York's battling Hebrew fighter, with a view to the American holder of the world middleweight crown coming over to defend his title against Mac. Krieger, from the tough district of Brooklyn had beaten Al Hostack for the championship, and had ended a long winning streak of the up and coming future champion Billy Conn. Wembley and Belle Vue were trying to secure the match. Meanwhile, Johnny Best the Liverpool promoter offered £2,000 if McAvoy would fight Ernie Roderick at Liverpool's football ground Anfield. Mike Jacobs the famous New York promoter, also sent word that he would like McAvoy to go to New York to fight Fred Apostoli.

Mac's last contest of the year took place just a week after his punishing bout against Frank Hough, on 6th December, at the Granby Halls, Leicester. He was matched with Jack Robinson, a Nottingham cruiserweight, but a fighter of limited experience at top level. Poor Robinson soon realised he was way out of his depth as he was floored four times in the first and four times in the second. The crowd were yelling at the referee to stop it and save the Nottingham boxer from being totally destroyed. The third man did just that and nobody was more pleased than Robinson.

Last Of The Peak Years

By the time 1939 came in, the volcano in McAvoy was much calmer and his career would now enter into a slow decline. Also, there were rumblings in Europe of a much bigger fight ahead that would bring death, destruction, and heartbreak to millions world-wide. The middle and light-heavyweight champion would only box five times. He would also suffer from a bout of diphtheria which would put him into Altrincham Isolation Hospital for a few weeks. Once out of hospital, Mac was back in training and his proposed middleweight title defence against Ginger Sadd, the Norwich hard-man. It was decided Mac needed to test himself out before defending his cherished middleweight title against Ginger Sadd. This was a sensible decision because his stay in the hospital had weakened Mac more than he at first imagined. After gradually getting himself back into full time training he was booked to fight in February against Emile Lebrize, of France, at Belle Vue.

The Frenchman was a leading contender for the European light heavyweight title, but it took McAvoy precisely 97 seconds including the count to knock out Lebrize, who had a ten-pound weight advantage. McAvoy was suffering with the sniffles before the contest began. The French fighter stormed out of his corner at the opening bell throwing right hooks to Mac's head, though the British boxer easily evaded these blows by the clever use of ducking and weaving. Lebrize tried left jabs all to no avail. Slipping Lebrize's left lead, Mac caught his man with a wicked right smash to the body. The foreigner was slow-footed, and slow-thinking. McAvoy was remorseless and drove his opponent into a corner. Then, rolling underneath the flimsy punches of the European contender, whack, another right to the body landed with a thud. This was immediately followed by a thunderous right cross to the chin that landed with full force and saw Lebrinze hit the floor with a resounding bang.

After his knockout victory over Lebrinze, Harry Levene sent a message to Sidney W. Ackland at the Boxing News offices. Levene asked why promoter Sydney Hulls was wasting his time and money going to America to sign Red Burman, a leading top ten heavyweight contender to come to England to box Tommy Farr? Mr Levene stated: "Jock McAvoy will box Farr. Everyone knows that Burman was knocked out in two rounds by John Henry Lewis, so what's the point of this contest?" Then McAvoy said: "I fought Lewis for the world's light-heavyweight title in the States, and, despite two injured hands, I lost only by the narrowest of margins over 15 rounds. I am the man to fight Tommy Farr."

Ten days later, McAvoy was back in action, this time in the Liverpool Stadium ring. Johnny Best, the well-known matchmaker, featured Mac against Gino Rolando, an Italian. The Italian was considered one of the leading European cruiserweights and was fully expected to give McAvoy a stiff workout. The contest lasted nine rounds, and Rolando, gave a good account of himself though coming off second best to the Rochdalian. He also took an unmerciful hammering for those nine rounds. He was, in truth, a big, awkward type of fighter, strong, but with little skill, yet an abundance of courage. McAvoy's potent body punching was awesome and had the Italian appealing to the referee that these blows were fouls. The official took no notice and Mac continued to blast away.

At the start of the ninth, McAvoy moved in for the kill, throwing a tremendous right cross to the pit of Rolando's stomach. The impact of the punch could be heard around the ringside and the game Italian fell to his knees, and he was in obvious pain and distress, he then he fell face forward. However, he was up before ten could be counted over him. McAvoy though, had seen an opening and another right hander decked him again, and he regained his feet slightly after the referee shouted "out."

A few days after beating Rolando, Jack Madden the Belle Vue matchmaker, announced 24th April as the new date for Mac's title defence against Ginger Sadd. Everything seemed set for the championship showdown when a couple of weeks before the bout McAvoy suddenly disappeared from his home in Navigation Road in Altrincham. His wife had no idea where he was and was frantic with worry. Harry Fleming and Jack Madden told the press they were searching for the fighter but had not got a clue as to where he might be or what was wrong with him. Madden pleaded with McAvoy through various newspapers to contact him urgently or he would have to postpone the fight and set a new date. After eight days Mac appeared back home. Friends said he had injured his knee and didn't want to cause any fuss so he slipped away to Blackpool for a bit of quiet by the sea. The new date for the championship clash was 22th May at Belle Vue, of course. Nobody ever found out the exact truth why McAvoy had disappeared for eight days and the incident was soon forgotten as he buckled down to training in readiness for Ginger Sadd. Whatever the reason for Mac's disappearing act, nobody could be in any doubt as to his whole hearted commitment while preparing for his title defence.

A couple of weeks prior to the fight a few London reporters travelled down to Manchester for a first hand glimpse of McAvoy in training. Among them was a journalist from the trade paper Boxing. They got out of their taxis at Belle Vue's main entrance, looked up at the billboard that declared they were visiting the show ground of the world. They then proceeded walking through the fun fair and into a building where there was a loud sound of music and grunts and the sound of a bag being punched. Going along one of the corridors in the pavilion, through a little side door, up a flight of stairs, and, on the other side of a partition, they heard somebody working out quite lively to the sound of a jazz-tune. The punching was done in perfect time and rhythm. It was all different, so to speak, from first what sounded like a few thumps on a bag of sand, then a rattle-bang-bang on what was quite obviously a punch ball, and then crash-biff-bang again on the sandbag again. After poking their heads round the partition they saw a sight which was something new to them. The bloke doing the banging was none other than Jock McAvoy, dressed in tights and a maroon coloured jersey, his dark hair all tousled about his cranium, and his face flushed with perspiration from the glow of fast and hard work.

A gramophone was playing a lively tune while Jock was performing on two bags and two balls in succession. One bag was a long and obviously heavy sandbag, the other was about half its size and obviously lighter, while one ball was of the kind built on a stand with a spring at the base, and the other a ball suspended between the usual elastic ropes. But to see Jock at work on them was an eye-opener. "I don't think I need bother much about giving his secret away, because it would seem impossible that anyone else could master what the middleweight champion was doing and the manner in which he was doing it," remarked the correspondent from Boxing.

Skipping around like a dancing-master in perfect time to the music, he would next punch away at one bag, then at a ball, then at another bag and another ball. And then suddenly pivot round on to another one and give it a clout as if to say: "You didn't expect that one, did you?" Not only was Jock punching with plenty of power, he also never seemed to stop, and another record was switched while he was just skipping around as if waiting for it. The reporters were suitably impressed and one said: "Good God, I've never seen a fighter have such a long spell in all my life," and he whispered to a bloke standing just inside who had caught his eye, "Good lord, isn't he ever going to stop?" And the bloke answered, "Nay, lad, he can go on for ever." And it certainly did seem like that. "I have never been so impressed with a boxer's workout before or since. As I watched McAvoy at work in this gymnasium I wondered where he stored all his marvellous energy. Speed and punching power. He was in truth a human dynamo. Now I'm not going to tell you about all the other things which Jock did during his training session, but I can tell you this, that if his present condition is any criterion then the 'Rochdale Thunderbolt' is going to give his challenger, Ginger Sadd, plenty to think about when they clash at Belle Vue", said The Ringsider in Boxing.

After training Jock was asked how he felt, he replied, "Oh, fine, fine!" and he certainly looked it. Then about three-o'-clock, the gym began to fill up and very soon there was Jackie Brown, the former world flyweight champion doing a spot of skipping and ground work, and then he donned the pillows and a headguard and had a real lively round or two with Phil Milligan. Later that afternoon, the gym came to a stand still as McAvoy readied himself for a session of heavy sparring with Scottish light-heavyweight, Tommy Henderson, a good fighter. The Scottish lad had been engaged for a guinea a round and Mac had told the gym regulars that he intended to make sure that Tommy earned every penny. When Tom Hurst shouted: "off you go" to commence the spar, Jock, in typical fashion launched a ferocious onslaught at Henderson. His pulverising punches to the Scot's body started taking effect almost immediately and big red blotches could be seen around Henderson's middle.

Showing no mercy whatsoever, McAvoy switched his attack to his partner's head. Jackie Brown turned to Pierce Ellis and said: "This won't go much longer." By this time there was a deathly silence in the place as everyone present was hoping Hurst would call time. One or two of the fighters in the gym wanted to tell Jock to take it easy, and get a few rounds under his belt in preparation for his up-coming fight. However, they were wise enough not to utter a word, knowing full well that to do so would bring McAvoy out of the ring and having a confrontation with themselves.

"I looked at Henderson as he came out of the ring," said Bert Daly, "and I noticed his face had turned a yellow complexion, as though he had a touch of jaundice. Mac's awesome body punishment had damaged his liver and kidney. He was sick in the toilet and could barely bend down to untie his boxing boots he was in such a shocking state and had certainly earned what little money they paid him. Afterwards, I heard Mac gloating about the pounding he had handed out to Henderson. I looked at him and, without realising it, a look of disgust must have been etched on my face. 'What's the effing matter with you?' he shouted. I knew better than to answer him back and replied 'nothing Joe, nothing.' This was typical of the man."

McAvoy, as we know, was a cantankerous fellow at the best of times but while preparing for a fight he would often fly into a rage at the slightest whim. This was one of the reasons he liked to train in solitude. Of course, when he had to spar then other people would be in the gym. Sparring partners, trainers, onlookers and at times members of the press. On these occasions Mac would try and bottle up his anger and frustration. However, many times when in one of his sulky moods, he would snap, and turf out reporters and spectators from his training quarters. Jack Bates knew how to handle the quick-tempered Mac, and Jock liked and respected Bates. In fact Bates had saved many a person from being clouted by a McAvoy right hand during one of his violent moments. "He would turn nasty with the blink of an eye," said Jack Bates.

Jeff Barr was a boxing journalist for the popular Topical Times, and before the title fight he went to the Cathedral city of Norwich to watch Arthur 'Ginger' Sadd preparing to fight McAvoy. He found everyone in high spirits and predicting a victory for the local boy. "They all firmly believe that Arthur Sadd will return here with the championship and McAvoy's Lonsdale belt," said the journalist. He visited Ginger's public house, which was a few hundred yards from the market Square. It was a cosy little pub with scores of photographs of Sadd's fights hanging on the walls. Ginger was quite a character. Auburn-haired, with thin sharp features, and eyes like a cat, never missing a movement. From the commencement of his career his foster mother and two friends had accompanied him, and they would be sitting in the Belle Vue stadium when their man took on Mac. They always travelled in Ginger's car everywhere he fought. Sadd told Mr Barr. "Come and see me in the dressing room after the fight to congratulate me. You can be the first reporter to interview the new middleweight champion." That was confidence for you. Ginger said he had waited a long time for the opportunity to fight McAvoy, and he was going all out to win. His wife was also confident he would win, although she also told her husband not to count his chickens before they were hatched. "Arthur has boxed many heavy hitters like McAvoy," she said. "And you saw how he handles them. He is boxing much better and punching much heavier. Harry Ware, the Norwich City centre forward, had been helping our Ginger in his training sessions. The soccer star's wife embroided Sadd's initials and a canary motif on the shorts he was going to wear when he fought Mac. He has the support of the whole

McAvoy in the Belle Vue ring – training for Ginger Sadd.

Eastern counties. They have been loyal to him for years." Ginger was the idol of the Norwich Boys' Club where he was a boxing instructor. The Chief Constable of Norwich was also a supporter and said he would be at the ringside for the fight.

There were over six thousand spectators seated in the King's Hall in Belle Vue, on Monday night the 22nd May, with plenty more standing at the back of the arena and at the side of the isles. Ginger Sadd was first into the ring, quickly followed by McAvoy. Although this contest went the entire fifteen rounds, it was brilliantly contested by both champion and challenger. Normally, when a contest goes the full fifteen rounds there are a few dull periods, however, this contest was an exception because each round contained excitement and good boxing and punching. It was a classic confrontation between the aggressive Rochdale Thunderbolt and the neat, subtle boxing of the Norwich boxer. Both men were in marvellous physical condition. For round after round Mac attacked ferociously and Ginger countered superbly and kept calm under the bombardment. The challenger gained the sporting Belle Vue crowds respect with his clever boxing and courage as he evaded the champions non-stop two-handed attacks.

Referee Moss Deyong handled the contest superbly and had very little to do as these two boxers fought a wonderful sporting bout. Both boxers made this a contest the fans would remember. It was close all the way with McAvoy's persistent attacking catching the referee's eye more than the clever left jabbing done by Sadd. There was a great deal of hard punching and beautiful boxing from both men, and the crowd applauded the skills of both boxers throughout the fifteen rounds. Mac, as usual, tried for a knockout, but on this occasion he was thwarted by the masterful defence of the Norwich craftsman. At the end of the fight Moss Deyong walked straight to the champion and lifted his arm aloft as the winner. However, it must be stressed that this was an extremely closely fought contest. The crowd cheered both champion and challenger for several minutes. Sadd never complained, and McAvoy stated that Ginger was one of the toughest opponents he had ever faced, praise indeed for the Norwich lad.

Bert Daly recalled an incident that occurred a couple of weeks before the Ginger Sadd fight took place and which, because of McAvoy's recklessness, could have resulted in the championship match being cancelled and typified McAvoy. "I well recall the occasion, I was always in the Belle Vue gym, and Mac would ask me to put the records on the gramophone player while he trained," said Bert. "One day after he had finished training at Belle Vue, McAvoy asked if I fancied taking a stroll with him. He had been banned from driving for some reason or other, and he had to pay a fellow to drive him about. However, on this day the driver wasn't due to pick him up for a couple of hours. It was a beautiful day, boiling hot. Of course I said yes straight away. To be seen walking in the company of a famous boxer like Mac was a great honour for a teenager like myself and brought me a great deal of personal prestige.

"As we walked down Hyde Road the passing motor cars and trams were hooting their horns and the tingling of bells from people on their bicycles and shouts of 'Good old Jock,' from pedestrians. Mac loved this adulation and I must admit I felt quite important just being seen with him. I had no idea where we were walking until we got near a large croft in Ardwick. Jock loved horses and took part in a lot of show jumping events. I liked knocking about this croft which was a hive of activity with poultry, dogs, cats, horses and donkeys being bought and sold. All the villains and petty crooks of the day converged on this ground and it was like a meeting place for them.

"Anyhow, on this particular day as I accompanied Mac to the croft, I thought he was just going for a look at some horses. There was always a lot of gypsies deal-ing here and these men were big, physically hard fellows, very tough and more than capable of handling themselves against anybody. In fact, they took great pride in their bare-fist fighting exploits. As we were strolling casually around the croft, sauntering around the dozens of horseboxes, Mac spotted a fellow he obviously knew and his face changed colour. He bolted over to where this fellow was stand-ing holding a conversation with a few friends. They were all gypsies, all huge, hard men who looked very intimidating. I walked slowly toward where he was arguing and the language was choice. Mac was pointing his finger at this particu-lar fellow, a big, rough unshaven man. As the argument raged on, the gypsies had made a circle round the two of us. I was frightened, but Mac was fearless - in fact he looked as if he was in his element. The next thing was that they both went into an empty horsebox, and everyone could hear the two men going at it hammer-and-tongs. I was more than a bit concerned because by this time there was a couple of hundred people around the vicinity and the other mean looking fellows were eye-ing me up. A couple of policemen passed by and upon seeing who Mac was knock-ing seven kind of bells out of, they turned a blind eye and carried on walking. I was told later that the fellow Mac was fighting was a known 'dead-leg' and a well-known liberty taker and was well acquainted to the police. Mind you, he wasn't taking any liberties with Mac. In fact, he was on the receiving end of a fearful past-ing.

"When he finally emerged from the box Mac, who hadn't a scratch on his face, walked straight up the biggest of the gypsies and swore obscenities before he cuffed the man with the back of his hand, then swiped a couple more of the gang. The crowd waited with baited breath for the three men to tear into Jock, but they must have thought better of it and turned away from him. Christ, he was frighten-ing when in this mood, he would have fought the whole bloody lot of them. I was terrified. Those gypsies were mean blokes, they certainly were. Mind you, I felt confident in his company knowing that he could look after both of us. Later, He told me that the fellow he belted had swindled him out of some money on a horse he, (Mac) had sold him. He'll think effing twice before he ever tries that effing stunt on me again," he said in a very casual tone of voice.

"I later found out that the fellow Mac had walloped was a brother of the acclaimed 'King of the Gypsies', Uriah Burton. I admit I was worried when told this. The rea-son for my concern was because this man was a very well known character not only among the gypsies but also the hard men of Manchester and other towns and cities in Lancashire and North Wales. 'Big Just' was a man to keep at a distance. Burton was a mountain fighter and feared by everyone. I had the uneasy feeling that the gypsies who saw me on that croft with Mac might take revenge on me if I ever bumped into any of them somewhere or other. Thankfully, I never had any trouble from any of them, I suppose they had completely forgotten me. This however, was not the case with Mac. In later life he had many confrontations with Big Just. Even when he was on walking sticks and wearing callipers Mac was ready to have a go at Burton. They ended up in court. Seriously, though, in his prime Mac feared no man and when he was crippled with polio even then he remained basically the same person."

Because his driving ban was still in force, Mac was still reliant upon someone to drive him to and from training and wherever else he wanted to go. One day at Belle Vue, while his driver was waiting for McAvoy to get showered and changed, the fellow decided to light a fag. As he stood outside the gym having a cigarette, out walked Bert Daly. The two men got talking and during the conversation the driver told Bert he was absolutely fed up and said he dreaded ferrying Mac about. He was getting paid of course, otherwise, he told Bert he would be off like a shot. The driver was exasperated with the situation and began pouring out his grievances about the way Mac was treating him. He said in a very agitated tone: "The cheeky bleeder tells me how to drive the car. Can you believe it?" He explained to Bert he had been driving trucks and cars for a number of years and was a very experienced driver. "He's picking faults all the time," said the man. "When I first drove him, I lit a cigarette in the car and he went absolutely berserk. He made me stop the car and throw the fag out then open all the windows and let fresh air in."

Realising Bert knew McAvoy intimately, a worried expression came over the driver's face and he begged Bert not to breathe a word he had told him about McAvoy. Bert assured the man his revelations were safe with him, and the worried frown left the driver's face, and he thanked Bert profusely. Walking home, Bert laughed to himself, "I could imagine what the poor soul went through. Sometime after my conversation with the driver I happened to be in the car with Mac and I heard first hand what he was going through. Mac was telling him how to change gear; turn right; turn left, go faster, now slower. The poor man must have been dizzy trying to listen to Mac barking out instructions. I couldn't drive, but even if I could I would never have driven for him. He was so bombastic it was unreal."

Bert recalled the time McAvoy owned a butcher's shop on Hyde Road, near Belle Vue. "It was during the war and everything was on ration, especially meat. Customers had to have ration books in order to purchase what they were allowed because of the war restrictions. Mac's first wife, Eliza, ran the business for him and did most of the serving. However, Mac being what he was, insisted on cutting the joints of meat. I'm certain he knew nothing about being a butcher. It was comical to watch him attired in his butcher's apron, sawing or hacking away at the meat on the chopping block. I don't honestly think he had a clue what he was doing, he was swinging a cleaver over his head and the pieces of meat were flying in all directions. Eliza didn't say a word to him, she knew better. Everyone in the shop stood frozen-faced, not daring to say a word or laugh out loud."

Having defended his British middleweight title successfully against Ginger Sadd, McAvoy was matched with Len Harvey in a contest for the vacant world lightheavyweight championship as recognised by British Boxing Board of Control. Harvey's British and Empire light heavy titles were also on the line in this, the fourth and last, fight between these two legendary warriors. This contest, staged at the White City in London, was the high water mark in the careers of both McAvoy and Harvey, and both men's glory days would soon be eclipsed by the outbreak of World War Two on September 3rd. This contest, a close points win for Harvey, is covered in the special Harvey - McAvoy chapter.

McAvoy's last ring outing of 1939 was another contest with Jack Hyams, on 20th November at Belle Vue. The fight, a non-title ten round affair, with Hyams was a truly dreadful affair. Mac had a genuine excuse for his below par performance as his father was seriously ill in Rochdale Infirmary, and was not expected to live. The Londoner however, could offer no reason for his over cautiousness apart from the fact that he had sampled McAvoy"s ferocious power in their previous encounters and decided to play it safe. Mr Bamford Senior, died the day before the contest, the news was kept from McAvoy and in fact he was told in his dressing room only after the fight. He was extremely close to his father and was obviously distraught upon hearing of his death. He took his loss badly and was inconsolable for weeks afterwards.

Len Harvey: A Classic Rivalry.

If you examine the history of boxing throughout the 20th Century, you will see that occasionally there are rivalries between great boxers whose careers coincided and who had a notable series of memorable battles. The Willie Pep/Sandy Saddler four fight series involving the world featherweight title in the late 1940s and early 50s is a prime example. More recently, the Ali/Frazier heavyweight fights is another example which springs to mind. The four Jock McAvoy/Len Harvey contests from the 1930s are similarly remembered as a special fistic rivalry, and as such, in which two great rivals faced each other at the peak of their respective careers.

Jock McAvoy (left) shakes hands with Len Harvey as they weigh in for their light-heavyweight title fight at Harringay.

Harvey and McAvoy were from the same era of boxing but were like opposite sides of the same coin, so to speak. While McAvoy was an openly aggressive fighter who traded on his hitting power, Harvey was a defensively minded technical boxer who hated taking punishment in the ring. Outside the ring, McAvoy was involved a lot of petty incidents of one kind or another. Harvey, on the other hand, avoided getting into scrapes and was, indeed, the "blue eyed boy" of the British boxing establishment. However, while Mac was a big hit with the American fight fans in his contests over there, Harvey was much less successful Stateside - and the fans there mostly thought that he was both boring and over rated.

Although this book is mainly concerned with Jock McAvoy's spectacular record-breaking knockout career, it would not be right or proper if we failed to give special consideration to his classic four fight series with his arch rival, Len Harvey. These two fought on four occasions in British championship contests, twice at middleweight and twice at light-heavyweight with each of the contests going the full distance. Though Harvey was adjudged the winner of three of their bouts, there was really hardly anything to separate them at the conclusion of their epic series, many good judges firmly believing that Mac won at least another one of their classic encounters.

Len Harvey, born in Cornwall in 1907, has a unique place in British boxing history. He is the only boxer to win the British middleweight, light heavyweight and heavyweight titles, and he must also be one of the few fighters who fought professionally in every weight division from flyweight to heavyweight. As a youngster, he regularly watched fighters slugging it out at the Cosmopolitan Club in Plymouth, and made the conscious decision that as and when he took up boxing, he would acquire and use good technique to make progress rather than rely on brute force. In addition, Harvey also developed a superb physique designed to enable him to cope with the rugged side of the boxing business. Len's approach certainly paid off as he went through a 20 year ring career involving 134 contests, and emerged mentally unimpaired and without a mark to show for all his various ring encounters.

Harvey lost wafer thin points verdicts against Marcel Thil for the world middleweight title, and against John Henry Lewis for the world light heavyweight crown. Perhaps his greatest victories were points wins over Jack Peterson to take the British heavyweight title, and Canada's Larry Gains for the British Empire heavyweight championship.

The first Harvey v McAvoy clash, at Manchester's Belle Vue on 21st March 1932, turned out to be a bitter rivalry with the immaculate boxing master Harvey successfully defending his middleweight crown against the aggressive Lancastrian, albeit by a close decision. The pattern of the fight saw McAvoy pressing forward, relentlessly throwing hooks in combinations, with Harvey nullifying the challenger's attacks by using every defensive trick in the book and firing back with stiff jabs and combinations of his own. In the fifth round, the boxers became entangled during an exchange on the ropes, and McAvoy suddenly found himself crashing out of the ring and sprawling on the floor amongst the spectators. Somehow, the Rochdale man climbed back before the referee reached the count of ten, then launched a ferocious counter attack as Harvey tried to finish him off. This contest, fought between two of the middleweight division's physically strongest men, was a battle of styles and strength, and ended with Harvey edging out the action at the end and catching the referee's eye in the process. The faultless Harvey, the Prince of boxers, had an almost impregnable defence and he was brilliant at tucking up and smothering his opponent's punches while clutching on the blind side of the referee. In the end, Harvey's greater experience probably was the deciding factor between two first class combatants.

For this fight Mac had moved in to Harry Fleming's house in Whitley Street, in the heart of Collyhurst. Mac did the bulk of his training at Belle Vue. McAvoy's sparring sessions were eagerly watched by those lucky enough to be permitted into the inner-sanctuary of the gym. Fred Shaw, Tim Ryan and Bud Larney certainly earned their money by sparring with Mac, who was spiteful and extremely ruthless with them.

It is a little known fact that McAvoy had to box Harvey on the first occasion for little more than his expenses. When Harry Fleming and Jack Madden travelled to London and negotiated with Len Harvey and Dan Sullivan, who looked after Harvey's interests at this time, they were shocked at the champions pay demands which were reputed to be a four figure sum. This was a tremendous amount of money in those days. In order for them to bring this fight to Manchester Jock had to accept a big reduction in his expected purse, with the remainder going to Harvey. The reason for this was quite simple. The King's Hall in Belle Vue could only hold around seven-and-a-half-thousand spectators, and times being severely harsh and money tight for Northerners, Jack Madden, said he couldn't charge any fancy exorbitant ticket prices. They were prepared to give Harvey what he wanted if Mac boxed on a percentage. The fighters of the 1990s should think about this for a few moments.

McAvoy, incidentally, had taken part in over seventy professional contests to get to the stage of challenging for the British title, and he had certainly served his boxing apprenticeship. Harvey, on the other hand, was looked on by the London news-papers and the powers that be in British boxing, as a sort of royal figure in the sport. There was no doubt about it - this was set to be a middleweight championship between an exceptionally well qualified challenger and an experienced and gifted champion. By the time the fight drew near McAvoy was in superb physical condition. He had however, suffered agonies with his left hand, though he couldn't possibly ask for a postponement.

Harry Fleming, talking about the first Harvey fight said: "McAvoy had taken part in plenty of tough battles, though the opposition was not the brainy, ringwise class of Len Harvey. Jock wanted that coveted Lord Lonsdale belt, and on the day of the fight he was as touchy as a keg of dynamite. He was straining at the leash, impatient to hear the bell for the start of the fight. There was a big crowd from London to support Harvey, but their cheers were drowned by the Lancashire roar that went up for the Rochdale lad. I tried to keep Mac calm but realised I was wasting my breath. He was bouncing up and down and biting the thumbs of his gloves. Many reporters said he did this in a fit of temper, well there may have been some truth in that, but the truth was both thumb bones had been broken at work when he was a youth. The bones had not knitted together properly and he found it difficult to fit his hands smugly into the gloves."

The first Harvey - McAvoy meeting, as already stated, was a very closely fought contest in which many of the nearly eight-thousand spectators thought should have gone to the Rochdale fighter, but referee, Jim Kendrick, the former flyweight champion, raised the champions arm as soon as the final bell rang. This was a successful defence by a beautiful boxer who seemed to pre-occupied with defence. During the contest, Harry Fleming loudly complained to the referee about Harvey's holding and pulling McAvoy on to punches. Mr Kendrick however, failed to issue one warning to the champion. In his dressing room after the contest McAvoy told the press: "It was a great fight. I learned a lot from Len, more, I bet, than he learned from me. Get me plenty of fights then try and get Harvey again. You will see a different Mac, and a different ending."

A disappointed Harry Fleming told everyone: "Jock forgot our campaign plan and from the first bell rushed at Harvey as if trying to sweep him out of the ring. We wanted Mac to slip Len's left lead and get inside and punch hard to the body. That seventh round was a corker. McAvoy's vicious left hook hurt Harvey and he clinched, and as they broke free Mac connected with a right to the jaw which again shook Len. Harvey struck in the thirtieth round and his pile-driven right cross caught Mac flush on the whiskers. It was almost a knockout punch, but McAvoy fought back courageously."

After a quick four fight demolition of Glen Moody, Les Ward, Ernie 'Red' Pullen and Belgium's Leornard Steyaert in January and February 1933, McAvoy received the news he had been hoping and praying for, the return contest with Len Harvey for the British middleweight championship. There had been a number of disappointments and set backs before these two brilliant boxers climbed into the King's Hall ring at Belle Vue in front of another sell-out crowd of nearly eight thousand. The original date set for the fight was 27th March 1933, but a fortnight before Harvey had boxed a draw with Eddie Phillips in an eliminating contest for the British cruiserweight title and damaged his hand. Len requested a postponement which the Boxing Board readily agreed. The new date was set for 10th April.
Mac was busy training hard and when he was given the news of the cancellation, he went berserk and became very irritated and flew into a frightening rage, pushing other fighters out of his way and being absolutely nasty to anybody who tried to console him by telling him that April would soon arrive and he would get his revenge. He was in a fierce temper and as destructive as could be with the sparse equipment hanging in the gym. Harry Fleming and Jack Bates were both trying to calm him down but their words were falling on deaf ears.

Luckily, once McAvoy started preparing again for Len Harvey, Norman Hurst came up with an ingenious idea. He suggested to Harry Fleming that they should bring over Rene Devos, a former Belgian middleweight champion, who had fought in America, and spent a considerable amount of time over there learning everything about the American training and fighting system. He had also fought Len Harvey, though only lasting one round. However, he was a brilliant, astute teacher and it was a wonderful far seeing idea of both Hurst and Fleming's to have Devos spar and coach McAvoy. The Belgian stayed with Harry Fleming's family in Collyhurst. He proved a real cheery fellow and being very well educated was able to speak English perfectly beside a number of other languages. He was a unique coach, to say the least, believing that every fighter had his own particular style, and he polished that style rather than interfere too much and cause his pupil to become confused. Devos thought it was a bad idea to try and convert a boxer into a completely new method of fighting. He had helped the formidable Frenchman Marcel Thil a great deal.

Soon, Rene Devos became a popular, well-known character around the Collyhurst

HARVEY (right), lead

A fierce looking McAvoy looks for an opening in his winning fight against the master boxer, Len Harvey.

area, where, when not working with McAvoy, he loved visiting the many public houses and having a good old-fashioned sing-song. Mac, though, was far from impressed when first told about Devos. In fact he was downright rude about the Belgian. Jack Bates, Harry Fleming and Norman Hurst spoke at length to him. "Look Joe," said Fleming. "You have worked exceptionally hard for this opportunity. We believe that Rene Devos can add the finishing touches to your fighting style. Give the man a chance, listen, practice and see for yourself if he can improve you in any way." Reluctantly, McAvoy agreed.

After just a few days in the gym one could see the change in McAvoy. Devos showed him little moves which were new to him, and he was so clever at parrying, blocking and generally nullifying blows that McAvoy was very impressed and was soon picking up on these ideas. Rene was a superb ring artist and he spent endless hours working with Mac on his in-fighting technique. The Belgian knew all the tricks of the trade and taught the Rochdale lad a tremendous amount. Things such as how to move by dropping side to side, how a tap or a slight push could throw his opponent off balance - the elbow block. He was a patient instructor and McAvoy began to take a liking to him. One day McAvoy jokingly said to him: "You know Rene, you shouldn't teach me so much just in case we have to fight each other." The shrewd Belgian smiled and replied: "Don't you worry about that. Because after sparring with you, there's no chance of me ever fighting you for real!"

Beside other sparring partners, Norman Hurst and Harry Fleming had hired an American boxer named Harry Smith to give Mac a different slant on things. Smith, like Devos, became very popular around the Rochdale Road area and because he was black, he became more a focus of interest than anything else. The reader must understand that there were very few coloured people living in England in those days, hence the novelty of having a black person living in the vicinity. Smith, incidentally had a wonderful time in Manchester where he said, he found the people friendly and courteous. He and Mac had some terrific sessions in the gym. At first the New York fighter held his own, however, after a few days Mac was giving him a tousing. There is a little mystery connected to the story here. In Denis Fleming's excellent book ñ The Manchester Fighters, Denis mentions one of McAvoy's sparring partners, a coloured American cruiserweight, who was brought over to shapen up the Rochdale fighters reflexes. After a few gym sessions with McAvoy, the American complained of feeling unwell, and was taken to the Collyhurst surgery of Dr Yule Laing. Dr Laing was a big supporter of boxing and the Collyhurst stable in particular. He examined the American. After the examination the doctor took Harry Fleming to one side and explained that the fighter was seriously ill and would be dead within six months. Fleming hurriedly made arrangements for the American to go back home. After a few weeks, news came through that the poor man had died. No one is quite sure whether this boxer was Harry Smith.

As the date of the fight drew closer, Devos predicted that McAvoy would beat Harvey this time and, he said, McAvoy would attain even greater heights. Of course, McAvoy himself was supremely confident of beating Harvey. There again, he was always confident of winning no matter who he fought.

On the night of the fight the King's Hall was packed to capacity and the atmosphere electric as Arthur Myers called the two fighters together for their final instructions. The champion was the betting favourite and he boxed like the ring master he was, though also rather negatively. After a few rounds which were lack-

Len Harvey defeats Jock McAvoy and wins British cruiserweight championship at Harringay. McAvoy (left) and Harvey spar for an opening.

ing in action, referee Myers brought the fighters together and called for more action. McAvoy then took the initiative, pressed forward and threw a lot more punches, gained his revenge and won the title with his non - stop aggression. After he was declared the new champion pandemonium broke out, with people pouring into the ring. McAvoy was carried on the shoulders of friends and the whole hall was clapping and cheering hysterically. The din was terrific. Photographers snapped their flash bulbs for endless pictures. Hundreds of fans were jumping on the ring apron to shake the new champions hand. It was complete bedlam with everybody gloriously happy. It took a posse of big, burly policemen to escort Mac back to his dressing room. As Harry Fleming was making his way back to the dressing room he felt a slap on the back, turned round and saw it was Jack Madden. "This is your third champion. What a great achievement, and all from that dingy little coal yard in Collyhurst." said the matchmaker. "I think we ought to give you a medal."

The Collyhurst changing room was a hub of singing and loud noise. Everyone was gloriously happy. Three champions all from the same little stable. While McAvoy was getting cleaned up, a knock came on his dressing room door and in walked Len Harvey. He shook Mac's hand warmly and was sincere when congratulating him on becoming the new champion, and said farewell. McAvoy told everyone he was proud to be champion and a Lord Lonsdale belt holder. Looking cold-eyed he said: "Believe me the fellow who takes it off me will have to fight like hell for it!" Well, those who tried did fight like that, but no one even came near taking it from the Rochdale Thunderbolt!

In 1938, Harvey took the British light-heavyweight championship from McAvoy, which Jock had won in 1937 with a spectacular 14th round knockout of Eddie Phillips, and their final fight in 1939, when Len made the score 3-1 in his favour was billed as the British version of the world light-heavyweight title, as well as for the British and Empire titles.

Jock and Len were totally different men both in and out of the ring. Harvey was perhaps a deeper thinker, more methodical in his approach to boxing than Mac. He always had a sallow complexion and looked nervous before a fight. He studiously observed his opponents and also the referees who were officiating in his bouts. Everything Len did inside the ring was planned to the minute detail. He took no chances whatsoever. Having started boxing at a very young age, he knew every clever dodge that was worth knowing. He was the ultimate master craftsman of the ring, a defensive genius.

In the 1930s he was perhaps one of the best-known sportsmen in Britain. Though Harvey is still regarded in this country as one of the best boxers we have ever produced, his style of boxing was not the kind that would normally win a world title - and especially not in America, where an aggressive approach carries a lot of merit. If anything, he was much too negative in his boxing for that, and in an age when the emphasis was on the knock-em-out-at-all-costs style of fighting, Harvey's over-use of his brilliant defensive technique did not meet with the world boxing officials' approval. The Americans, especially, considered him a boring fighter. Outside of the boxing business he was quiet with a good sense of humour, also a very intelligent and a considerate man.

As you will have gathered by now, McAvoy was everything that Harvey was not. Mac, of course, was an adventurous fighter and a punishing hitter. Mac's life outside the ring also, to a large extent, mirrored the manner in which he fought.

Jock McAvoy after taking the British middleweight championship from Len Harvey.

In 1938, as stated above, Harvey took the light-heavyweight championship which Jock had won in 1937. After demolishing Jack Strongbow, McAvoy had a few weeks to prepare for his third contest against Len Harvey that was to be staged at Harringay Arena in London, on 7th April. Fans were keen to see these two grand warriors battle it out once again, and the newspapers were full of articles and information about the contest. There was a great deal of interest shown by everyone concerning these two grand men of the ring. Jock started his training at Belle Vue before moving out into the countryside of Knutsford, in Cheshire. He got himself into marvellous physical condition and had no weight problems, but what pleased him most of all, his fragile fists seemed to be getting better by the day. One of his sparring partners in Knutsford was Dan Gillespie who was a former amateur middleweight champion of Scotland. Gillespie had been living in Ireland for a couple of years. He replaced another Scottish boxer, Tommy Henderson from Dumfries, the Scottish light-heavyweight champion, who cracked a couple of ribs while working as Mac's chief sparring partner. Mac wanted dearly to beat Harvey once again. The champion was annoyed about the politics of the boxing business. As the

Len Harvey meets McAvoy at Belle Vue, Manchester.

champion he was getting a purse of £1,440, while Harvey was on a guarantee of £960. Mac said: "Considering that Harvey relinquished this title three years earlier because he wouldn't accept £750 to defend his crown, it now seems strange to me that he should now be offered over two-hundred pounds more for the opportunity of winning it back."

Every seat had been sold and that meant 10,000 spectators, so the promoter was delighted of course. The fight made history as the first ever to be shown on television in this country. There were the usual sporting, show business and political celebrities seated around the ring. Percy Moss was nominated as the referee. The contest itself was closely fought, and was another encounter between Harvey's wonderful ringcraft and subtle defensive qualities and McAvoy's relentless aggression. Opinion at ringside was sharply divided about the points win for Harvey, a master at his craft. McAvoy, disappointed at the loss of his titles, commented afterwards:

"I believed that I won this fight. The referee thought otherwise, however, and to my surprise and great disappointment he gave the verdict to Harvey. He did so without consulting his score card, but the decision caught the newspapermen and the fans in a mixed frame of mind, and while there was no actual outcry there were many who considered I was more than a trifle unlucky."

The fourth and final meeting of these two legendary boxers was staged on Monday the 10th July 1939, at the White City Stadium in London, and witnessed before a crowd such as had never been seen before in Europe or this country, more than 80,000 spectators. Mac, as we know was still the British middleweight king, while Harvey held the British and Empire light-heavyweight championships, and was also the British Empire heavyweight champion after having stopped Larry Gains in 13 rounds a few months before. If Mac were to beat Harvey he could quite rightly claim the champions British Empire heavyweight crown.

Originally, the plan was for Len Harvey to have a return bout with world light-heavyweight king, John Henry Lewis for his title. However, in May when the American arrived in London he had suffered a one round defeat to the Brown Bomber, Joe Louis, there were rumours circulating that John Henry was having eye problems. The National Boxing Association of America sent word over that there was nothing wrong in allowing Lewis permission to defend his world title and to go right ahead. The British Boxing Board, however, insisted that John Henry undergo a thorough eye medical while in London. Sadly, he was told by two eye specialists that he should never box again and he returned to America. A short while later, Lewis announced his retirement from boxing due to failing sight in one of his eyes. The Americans, meanwhile, were pushing the claims of two of their own men, Billy Conn and Melio Bettina to box for the vacant title. However, the British Boxing Board of Control declared that the winner of Harvey and McAvoy contest should be the legitimate world champion. It must be emphasised that Len Harvey held considerable influence over British boxing at this time, and it was on his suggestion that the British Boxing Board of Control sanctioned the match between Harvey and McAvoy as for the vacant world title. Harvey, a highly astute businessman, even had a hand in getting the cheapest seats reduced from five shillings to half-a-crown.

Once contracts had been signed Mac made plans to prepare for Harvey. He caused his usual pandemonium, this time about where he would train. At first he decided he would train at the 'Green Man' at Blackheath, however, after a brief visit there he changed his mind for some reason. He then set his mind on preparing at Sam Carter's hotel at Shoeburyness, which was a place most of the south's leading fighters used. After only a few days there he suddenly said the air didn't suit him and packed his bags and left for Manchester. He preferred to train at his old love, so to speak, Belle Vue.

"Harvey connects with a left lead," in this final encounter between McAvoy and Len Harvey, July 1939.

Len Harvey's preparations, meanwhile were going strong at Jack Straw's Castle, a hotel on London's Hampstead Heath - not the house of the Home Secretary, I might add! While training in the Belle Vue gym, Mac put himself under the supervision of Tom Hurst, and tried out several new tricks while sparring. Against one sparring partner he boxed using only his left, jabbing and hooking to head and body, the following round he then used only his right hand. He did eight fast rounds like this and he looked tremendous. This was a disciplined McAvoy - usually he was very impetuous, wanting to let fly at his sparring partners with wicked two-handed punches. Hurst was concerned about Mac's weight as he was well under the 12 stone mark, and Hurst wanted him coming to the scales weighing at least over 12 stone. There was no doubt that Mac was in marvellous condition and ready to fight until he dropped. He planned to set a fast continuous pace and punch with all the power he could muster

Manchester and Rochdale supporters were travelling to watch the fight in large numbers on special trains organised by Harry Fleming, at a cost of ten shillings and six pence.

On the night of the contest, there were amazing scenes inside and outside the Stadium the like of which had not been witnessed before. Hours before the doors were due to open thousands of spectators converged on the White City Stadium. All roads were packed with people making their way to the venue and every available means of transport was being used. Apparently, even horse drawn, rag and bone carts were ferrying fans to the White City and news reporters on duty that evening were raising their eyebrows in astonishment at the scenes which resembled an Wembley FA Cup final day. It was later estimated that over a quarter of a million people were outside the stadium. Len Harvey, not allowing for this vast throng of people was caught up in the huge traffic jam and was mobbed by hero-worshippers, making him late into the stadium. Because of the traffic hold up and Harvey arriving late, the Harvey/McAvoy main event was delayed for forty minutes, and a preliminary bout put on in the meantime in order to keep the huge number of spectators happy, something present day promoters would do well to heed. Things looked to be getting out of hand at one stage when hundreds of people charged at the gates in order to get inside, causing the police to move in quickly and restore order. On the other side of the stadium, another large section of people broke through a barricade. Fortunately, the crowd were in good spirits and hardly any serious trouble was reported. It made one feel proud of our British nationality to see the manner in which a situation, which could so easily have gotten totally out of hand, was averted because of the sportsmanship of the crowd and the manner in which it was dealt with. Seeing the magnitude of the crowd, the chief publicity man, Lorne Bartram, remarked: "I would say there is between 90 and a hundred thousand here tonight."

Len Harvey was by this time reaching the twilight of his career, yet he was still one of the fittest men in the world at his age, and would celebrate his thirty second birthday the day after his fight against McAvoy. Always a well conditioned and physically powerful man, he certainly needed all of his attributes on this night. The fight itself turned out to be one of cleanest and sporting contest ever witnessed in a British ring. Neither man gave any quarter or asked for any. Many boxing connoisseurs maintain it was one of Harvey's most brilliant performances. Mac gave everything he had and the bout was fought at a hectic pace and on a knife edge throughout the entire fifteen rounds. Harvey's boxing was indeed masterful, though McAvoy matched him with his aggression and was the more exciting of the two. The spectators were in a state of suspense, expecting at any second that the Rochdale Thunderbolt would connect with one of his ferocious punches and bring the elusive bigger man down. Whenever Len needed a breather he would go into a clinch and hold and frustrate McAvoy until the referee, Mr C. B. Thomas, broke them up. Harvey had this aspect of his skills off to a fine art and it gained him valuable time in which to re-organise himself. This was a contest in which both boxers fought their hearts out and gave everything they had. At various stages throughout the contest one would take the initiative only for the other to storm back and take the upper hand. Hard punches were given and taken by each man. There were also occasions when each boxer looked on the brink of a knockout defeat but used their defensive tactics and courage to hold on and recover to come back into the fight. The crowd were in raptures at this thrilling, all-action contest between two evenly matched champions.

At the final bell, Mac believed he had done more than enough to win. The referee however, hesitated, before lifting the winner's hand aloft. He pulled his scorecard out of his pocket and checked it closely. The crowd were holding their breath, and finally Mr Thomas walked toward Harvey's corner and declared him the winner and new World, British and Empire champion. Mac was upset and deeply disappointed at not being acclaimed as the victor. There couldn't have been much in it, but many reporters and spectators thought he had done more than enough to have clinched it.

Later, in Harvey's dressing room, his wife Florence, presented her husband with a big kiss and handed him a silver Victorian beer tankard, which had the inscription: Len Harvey - The Light-heavyweight Champion of the World. Harvey's victory over Jock McAvoy really was the climax of his career. A few weeks later, war was declared with Germany, and Harvey joined the RAF on active service. He would fight only once more, when three years later in 1942, he put his titles on the line against the challenge of the up and coming Freddie Mills, at White Hart Lane in London. Mills, at his most tigerish, overwhelmed the ring rusty 35 year old Harvey in just two rounds. Len Harvey, a proud champion, suffered the indignity of being knocked out of the ring and counted out - the only knockout defeat he ever suffered in his long and distinguished career.

Fiery Freddie & A Fistic Eclipse

The night Jock McAvoy ducked through the ropes to fight Jim Berry of South Shields in the King's Hall in Belle Vue on 29 April 1940, little did he realise that this would be his final ring appearance at the famous old stadium. This was the venue where he been hailed as a future world champion by adoring Lancashire fight fans, the hall where he had built his reputation and engaged in his most famous and exciting victories. Over the years he had often said that the King's Hall was his favourite fighting ground.

'Fiery' Freddie Mills

Away from boxing, Mac was having more domestic upheaval as he was in the process of leaving his second wife, Joan Lye. Another cause of concern was that the war was now underway and sport was being pushed into the background as the country came to grips with the situation, which by mid 1940, was extremely serious. Boxing shows would be few and far between, and the majority of boxers joined the armed forces - in other words, pro boxing almost ground to a halt in the early years of World War Two. Jim Berry was one of those extremely tough, rugged and awkward southpaws, who on any given night, could and often did make life uncomfortable for any orthodox boxer, and make them look bad. This is exactly what he did to McAvoy in the King's Hall.

The South Shields boxer was fit and ready for the fight of his life. He was in fact as sharp as a razor and proceeded to pick up the points by the use of his educated right jab and constant movement. Mac at times looked bewildered and didn't seem to know how to deal with this elusive southpaw, who would grab hold of the Rochdale man's arms as soon as there was any sign of danger. Mac huffed and puffed and snorted his defiance when he missed with his intended punches, which was often, and Berry countered him with snappy two-handed blows to head and body. The South Shields man was gaining the upper hand as round after round went by, he was well in front on points coming into round six. The round started with McAvoy again falling short with his punches while Berry was beginning to get more leverage behind his blows. The Belle Vue fans were beginning to think this was perhaps the end for their hero when suddenly Mac unleashed a vicious left hook to Berry's chin, the blow landing smack on the South Shield's man's mouth. He stopped in his tracks and his whole body shuddered like a train smashing into an express. He was hurt badly and his lip seemed to be hanging off his mouth, there was blood everywhere and the referee wisely waved his arms and halted the bout.

Later in his dressing room Berry had stitches inserted in his lip. He told the reporters that he thought he could have beaten McAvoy and stated he hoped Mac would grant him a return. Mac, as always, said he was more than willing to oblige, though he knew in his heart that these tough, awkward southpaw types should be avoided if at all possible.

On the eighth of August 1940, The Rochdale Thunderbolt met Britain's new fistic star when he tangled with the up and coming 20 year old Freddie Mills, at Liverpool Stadium. McAvoy was 31, and considered by many sceptics as being way past his peak, while the younger Mills, who was a corporal serving in the Royal Air Force, was one of the most promising fighters in Europe. 'Fiery' Freddie had been guided brilliantly by his manager, Bob Turner, a Manchester man born and bred who had moved down to Bournemouth and ran a stable of fighters. Mills had been boxing as a middleweight but was finding it difficult to get down to the championship poundage of 11st 6lb. He made his official light-heavyweight debut against Ben Valentine of the Fiji Islands at Bournemouth on 22nd May 1940, when he weighed in at 12st 9lb. and stopped his man in the third round after Valentine

McAvoy versus Jim Berry, from North Shields. Note the pressure being administered to Berry's wind pipe from the thumb part of Mac's left hand. He used to punch illegally on the blind side of the referees and so cunningly got away with it. It was named 'The Choker'. The famous Harry Greb also used it. Mac had a few of Greb's manners in fights.

sustained a nasty looking cut eye. Though the McAvoy-Mills match was only a ten round non-title contest it created a great deal of interest. If Freddie could beat the legendary Rochdale fighter his prestige would soar enormously. Mills had his sights on Len Harvey, who was by then a serving officer in the RAF, for the British light-heavyweight crown and who also held the European version of the world title at this weight, and also Billy Conn, the classy American recognised world champion at 12st 9lb. For this encounter, Freddie was only getting a purse of £50 to oppose McAvoy, though this was his last consideration.

Liverpool Stadium was packed to capacity despite a roped off area near the ringside where an incendiary bomb had landed. After ten tremendous and exhilarating

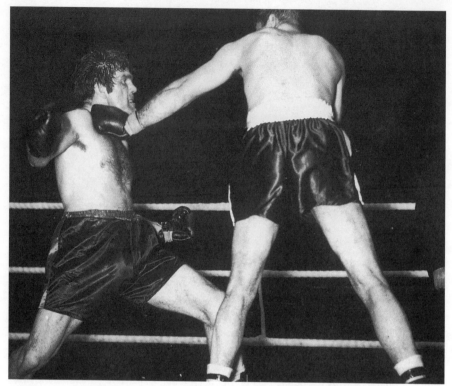

Freddie Mills losing his World title to Joey Maxim, January 1950

rounds of toe to toe slugging, the younger man was declared the victor - edging out a close decision. Mac thought he had done enough to merit the referee's decision but accepted the loss by showing true sportsmanship to his young conqueror. Losing a points verdict to the rugged but comparatively unskilled Freddie Mills caused many experts to express the view that McAvoy was now largely a spent force as far as big time boxing was concerned, and that he ought to consider retirement from the ring.

Eighteen days after the Mills defeat Mac fought 'Battling' Charlie Parkin of Mansfield, the Northern Area middleweight champion, at Nottingham. Parkin was an extremely good boxer, and though not possessing a heavy punch in either hand, he was quite nifty on his feet and his defence was sound. From the start of the bout Mac did all the forcing and Charlie blocked, slipped and evaded the Lancashire fighters heavy artillery. If anything, McAvoy looked slow and sluggish. He was, as always looking to land the pay off punch but Parkin was doing fine while poking his left jab into the champions face at every opportunity. Mac grunted every time he missed with a punch, which was quite often. "Has he lost his punch?" Parkin's seconds were thinking. That might well have been a good assessment when talking about the majority of big punchers, however, it certainly wasn't the case as far as McAvoy was concerned. Coming into the sixth round the Mansfield boxer was confident that he had Mac's measure, and certain he was about to cause an upset. The next second he was spark out on the canvas. The Rochdale fighter had been patiently waiting for that one opportunity to land the knockout blow on his opponent.

"Charlie was very clever," said McAvoy after the fight. "He ran up the points, but I knew that sooner or later I would catch up with him and hit him really hard when I did. He made a false move in the sixth round, and I didn't need a second chance."

McAvoy's last contest of 1940 was a re-match in October with the South African Eddie McGuire, an opponent Mac had knocked out in just two rounds back in 1934. This time, however, matters were very different. A much improved McGuire used his foot speed and fast combinations of punches to take the initiative, and to keep away from most of McAvoy's heavy artillery. At the end of the scheduled ten rounds, McGuire was awarded a points decision on this rare wartime boxing promotion in Nottingham. By his own admission, this was a poor performance by McAvoy - being outmanoeuvred by a man he had once blasted away in double quick time. This unexpected defeat, coming only two months after the loss to Mills, really did suggest that the writing was now on the wall for Mac's ring career.

Boxing's Bleak Years

The world events of 1940/41 left very little scope for entertainment in general, and sporting activities in particular. Britain was so pre-occupied with the Battle of Britain and the Blitz that hardly any boxing promotions were staged anywhere. The constant danger of air raids plus the fact that most boxers were now away from home on active service in the forces made promoting and matchmaking an awkward proposition, to say the least. Although not in any of HM forces, McAvoy had no fight offers at all for months after his defeat by Eddie McGuire, and it would be a full twelve months before he fought again.

On October 28th, a month short of his 34th birthday, McAvoy climbed into the ring at the Seymour Hall, Marylebone in London for yet another contest with Jack Hyams. The purse money for this bout was much less than Mac was used to, and the venue was relatively small time by his standards, but at least it meant he could keep active - a sort of 'beggars can't be choosers' situation. Although Hyams showed considerable skill, toughness and a good fighting heart, the decision after ten action packed rounds went deservedly to McAvoy. Mac scored the only knock-down in the fight - in the ninth round - and Hyams did well to last the distance against an opponent who was clearly anxious to get back to his winning ways of old. Jack Hyams, then serving in the army, lost five times to McAvoy, and has the unique claim of facing the great man at virtually every stage of his career over a ten-year period.

Twenty months after their first meeting, Mac and Jim Berry crossed gloves again. It was 8th December 1941, and Japan had gone to war with Britain and America (the Japanese attack on Pearl Harbour having taken place the day before, on the 7th). Mac's friend and one time stablemate Johnny King was by now in the Royal Navy serving on the ill-fated battleship, The Prince of Wales. Topping the bill at the Royal Albert Hall for this Monday afternoon promotion was a bout featuring Freddie Mills and future British heavyweight champion Jack London, a contest won by Mills via a ten rounds decision. Jim Berry told the press that he wasn't sat-isfied in the manner in which his previous bout with Mac had ended, and said he would reverse the loss. It turned out to be a cracking contest with the South Shields southpaw taking an early lead. Mac seemed bemused, and was caught often by Berry's right lead, which the clever southpaw turned into a hook. The Rochdale man was rushing after his tormentor in an attempt to corner him and then land his heavy punches. The spectators were treated to a cultured boxing display from Berry and Mac was receiving a boxing lesson. At on stage after McAvoy had caught him clean on the chin with a solid punch which sent him through the ropes, Berry grabbed the ropes and did a back flip and landed back in the ring to a great ovation from the crowd.

McAvoy was raging, and he didn't like the way the South Shield's boxer was making him look bad. In the fourth round he bit down on his gumshield, closed his gloves, and left his corner determined to do something about the situation. Berry was winking at ringside spectators when Mac caught him with a power driven left hook to the liver. The colour drained from his face and this was the chance Mac had been waiting for. The Lancashire fighter was now in his element as he bombarded Berry with a fierce body assault. Bang, a short left hook to the body almost lifted Berry off the canvas. He dropped to his knees, the crowd were now silent as he struggled to beat the count. McAvoy gave him no chance to recover and delivered another hook, which again sunk into Jim's liver with a sickening impact and dropping him again. He gamely beat the count but the tide had turned and Mac was like a tidal wave, unstoppable! The fifth and sixth rounds were fought at McAvoy's dictate. It was sheer agony for the brave South Shield's man as Mac, bobbing and weaving dug hurtful body punches that had Berry doubled over in pain. He went down for a nine count from a body blow, though hurt badly he courageously tried to fight back but was dropped again by another murderous left hook to the liver, he couldn't beat the count and the massacre had ended.

When McAvoy was matched in a return contest with the in-form Freddie Mills in February 1942, it created enormous interest throughout the British Isles. Most of the country was too busy protecting itself from Hitler's bombing campaign to worry about sporting events. But the McAvoy versus Mills battle would give folk something else to think about for a while other than war restrictions. The pair were matched in a final eliminator for the right to challenge Len Harvey for his three light-heavyweight titles, the British, British Empire and ' World' crown, though the world title was recognised only by the British Boxing Board of Control. Mac had been thirsting for revenge over the highly popular former milkman, Freddie Mills, after losing a very close and disputed points decision to him eighteen months before in Liverpool.

The promoter was John Muldoon and he booked the Royal Albert Hall in London for this eagerly awaited scrap. From the moment the tickets went on sale there was a stampede to buy them and every ticket was sold within hours. Mills had knocked out Tommy Reddington, a Manchester boxer, in his last fight four weeks before facing Mac so he was sharp and ready for action. The famous old arena was packed to the rafters as the two fighters entered the ring. There was a clamminess throughout the hall, a buzz of expectation. The fans knew these two men didn't mess about, expecting full-blooded action from the first bell. What transpired was unreal and horrific, and altogether unexpected. The fight started with both men going at each other, and the now veteran Lancashire fighter scored first with his left. After a few brief exchanges, Mac caught Mills with a powerful right cross to his stomach. Freddie, hurt, charged after Jock with fire in his eyes. McAvoy stepped back to avoid Freddie's surge when all of a sudden the Rochdale man was down on one knee. It was thought that he had slipped on a wet part of the canvas or caught his foot on the canvas, however Jock was embarrassed to say the least. A few moments later, having regained his feet, McAvoy was in agony as he turned away from his opponent with his face screwed up in pain and his left glove pressed against his side in an effort to relieve the pain. "I felt a burning pain in the small of my back," said McAvoy later. "It was like a red-hot poker had been thrust into my back."

The crowd went hushed and looked on spellbound as Freddie stood back, looking on in amazement. The referee also seemed as if he was bewildered as to what to do. "Hold it, Freddie - my back's gone," McAvoy shouted to the bemused Mills in front of the still bewildered referee. Ted Broadribb was screeching at Mills, telling him to go in and finish off McAvoy. Freddie, ever the sportsman, sensed something was seriously wrong and stood back without throwing another punch. A few seconds later, the bell to end round one sounded. The short-lived fight was over, and with a most unsatisfactory ending. Mac had to be helped to his corner but could not sit down and was lifted over the ropes by referee Ben Hardwicke and other ring officials and carried back to his dressing room. It took a couple of big, burly fellows to hold Mac down as Dr Phil Kaplan gave McAvoy an injection between his spine and kidney. He was in terrible pain but his only thought was that he had let the spectators down badly. He was taken directly to St Bartholomew's Hospital for treatment. It was a freak accident. The doctor told McAvoy that a strained muscle at the back of his left kidney, a one in a million accident, caused the injury. The return journey home to Manchester was full of despair. Once home he was laid up in bed for weeks.

It was a couple of months later when McAvoy took stock of his future. He was now out of the picture as far as the light-heavyweight title was concerned. Though he pleaded with promoters to secure him a return with Freddie Mills, nothing came of it. He still had his middleweight title, and only needed one more victory to make the Lonsdale belt his second trophy. With the war now at its height, however, there were no challengers forthcoming and neither were there offers for any other fights.

Four months after his bizarre victory over McAvoy, Freddie Mills knocked out Len Harvey in two rounds at Tottenham Hotspur's White Hart Lane ground and became the new British, British Empire and 'World' light-heavyweight champion, though it must be pointed out that the world title claim was only recognised in Great Britain. This contest, incidentally, ended the long and illustrious career of Len Harvey. In 1948, 'Fiery' Freddie did win the universally recognised version of the world light-heavyweight crown when he outpointed the American Gus Lesnevich. After Mills retired from active boxing he tried his hand as a boxing manager, and a promoter. An outgoing personality, he was also much involved in showbusiness, appearing on various television programmes such as the rock 'n' roll show 'Six-Five-Special' and in comedy shows, in panel shows on radio, in comedy films such as Carry On Regardless; he also played the part of a stooge with the famous circus clown, Charlie Cairoli. Freddie appeared around the country on several occasions in pantomime, where again he would do slapstick comedy sketches as a pantomime dame. One night during his pantomime performance in Cinderella at the Palace Theatre in Manchester, upon looking into the front row of the audience, he saw Jock McAvoy sitting with his arms crossed looking extremely embarrassed at what Freddie was doing. Shaking his head, and tutting, Mac was obviously thinking "How could a former world champion make such a Pratt of himself?" Later, when Mac was asked his opinion on Mills' performance and, if *he* fancied getting dressed up as a pantomime dame, he gave the person who asked the question one of his famous looks of utter disdain, and the conversation ended there and then.

It was about this time that Mac's private life was about to take another turn. He had been dealing in second hand cars, buying and selling. He was also doing a bit of taxiing for himself to earn a living. He had been going out with very attractive young lady named Renee Garrett who was 22. Soon he moved in with her, and in March 1942, the couple married. Mac was now 34 and it was his third marriage. They had one child, a daughter Josephine Patricia. One would have thought that his wayward streak would have been curtailed, after all, this was his third marriage. However, everything in the McAvoy household was most certainly far from rosy. He was his usual irksome, dogmatic self. Poor Renee found it hard going and though she had her own interests and opinions about things she quickly learned to keep them to herself. "Life was a constant battle with him. He let you know that he was the boss and hated it when I explained that I also had my own views," said Renee.

The war was taking its toll on everything. It was 1944 before Ginger Sadd was again nominated to fight McAvoy for the middleweight crown. Mac was pleased, and though not happy with the purse offered by a Norwich promoter, he realised it was the best he could expect under the circumstances. After a few weeks of training McAvoy received a request from the promoter asking him to accept a large cut in the purse he had previously accepted, because, the promoter explained he couldn't make the fight pay. Mac was fuming and felt belittled. "As a British champion I did not feel inclined to go through with the fight on reduced terms. I could earn more money applying myself to my business ventures," he told the press. He was still prepared to honour the original contract, he told the promoter, but would not consider fighting for less. The British Boxing Board of Control fined him £200 and deprived him of his middleweight championship as well. Mac felt bitter at this treatment by the ruling body and refused to pay the Board of Control a single penny. "They've had enough brass off me over the years," he said. Taking everything into consideration, it was a shoddy way to treat a proud champion who had brought glory to his country through his exploits in the ring, and things haven't changed much in this department.

Early in 1945 Renee, fed up with her husband's irrational behaviour and mood changes, packed a suitcase and with baby daughter Patricia, travelled to her brother's home in Torquay. She hadn't told McAvoy she was leaving or where she was going. Renee's brother, Reginald Garrett, was a fireman and made his sister and baby Pat welcome in his home. Back in Manchester, McAvoy was seething with anger and went berserk when he found out his wife and daughter had left him. He searched high and low for them throughout Manchester. He was like a smouldering volcano ready to erupt. When he heard his family was in Torquay, he immediately gathered a couple of so-called friends, jumped into his car and set off to locate them. This sad affair ended in another court appearance, this time in Devon, and he could consider himself extremely fortunate that he wasn't sent to prison.

McAvoy told the court in Devon that he went to his brother-in-law's home looking for his wife and daughter in order to take them back to Manchester. Reg Garrett told Mac he had no idea where Renee and baby Pat were. In evidence, McAvoy told the court he was hit on the head, and automatically struck Mr Garrett, damaging his brother-in-law's ear. His two companions moved in on Mr Garrett when, according to evidence, he was about to throw another punch at McAvoy. The court was told McAvoy had numerous convictions with three convictions for common assault. The outcome was Mac was sentenced to two months in prison and ordered to pay seven guineas costs. His two pals were fined £5, and ordered to pay three guineas costs. Mac's legal representative lodged an appeal against McAvoy's two months sentence, and it was later quashed. He was a very lucky man not to have gone to prison. Eventually Renee and Mac patched their differences up and got back together again.

1945 - Ring Comeback

In 1945 with the war at an end, Mac decided to make a ring comeback. He had watched the leading middle and light-heavyweights in Great Britain and decided he still had enough in him to once again become a champion. The public was looking for sporting heroes to help them forget the bleakness and heartbreak of the war years. Sporting events were attracting thousands of fans all over the British Isles. Jack Solomons was the leading promoter at this period and the biggest boxing star was Doncaster's Bruce Woodcock. It seemed that every man woman and child knew who Woodcock was. Solomons matched the young Doncaster boxer with Jack London, the British and Empire heavyweight champion and the father of Brian, who a few short years later would also hold the British heavyweight crown. The match between London and Woodcock was in the open - air on Tottenham Hotspur's football ground in London, and London's championships were at stake. A huge crowd was expected.

Having decided to resume his ring career, McAvoy met up with Harry Fleming, his former manager and trainer. The straight talking Fleming turned down Mac's request for his services, telling him: "I told you to retire in 1939, so I'm not likely to look after you now. Forget the whole idea, Joe." Undaunted, McAvoy hired the London based trainer, Wally May, and set about training for his ring return. Many people wondered why McAvoy never approached Jack Bates to look after him? Well the answer was that at this time Bates was still serving in the Royal Air Force.

Jolly Jack, as Solomons was known, matched the now 38-year-old Mac with George Howard of Finsbury Park, London. McAvoy was in superb condition and his weight was 11st 8lb, a tremendous achievement considering he had been inactive for so long and not fought as a middleweight for a number of years. Harry Levene was looking after his interests and Wally May, a well known and respected trainer, supervised his preparations. In later years McAvoy was high in his praise of May. "When I made my comeback I was past 37, but because of Wally May's training I had never felt fitter in all my life," McAvoy told the press. "I got down to the middleweight limit with ease and rested four days before the first fight of my comeback campaign. At no time during training under Wally was I either hungry or thirsty as I had been on many other occasions, when having to make a required weight. Of course I put myself entirely in his very capable hands. I was well past my best when I embarked on my come back but he helped a great deal."

When one considers that Mac was almost 38 years old when embarking on his comeback, yet he still got down to the middleweight limit speaks highly of his own determination and sacrifice. It also underlines what several people stated over the previous years and later, that Jock McAvoy always was a middleweight first and foremost. And it was true that he only tackled bigger and heavier men in order to keep busy and earn money.

There were over 38,000 spectators in the ground and everyone was relaxed and looking forward to a new beginning now the hostilities were at and end, what better relaxation than to watch a feast of good, exciting boxing. Bruce Woodcock put the fans in good humour when he became the new champion, knocking out London in six rounds. The crowd gave Mac a tremendous reception as he made his way to the ring. He was tingling with excitement and determined to show everybody he was not a spent force. He was impatient for the proceedings to be over. From the first bell it was the usual McAvoy - snorting like a bull; bobbing and weaving while looking for an opening to land the knockout drops. He mugged the classy London favourite. Unleashing a dynamic left hook that cracked against the younger man's jaw, he dropped George for a count of eight. The Finsbury Park battler got to his feet on rubbery legs and was soon on the floor again. Mac floored the cockney three times in this opening round and the fans were yelling for the veteran campaigner just like in his glory days. To all intents and purpose the fight was as good as over. Howard had been badly shaken up in that first session and the solid blows he had taken had taken their effect. McAvoy swarmed all over him and flattened his opponent for the full count. He received a chorus of cheering and clapping - shouts of "Good old Mac," and, "you can win the title again Jock," were shouted at him.

Mac was of course delighted with his comeback victory, though not very happy about his financial rewards. Still he knew this was now a different period and he was looked on as an old timer who was fighting for his last few purses. His next test was in Portsmouth three weeks after knocking out Howard, and he flattened Scotland's Johnny Clements in the sixth round of an eight round contest. Clements was full of pluck but lacked the experience to cope with the punching power of Mac, who had the fight well in control from the opening bell. In the sixth, the old timer went all out for a knockout and within a minute had his man down for a count. Clements rose on shaky legs and looked almost out on his feet, McAvoy was on him like a wounded tiger and finished him with power packed punches to the jaw and head. Again Mac was pleased with his performance though again less than happy with the purse money he received. He was starting to question whether it was worth all the effort for so little reward. The days of the big purses that he used to receive when fighting at Belle Vue were, without a shadow of a doubt, well and truly behind him.

A month later he was matched against the Welsh middleweight champion, Tommy Davies. The bout was held in Swansea in the open-air, and the weather was less than kind to the boxers and crowd because it was raining. In this fight, an eight rounder, Mac looked at times like an old, great actor who was trying desperately hard to remember his lines and just going through the motions. There were occasions in this bout where he seemed totally disinterested in the proceedings. He clipped the thirteen years younger man in the fourth, putting him down for a count. Davies, though, was full of fight in front of his own fans and rallied well to rock the Rochdale man on a few occasions. In the eighth and final round, McAvoy was down for a count but rallied back to make a fight of it, taking a close decision. Many believed he was rather fortunate to have been awarded the decision.

On the way home Mac thought long and hard about his future in the boxing business. For eighteen years he had been the best. He had tasted the sweetness of success boxed at top venues and been a worthy, proud double champion in an era which British championships were held in high esteem by the sporting public. He came to the sad conclusion that the fights were going to get harder and the money poorer, and with that in his mind he decided to quit while he still had his brains plus his health and strength. He had been cruelly robbed of his chance to become middleweight champion of the world by the American gangsters, and cheated out of his rightful fortune by a conniving, silver - tongued con man in Dave Lumiansky. And the great Jock McAvoy never fought again. Its likely that this little island of ours will never witness the likes of the Rochdale Thunderbolt again!

Retirement - and Trouble

The following years did not treat Mac too kindly, as we shall see. He was depressed at no longer being an active fighter. He couldn't believe how quickly his name had disappeared from the sporting headlines. Like many great fighters he could not accept that his popularity had waned. He became more and more irritable. On top of all this, a few months after his last fight his beloved mother died. All his success in the ring had certainly not brought his mother the luxury and money he envisaged it would bring her from his exploits in the ring, though he had always seen to it that his mother didn't go short of anything. Although he had retired from active fighting, he could still be found in various gymnasiums in and around Manchester and Rochdale. Mac was a spectator now, watching other boxers going through their paces. He was particularly keen on a couple of brothers and spent hours watching them train. Jackie Williamson and his brother Frank both became top class professionals. Frank, using the name adopted surname Johnson, went on to become the British and British Empire lightweight champion in the early 1950s, while Jack who boxed as Jackie Braddock, became a top class professional boxer and, though he never secured a title chance, had the ability to become a British champion.

Mac had no intention of ever working for anybody and was determined to be his own boss, trying his hand at various business ventures, mainly involving buying and selling cars. He also owned a couple of butcher's shops and a wool shop. Mac, however, lacked any real business acumen, and none of his money making schemes ever amounted to anything. Somebody as well known as McAvoy would meet all kinds of people during and after his boxing career, after all he was a legend and his exploits both inside and outside the ring were well documented. Most were genuine, honest fans and people who simply admired him for his boxing achievements. But he would also brush shoulders with various rogues, vagabonds, con men, thieves, and undesirables. Unfortunately, McAvoy was prone to attracting the kind of 'friends' whose company he would have been better off not knowing, leading to further brushes with the law. In fact, in 1947 he came very close indeed to being imprisoned.

On Monday 3rd February 1947 McAvoy's name was in the newspaper headlines again, but not the kind of headlines his most ardent admirers wanted to read about. He was fined £5 and ordered to pay two guineas cost when appearing at Stockport

Magistrates Court. McAvoy used a vacant plot of ground on Wellington Road North in Stockport to sell cars. The plot was in the front of Mrs Margaret Manifold's home, and she owned the property. McAvoy also used a room in Mrs Manifold's house as an office and he had various items of furniture stored in the house. What happened, according to the owner, was that one particular day Mac, accompanied by another man, called and said he was collecting a display cabinet from his office. Mrs Manifold confronted McAvoy and asked him if he would be kind enough to settle the rent account, which was outstanding. What happened next, according to Mr G.R. Duck, acting for Mrs Manifold, was that McAvoy pushed the lady on the right shoulder, sending her staggering across the room. Mrs Manifold's 14 year old, son Alan, was present in the room, and on seeing his mother pushed, he picked up a chair, and McAvoy told him to put it down. As she walked across the room, Mrs Manifold alleged that Mac pushed her in the chest with the flat of his hand and, as he was going through the door, carrying the cabinet, he kicked her on the right leg. He was summoned for assault for punching and kicking the woman. He denied the charge and appealed. It was distasteful, to say the least, but worse was to follow.

"McAvoy Is Sent For Trial," was the headline in the Manchester Evening News on 21st of June 1947, while the Manchester Evening Chronicle headline was "Two For Trial On Car Charges." McAvoy and a friend, 34 year old Wilf (Bunny) Hughes of Fenton Street in Rochdale, appeared at the Manchester Assizes on a charge of intent to defraud. The newspapers were full of the story of how the famous ex-boxer and his conman friend had bought a Rover car from the Davenport Garage. When it came to paying for the car, Hughes, masquerading as a doctor, told the salesman, Mr Harry Lane-Smith, he would pay for the car by cheque. The salesman, who knew McAvoy well, did not feel comfortable accepting a cheque from Hughes, a complete stranger and also a shady looking character, and went outside to speak to McAvoy who was sitting in his car. Mr Lane-Smith told the former champion that 'Doctor' Hughes, wanted to pay for the car by cheque and did he (McAvoy) think this was safe to accept payment in this manner? Mac told him it was all right. The 'doctor's cheque was, of course, a counterfeit and within a couple hours the car was sold to another garage in Manchester - for cash.

In court McAvoy denied that he would have found the money to pay for the car if the case would have been dropped. It was a silly and very stupid thing to do especially for someone as well known as McAvoy. More bizarre was the story Hughes told the court. He said he sold the car quickly because he needed money to buy a mill for £650. He then claimed he already had a buyer for the mill, the buyer was going to pay him £1,250 for the mill he was going to purchase for £650. The outcome was that 'Doctor' Hughes was found guilty on charges of fraud and deception and given an 18-month prison sentence. It was revealed that Hughes, who had a criminal record, and had the 'gift of the gab,' was a criminally inclined 'chancer' who lived on his wits, and was also a gambler and drinker. The judge, Mr Justice Staples, was scathing when sending the conman to prison, telling him that his criminal record was shocking and also mentioning his poor Army record. He also told the court that Hughes had accepted the blame for the fraud. "You got hold of this stupid giant and found him very useful for your purposes," the judge said while looking directly at McAvoy. The man who had defied some of the world's hardest punchers without as much as a shrug of the shoulders was now quaking in his shoes as he stood, ashamed of himself, in the dock. He was expecting to get a prison sentence. Mac told Mr Basil Nield, K.C prosecuting, that all he was expecting from introducing Hughes as a buyer, to the salesman at the Davenport Garage, was £25 commission

The judge bound him over and told him. "You are a man with reputation known all over the world, and you have thrown it out of the window by getting involved with this sort of business. I know you boxers are much easier to lead astray than to knock out, because you have more in your fists than you have in your heads. You have been a fool, but I am going to give you a chance by binding you over. Don't come here again." McAvoy couldn't believe his good fortune at not being sent to prison and he thanked the judge profusely. Mac could consider himself a very fortunate man indeed not to have received a custodial prison sentence for his part in the fraud case. He knew it as well. His wife Renee could tell her husband was relieved by his behaviour at home. He spent more time with his baby daughter Patricia who was now walking about and getting up to mischief.

Disaster Strikes

A few weeks after the trial with Bunny Hughes, a blow from which he would never fully recover would hit Jock McAvoy. It was a blow much more devastating than anything he had delivered or endured throughout his long and illustrious career. "He complained of not feeling well," said Renee, who told him to make an appointment to see the doctor. Mac's illness began with influenza like symptoms i.e. headache, sore throat, aching limbs and a high temperature. After a few days, the symptoms worsened and Mac's legs began to feel very weak. The doctor suspected infantile paralysis - the much dreaded polio - a condition which was rife at that time, and very difficult to cure. Those who knew Mac intimately were aware of him always complaining about illnesses and they knew him to be a hypochondriac. Little did any of them know that he was in the process of becoming permanently disabled.

On Wednesday 16th July, the Manchester Evening Chronicle reported that McAvoy was confined as a patient in the Manchester Jewish Hospital. It was stated that he had all the symptoms of a nervous breakdown. The hospital said a nerve specialist was going to examine him, and Mac was feeling far from well and only his family was allowed to visit him. Once news spread that he had been confined to hospital all sorts of rumours were going the rounds. Many people were wondering if this was the after effect of his recent court case.

However, this illness was far more serious than anyone, least of all McAvoy, could ever have visualised. Once the doctors diagnosed polio and Mac became truly aware of what its consequences were, he sank into the pits of despair, wondering how and why he, of all people, should have been stricken with it. For quite a while he was filled with self pity, and could not think straight about the future.

After a few weeks, McAvoy's mental state improved and he announced to friends that he was determined to beat his illness and walk again. To this end, he had a set of parallel bars installed in his house in a desperate and determined attempt to regain the use of his legs. Mac then spent hours on end straining away in his bid to walk - an effort that was totally admirable but, sadly, quite futile. The disease had permanently damaged the nerves in his legs, leaving him wheelchair bound or walking unsteadily with the aid of leg callipers.

At home, back in Rochdale, with his good friend, Bert Hulme.

"Help Me" was the headline on Monday 5th January 1948 in the Manchester Evening News. Jack Hutchinson, a journalist on that newspaper, had called to see Mac in his house 371 Wellington Road North in Heaton Chapel. The journalist said McAvoy was sitting in a wheelchair, wistfully watching the world go by. "The world that once cheered his triumphs and which he now feels has forsaken him in adversity. This is the man who ruled the middleweights for eleven years" added Mr Hutchinson, who went on to say that McAvoy was upset that hardly anybody called to visit him at his home. "Only a scrapbook of newspaper cuttings and the memories of hundreds of fights light up the dark shadow of his dreaded affliction. The story of Jock McAvoy is a moving human documentary. This wonderful athlete, the greatest puncher since Ted 'Kid' Lewis, has been stricken with Infantile Paralysis." Mr Hutchinson said McAvoy's only companion was his wife, and his only glimpse of the outside world was when he sat at the open door in his invalid chair. "He has borne his misfortune with fortitude, but his nerves are becoming frayed," added the journalist who went on to say that few of Mac's old friends think of calling to see him, and fewer still bother writing to him. It appeared the only person who kept in touch with McAvoy to any great extent was the man who he defeated on five occasions and prevented from winning the British middleweight title, Jack Hyams. Mr Hutchinson said McAvoy was existing on an allowance of £3 a week, which he received from the Sportsmen's Aid Society in London. "This measly £3 a week is supplemented by the sale of his furniture," added the journalist. "To be struck down like this at the age of 40, with no means of support, is a calamity." The journalist also said that he thought fans should approach the Manchester sportsmen, and he felt they would respond in the same spirit as the London people. Gus Demmy, the well-known sportsman and book-maker said: "Something will certainly be done."

Renee, besides looking after young Pat, had to bear the brunt of her husband's mood swings as he became more and more irrational and depressed. "It was terri-ble and distressing to watch him," she said. "He had prided himself on always being fit and healthy. He had certainly lived life to the full and now he was depen-dent on me to fetch and carry for him. And with him not being able to move about like any normal person, the reality of his situation hit him like a sledgehammer. People who haven't been through this sort of heartbreak will not really understand how very, very difficult it was for both of us. He took it badly. He couldn't under-stand why it was him who had caught this disease and he was in no mood to accept people's sympathy." Renee said that Mac was in the hospital for quite a few weeks and was distraught and not in the mood for visitors. She said after what seemed an eternity, her husband stopped wallowing in self pity and started to fight the illness.

Renee said that her husband showed remarkable fortitude and determination to conquer his affliction. "He had a contraction rigged up in the bedroom where he would force himself to grab hold of these bars and move his body along them, it looked extremely hard work but I knew better than to suggest he rested or took it easy. I think he believed this would get his limbs functioning again and he would eventually get better. When he got the wheelchair he seemed to sink a little lower in spirit and it was a problem getting him to sit in it. Unlike today, there was no house visits by hospital physios and other medical staff who could advise and help him, it was my responsibility to do whatever had to be done for Joe."

It was around this period when Mac in need of money, sold his pride and joy - his prestigious Lord Lonsdale Belt. This was a further blow to his self-esteem, how-ever, slowly but surely he accepted that he would never again walk without aid. And after going through the darkest period of his life he started to get about with the aid of callipers and walking sticks. He still looked a fine specimen of manhood, though many that remembered his fighting days felt a twinge of sadness when see-ing him walking ever so stiffly. Over the coming years he would also be able to

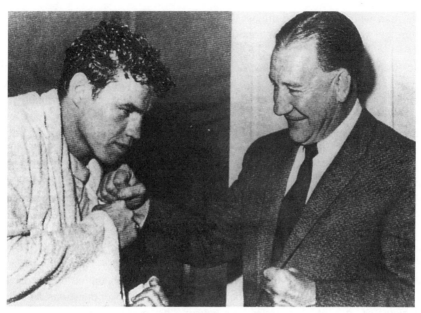

Terry Downes receiving 'sound' advice from 'Mac'.

get out and about because he had had his cars fitted with an automatic gear change. This helped brighten him up considerably. It got him out of the house and also gave Renee a bit of respite from him.

In 1950 McAvoy travelled to London to watch the Bruce Woodcock - Lee Savold heavyweight fight. On his way to the stadium he called on Wally May, the trainer who had trained him for his three comeback fights in 1945. On entering Wally's home Mac was struck by the plight of his former trainer. Wally was in ill health and dejected. He told the former champion his services seemed to be no longer required by the boxing establishment. He was down in the dumps and needed cheering up. Though on callipers and having great difficulty getting about himself Mac did his best to reassure May that his luck would change for the better. After saying good bye to Wally, Jock went to the fight and spoke to several reporters about May's plight. "It seems so wrong to me that a man with Wally May's undoubted knowledge and qualifications - the best trainer in this country, in my opinion should be unemployed," he said with emotion in his voice. "Some of our so called champions would be a lot better off if he was in charge of their training. I believe it is only right and proper that something should be done for this incredible man who has devoted almost the whole of his life to boxing, and, it would seem, got very little remuneration for it."

Vic Richardson was the nephew of Jack Madden, the famous Belle Vue matchmaker. Vic, was a keen boxing follower of the Lancashire fighters of McAvoy's era, being seated at ringside for most of the big boxing events. He was an avid follower of McAvoy during his career. He recalls his uncle Jack helping Mac, in the period after he contracted polio and was trying to get his life together again, obtain the necessary permission to sit on the seafront at Blackpool in an archchair, with his weighing machine and autographed pictures in order to earn a few quid. "Uncle Jack thought the world about Mac," said Vic. "He was always telling me about what a truly great fighter McAvoy was. He admired him as a fighter a great deal. My uncle had lived in Blackpool for a number of years. He had staged charity tournaments there and obviously knew the right people to approach on McAvoy's behalf."

Many people remembered being weighed by the former champion then receiving a signed photograph from him and he would smile and answer questions. Mrs Bell, of Newall Green in Manchester, was courting her husband at this time and she remembered seeing Mac sitting in his archchair weighing folk and handing them a picture. She turned to her husband to be and remarked. "Oh what a come down for him, a famous boxing champion having to do this to earn some money." Mrs Bell did not know McAvoy's desperate financial situation. When she spoke to me over forty years later she had read of his plight and told me she did let Mac weigh her and to prove it showed me her signed photo.

At the start of the 1950s, Harry - the Barbers, was a popular and well-known gentlemen's hairdressers on Rochdale Road in Collyhurst. A lot of footballers from Manchester United and City were frequent customers'. Harry had a young staff and the popular "Bop," 'DA' and 'Tony Curtis' hairstyles were the order of the day. The shop was always crowded, with customers coming from all over Manchester. Jack Bates had a small gym at the side of the shop, which was owned by a jovial, respected Jewish character known simply as "Harry" Training times were every night of the week and Sunday mornings. One wet and miserable Sunday morning the gym was packed with boxers training. Jack Bates was teaching young Bob Skinkiss while Tommy Fynan, a former fighter and helper in Harry Fleming's gym, was timing the rounds. All of a sudden there was a bit of a commotion and everyone stopped what they were doing and looked toward the back of the room.

It was McAvoy accompanied by a young man who turned out to be his youngest son, Jackie.

Bob Skinkiss, recalled McAvoy hobbling into the gym through the back entrance, with his son. "I was thrilled at seeing one of my idols," remembered Bob. "I felt sad watching him struggle with his callipers a sticks, though he still looked powerful. I visualised what he must have looked like in his prime. I had read all about his exploits and was brought up listening to the stories about this great fighter. Jack (Bates) and Tommy Fynan made a big fuss of him and they were laughing and joking and talking about old times."

A couple of years before, McAvoy's eldest son, Joe, had tried his hand as a professional boxer under the name of Joe Patrick, and had fought a handful of professional bouts before deciding that boxing wasn't for him. According to what Mac told Bates and Fynan, his younger son Jackie, fancied trying his hand as a professional and Mac wanted to try him out. He wanted his old trainer's assessment of young Jackie's prospects. Bates readily agreed to help in any way he could.

Bob Skinkiss who stood under five-foot and boxed as a flyweight, was in the ring moving about with his pal, a lad named Nobby Heppel. Nobby had boxed as an amateur and weighed about eleven stone but was limited. Bates decided that Mac's son could box a couple of rounds with Nobby, to which McAvoy readily agreed. Bob recalls speaking to McAvoy. "He feared me just by the way he spoke," said Bobby. "His eyes were like hawks and you could imagine what it must have been like facing him in the ring. He spoke coarsely and didn't seem to have any patience for anything or anybody. My pal Nobby was no great fighter and his knees were knocking at the prospect of boxing against the great Jock McAvoy's son. When they got into the ring for the spar, McAvoy edged his way down to the side of the ring and stood against the wall. I don't mean it disrespectfully but McAvoy's son was absolutely useless. They hadn't been sparring for more than a minute when Mac's booming voice was barking out instructions to his son. Jack (Bates) and Tommy (Fynan) looked very embarrassed, but said nothing. I felt sorry for McAvoy's son, it was quite obvious that he didn't even understand what his dad was telling him to do let alone follow his instructions. Because of his inadequacies as a boxer, he made Nobby look brilliant.

'When Tommy Fynan shouted 'time' to end the first round, McAvoy started berating his son unmercifully. The second round had not gone two minutes when McAvoy, who was red faced with anger. He was saying all sorts of uncomplimentary things to his son, then shouted: "That will do. Come out and get changed, you're hopeless."

Bates and Fynan tried to calm Mac down and take the heat out of his obvious anger at Jackie's inept showing. Jack Bates told him young Jackie could come down to the gym whenever he wished and he would help him as much as he could. McAvoy never said a word at this suggestion. It appeared he had already made his mind up that Jackie would never make it as a fighter, needless to say his son never fought as a professional. Though he appeared harsh toward his two sons, he did in fact love them dearly. Over the years Mac tried to help his children in any way he could. In 1969 Jackie was found dead in his mother's house in Rochdale. He was 38. His father took it badly and became very depressed.

In Conclusion-The Later Years

After McAvoy's weight guessing period in Blackpool came to and end, he diversified into market trading, selling suitcases, hand wallets, purses, etc. He had stalls on Todmorden, Ashton, and Oldham's Tommyfield Markets. Griff Williams, the only boxer ever to hold Mac to a draw, said McAvoy obtained his stock from a wholesaler in Whittle Street in Littleborough, Lancashire. Griff said the goods were 'seconds.'

During the 1950s period McAvoy spent a great deal of his time taking his daughter Pat who loved horses, to horse shows and events. Pat became quite proficient at horse riding and entered several showjumping tournaments. Mac was delighted at his daughter's progress and encouraged her with the same vigour he himself used to put into his own training when he was boxing, though it appears that at times he would become a little too enthusiastic and overbearing. Later, when Pat became a teenager she lost the zest for competitions and tournaments and wanted to pursue other interests. Talking of her early interest in horse riding Pat said: "It was an event whenever we went for a ride from our home, it was at times embarrassing. You can imagine what it was like on those small country lanes. It was very precarious when vehicles and horse riders were using the lanes at the same time. My Dad was very obstinate on these occasions, he would insist that he rode in front, and I and my mother would be behind him. Dad would hold the traffic up and drivers would be shouting insults and sounding their horns because of his actions. This would annoy dad, he would be infuriated and shout back at the drivers causing a scene."

Pat also mentioned occasions when she was taking part in various horse shows, and showjumping tournaments. Officials would be standing at the entrances directing the cars with horseboxes to designated parking areas. Mac would ignore the commissioner's signals, and park where he wanted. When he was approached and told he couldn't park in a certain place, ructions would ensue, it might be comical for the casual onlooker but highly embarrassing for his beautiful young daughter. Eventually Pat gave up the competitions though still a keen rider, something she still does to this day.

While driving his specially - adapted car, fitted with hand controls, through Middleton which was near Rochdale, Mac's mind was on a fight - a fight that Marilyn, his three year old grandaughter, was waging against the dreaded disease. Mac of course knew the peril she was facing because of his own situation. As he made his way along the road heading for the hospital where baby Marilyn lay with a cage over her legs he was doing 55 miles an hour. He was flagged down by the police and summoned to appear at Middleton Magistrates Court for speeding. Mac told the court that the family couldn't be sure how badly his grandaughter's legs were affected. "This is a first class torment for me," he said. "I have been a polio sufferer for ten years and I still have to use callipers and crutches to stand and walk. my mind was on my grandchild and I didn't sped knowingly. I was a victim of circumstances, for the word 'polio' strikes terror in all parents' hearts. It is a cold and cruel complaint." He went on to tell the court that the child had almost recovered. "Thank God," he added. "I am taking young Marilyn on holiday." He was nonetheless, found guilty and fined £5.

In the 1960s Mac suffered from various illnesses including a heart attack and mental problems and spent periods in hospital. He was frequently down in the dumps and becoming more and more depressed and in need of a boost. Tommy Burke, a taxi driver from north Manchester and a comical 'character,' was helping Mac sell a copy of his booklet - 'Photographic Panorama of Spectacular K.Os." It was a twelve page booklet with photographs of some of his exciting knockouts, and it was being sold for half a crown. I invited Mac along with Johnny 'Nipper' Cusick, to be the guests of Collyhurst and Moston Lads Club's amateur boxing tournament, which was being held at the Palladium Club on Collyhurst Street. Mac wanted to sell his booklet but Mr Noel Sykes, the club warden, said that as the tournament was a fund raising event he didn't think it would be fair to ask supporters to shell out any more money. When I explained the situation to Mac, he understood and told me he would still consider it a privilege to be our guest of honour.

The tournament was a huge success and both McAvoy and Cusick received a rapturous, sustained ovation, which almost lifted the roof off. There were over a thousand people crammed into the former cinema, which was owned by the comedian, Bernard Manning. After this, Mac would phone me regularly three or four times a week. The man was lonely and down in the dumps, with hindsight, he just wanted somebody to listen to his worries and problems. Unfortunately, I was a single young man in my late twenties and couldn't really comprehend Mac's cry for help. I listened to him, but I'm afraid I was in no way experienced or qualified to do anything for him.

He and Renee were now running a caravan business. It kept him busy and in the beginning he seemed happy and contented. However, this state of affairs would not last long. He had been in hospital with heart trouble and was plagued by bouts of depression. Things between him and Renee were not running smoothly and this made him worse. Then in the late 1960s, Mac was hit by news from which would escalate his own death. Jackie, his youngest son was found dead. He was 38 and left a wife and children. Jackie was separated from his wife and children and had been drinking the previous night. He was staying at his mother's house and it was she who found his body. Beside the drink he had consumed, it was revealed that he had also taken some sleeping pills. His mother, Eliza, was devastated and died a couple of years later. One can only imagine McAvoy's feelings about his son and then later about his first wife, whom he had kept in regular touch with over the years.

After his son, Jackie, and his first wife, Eliza, died, Mac found himself lonelier than ever. His ever-present need to be at the centre of everyone's life caused myriad problems for Renee and daughter, Pat. He began feeling a deep melancholy. When his friend, Jack Cassidy, a former wrestling star, called to tell Mac that he was off to wrestle in Europe for a few weeks,Mac became even more depressed. Cassidy had been a constant companion over the previous months, travelling everywhere with McAvoy. Mac pleaded with Cassidy not to go, even offering to pay him what he would earn wrestling in Europe.

Jack thanked McAvoy for the offer, but said he was contracted to go. Mac looking gloomier than ever told Jack that he wouldn't be around much longer. "I will not be here when you come back," said McAvoy. Cassidy trying to boost his friend's flagging morale told him not to be silly and, dismissed Mac's morbid notion. He decided that Mac was simply tired and, as he knew Mac was one to do, was feeling self indulgent and self pitying and wanting more attention.

An associate of McAvoy's, who asked for anonimity because he still has a close,0 long standing association with the family said: "At times Mac was impossible, just a difficult fellow. It was extremely difficult for Renee to put up with his behaviour. As he got older, he was exasperating, a real dictator. Mind you he always had been this way with his three wives. He would order them about, banishing them if somebody called to visit him, showing his disapproval in outrageous, immature ways.

Two of the all time greats – Jock McAvoy and Joe Louis in a picture taken at Belle Vue, Manchester.

He would throw things, have temper tantrums. Poor Renee. I think she had a dreadful marriage, but she was devoted to him."

At the start of the 1970s, Mac and Renee were living separate lives. It must have been a terrible burden for her to exist in such an hostile atmosphere, nevertheless, she continued running the caravan business. There appears to have been constant bickering and Renee had had enough. On the night of the 19th of November, all the constant arguments and bad feeling seemed to catch up with McAvoy and he started drinking heavily. His life, once overflowing with the grand emotions and vital juices of his existence, now seemed empty. He wondered if anything was worthwhile now. In other words, what was the point of being a has been? What pride was there in that for a man like Jock McAvoy? Desperate thoughts and unasweraable questions began to invade his mind. The fighting instinct that had always been an integral aspect of his personality disappeared. In the early hours of the morning on the 20th of November 1971, his 64th birthday, Mac was found dead. He had committed suicide. The cause of death was barbiturate poisoning. At his inquest, it was revealed that he had tried to commit suicide several times, even slashing his wrists in one attempt. Nobody believed that Mac would end his life like this. There had been previous suicide attempts but most people who knew him thought he really wasn't serious about ending his life. They were, however, cries for help, for attention.

"Things began to change for Mac when he fell prey to his illness," said one close associate. "He was ready to die. He was truly, truly tired. Tired of fighting his illness. Tired of fighting to save his marriage and tired of living".

Jock McAvoy, born Joe Bamford, was buried at Rochdale Cemetery on the 26th of November, 1971. The dignified ceremony, conducted by Father Murphy, a priest who had known Mac for most of his life, was attended by a large number of relatives, friends and members of the boxing fraternity. Amongst the floral tributes was a wreath from Len Harvey, inscribed: "I salute you, Mac – a great fighter".

The arguments were now futile as to why he took this course of action. However, one has to consider that for the past twenty or so years, this once great fighter, who always prided himself on his physical fitness had been confined to the life of an invalid, and suffered mental torture because of his illness and his inability to do the things. He had lost his mother, his son, his first wife and a few months before his friend and former stablemate, Jackie Brown had died. His third marriage had failed and he could see no future.

Just before we handed in the manuscript to the publisher for this book to be processed, I wrote a letter to a few newspapers requesting anybody who had any little anecdotes about Jock McAvoy to contact me. My phone rang on Good Friday the 2nd April 1999 and a well spoken man answered. His name was Steve Specterman. He told me that in the 1960s he was a manager for Thomas Mouget, a Civil Engineering Company. It transpired that Mr Specterman was in charge of work, which was being carried out on Irlam Steelworks, and a huge ten ton hammer was being used to demolish buildings and flatten the steel into scrap. The hammer made a loud, piercing noise, which could be heard, for miles around. One particular morning I received a phone call from a gentleman who told me his name was Jock McAvoy. "Are you in charge of the work that's being carried out involving all this noise?" he asked. I told him I was and could I be of any help to him? "Can I come round to see you?" he said. I told him I would be delighted to meet him. I had of course heard of Jock McAvoy, the famous boxer. There wasn't the slightest tone of anger in his voice. "Good," he replied. "I'll be there in a couple

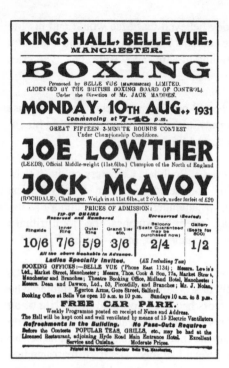

'The Good Old Days'– poster from August
1931.

of minutes." My office was a little house that had been converted into an office and it was situated on Atherton Lane, facing the George Pub in Cadishead. I got up from my desk and went outside to meet him. I was a little excited at the prospect of meeting him because I had read and been told so much about him. However, I wasn't expecting what happened. As I stood waiting to greet him, up walked this man clutching two sticks and callipers on both legs. "Are you the fellow I've just spoken to on the telephone?" he shouted at me. "Yes," I replied smiling, "what can I do for you?" "I will do something for you," he replied. "If you don't stop this bleeding noise I'll flatten you." I was flabbergasted. Later, I had to laugh when telling my superiors about meeting the great McAvoy.

In the 1960s Belle Vue had started promoting tournaments again after a long absence. On this particular night Terry Downes was topping the bill. Downes was a 'character' as well as being an exciting fighter. He would go on to win the world middleweight championship from the American Paul Pender in 1961 and go on to challenge Willie Pastrano for the world light-heavyweight crown, losing in the eleventh round. Before his fights Downes would be ready for action long before his contest was due to start. Spectators would be treated to Terry doing excercises, shadow boxing and jigging up and down while he would be watching the other fights taking place. John Kay of the Manchester Evening News was sitting in his usual ringside seat in the press section when he saw the Londoner doing his act. Turning to a younger reporter Mr Kay said: "Call me sentimental! Call me old-fashioned! Call me what you will, but please don't blame me for harking back to grand old-timers who fought and won titles in this Belle Vue ring in the glorious days when Manchester and Harry Fleming could boast three champions. It comes back to me now because Terry

Downes, the British middleweight champion ducks under the King's Hall ropes tonight for the first time.

John Kay went on to say that though Downes was a colourful character, and oozed pep and personality from the moment he left his dressing room and starts shadow boxing his way to the ring he couldn't be compared to Jock McAvoy. The journalist said that McAvoy in his opinion would always be the greatest fighter of the age. "I watched him win his British title from Len Harvey in this same King's Hall ring way back in the mighty 1930s. I also saw him give tough Jack Casey the hammering of a lifetime only to throw away his area title with an accidental low blow towards the very end of a memorable scrap. McAvoy had what it takes to pack any arena. He was also the light-heavyweight champion."

He went on to regale his younger contemporary with how McAvoy had challenged John Henry Lewis for his world light-heavyweight crown, and even fought Jack Petersen for the British heavyweight title. "He knocked Babe Risko cold inside a round when the Yank was the kingpin of 'em all. They told me at the time that America wouldn't let Mac fight Risko for the middleweight crown because he was sure to beat him." He made no apology for this diversion! He said he had started out with the intention of paying tribute to Terry Downes, but somehow or other the shadow of McAvoy was always in his mind. He meant no disrespect to Downes, a mighty good scrapper and a worthy champion. But said John. "It just so happens that he can never hope to oust the memory of Jock McAvoy from my fighting recollections. I'll raise my glass right now to Terry Downes, the British middleweight champion! But don't ask me to think about him in terms of Jock McAvoy. Downes is good - McAvoy was great!"

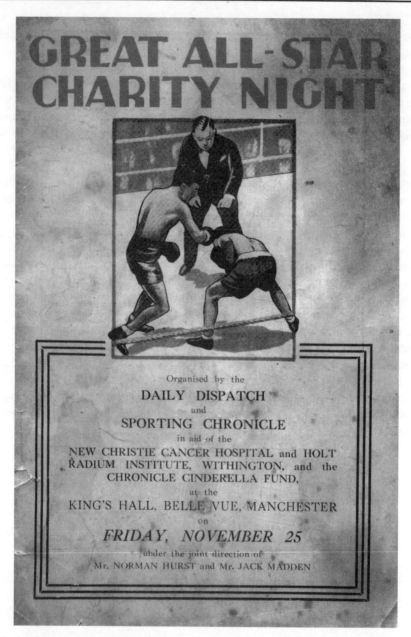

Jock McAvoy on the bill against the Romanian champion, Mihail Fulea, all in support of a local charity.

Mr Bert Daly

The man who should take the real credit for the writing of McAvoy: Portrait Of A Fighting Legend is Bert Daly, well known to many people in the boxing business as the one time Public Relations Officer for the Manchester Ex-Boxers Association. Bert, in his eighties at the time of writing, is also renowned as one of Britain's leading boxing historians-a man with an encyclopedic knowledge of everybody and everything connected with the boxing game.

Bert Daly knew Jock McAvoy intimately, both as a fighter and as a man, and probably knows more about the subject of this book than anyone else. When you read the story of the great McAvoy, for most of the time you are really absorbing the memories of Bert, as told to me.

Jock McAvoy's ring career began in 1927 and ended in 1945. For most of that time and most of Mac's 147 contests, Bert Daly was present-observing and assisting his training and watching him fight. Bert is therefore uniquely qualified to pass first hand comment on McAvoy, and his informed opinion forms the backbone of what you will read in these pages.

Bert's opinion is that Jock McAvoy was the roughest, toughest and most destructive of all of Britain's middleweight champions. Bert believes that McAvoy, at his best, could have taken on and knocked out Randolph Turpin, Terry Downes, Alan Minter or Chris Eubank - four men who became world middleweight champions - or any of the others at his weight who became national title holders. Our joint evaluation of McAvoy places this most meanest and hardest punching of fighters right at the very top of the list when it comes to discussing Britain's middleweight heroes.

This biography is an unashamed celebration of McAvoy's boxing career, with the emphasis on demonstrating to the reader just what a formidable knockout artist the man was in his hey day. 91 knockouts and stoppages in 147 bouts, mainly against quality opposition, is quite a record. Bert Daly saw McAvoy's legendary power close up on many, many occasions and is of the opinion that few men of his weight - at any point in boxing history - could stand up to the "Rochdale Thunderbolt" at his best.

A million thanks go to Bert Daly - the doyen of boxing historians - for making the telling of Jock McAvoy's story possible. God bless you, Bert.

Recollections of the Great Mr McAvoy

One dull, rainy morning in 1970 I stood with several others on Hyde Road in Manchester and watched with sadness as the bulldozers began demolishing the once world famous showground of the Belle Vue Amusement Park. Mancunians were told by the planners and architects that it was being demolished in order to make room for more modern inner-city developments, and in the long term it would prove to be all worth while. Nevertheless, many folk watching shed a few tears at Belle Vue's passing. Thousands of people who remember Belle Vue will never forget the many pleasures and pastimes this grand place offered them, especially families. It will always remain unique. I myself fondly remember with nostalgia those bristling, exciting nights when I watched some of the world's greatest fighters performing.

It was a proven fact that the city of Manchester once boasted more boxing halls within a ten mile radius of its Town Hall than any other city, possibly with the exception of London.

The King's Hall in Belle Vue was the Mecca for boxers and supporters. It seated 7,000 but a couple of thousand more people regularly stood at the back of the stadium, leaned against the walls on the aisles, or sat on the floor to watch their idols. It was the ideal stadium and was home to many great fighters from around the world. There were smaller halls, both licensed and unlicensed, within a stone's throw of this great northern showground. All have their own stories to tell and are part of Manchester's history. However, it was at Belle Vue where I saw some of the finest champions and contenders that boxing has produced. The name of Jackie Brown became the most popular during those nostalgic days of the 1930s. He was a brilliant boxer with the heart of a lion, noted for his speed and skill, however, he was also well known for his remarkable showmanship. He was the only one of Manchester's truly great fighters to become a world champion, but I assure you there were several others who could and should have gained world honours. Johnny King and Johnny 'Nipper' Cusick were among just a few who for one reason or another were unfortunate not to have become world champions.

I became interested in boxing while a schoolboy. As a youth I boxed as an amateur for Ardwick Lads Club, but realised I wasn't good enough to turn professional. I was a regular attender of thousands of tournaments throughout Lancashire in the Roaring Twenties and the depression of the Thirties. I marvelled at the skills and boxing ability of those stout-hearted boxers who became part of Manchester's boxing history. I am not one of those people who believe that fighters from my era were much better than the present day crop of boxers, but in my day there were so many more of them. And they had to be good at their trade or they wouldn't get bookings. In those times working class folk queued for everything: jobs, food, coal and coke, etc. It was no different on the boxing circuit, fighters would turn up at tournaments hoping to get a fight and if they couldn't get on one bill they would hurry to another area where another tournament was being staged. Hard times they were, but it produced great ringmen in abundance. However, as great as they all were, there was one particular fighter who became my idol. The incomparable Jock McAvoy! I was his number one fan, I hero worshipped him.

Jock McAvoy of Rochdale was boxing's number one newsmaker in the 1930s. This Burnley born but Rochdale raised man who brought glory to his home town and his country once he moved to the Collyhurst Gym in north Manchester, packed more excitement and drama into those few years than most people experience in a lifetime. His name was seldom out of the headlines, though not always for the right reasons. To many boxing followers, Jock McAvoy is still the greatest middleweight champion Britain has ever produced. He himself would not have denied it, but as a perfectionist was quick to recognise his own faults. His 'Rags to Riches' story is unsurpassed.

Jock McAvoy isn't a very long name - just ten letters. Yet boxing fans in Britain, Europe and America knew him simply by the name of 'Mac.' That was the accolade, the supreme honour. 'Jack' is still Dempsey, 'Joe' was Louis, 'Henry' meant Cooper, 'Ali' meant Muhammad, while in a similar fashion Brazilians (then the rest of the world) called their national soccer hero - Edson Arantes do Nascimento, simply 'Pele.'

During his peak years Mac was considered the most exciting middleweight in the world and, many an amiable Lancastrian would turn awkward with anyone who disputed that. McAvoy dealt in only one currency - Knockouts! And he scored plenty during his glittering career. During Manchester's palmy days of the 1920s and 1930s he was the most magnetic fighter of his generation. McAvoy was called

A very debonair, Jock McAvoy.

the equivalent of 'big head' from many boxing halls and arenas. He was always where the fighting was the thickest, and was tempestuous, robust and highly temperamental. When he was a teenager, critics who had watched boxing for years said he would burn himself out before he was 25, because of his restless pursuit for absolute perfect physical fitness and his chase for the biggest share of the action every time he ducked through the ropes to either spar or fight competitively.

He had cold, sharp eyes; these same eyes were open for sycophants, boxing tricksters and con men who came in all shapes and sizes at the heart and on the fringe of the business, and sometimes for fools. He wasn't in love with boxing in the same way as other champions like for example Len Harvey, or his stablemates Jackie Brown, the world flyweight champion, and Johnny King, the British and Empire bantamweight title holder. Mac, with his rugged good looks saw boxing chiefly as a way to make his fame and fortune. He never forgot his mother's advice. "Put your pennies in the bank, Joe. If you don't you'll find that most of the punches will have been in vain." His attitude to money was diamond hard and he wanted as much of it as possible in Jock McAvoy's bank balance at the earliest possible date. He was greedy for money, because he saw so little of it while he was growing up, and his desire was to live in untroubled comfort. The only snag with Jock was that his retirement age was set 30 years earlier than most. By his mid - thirties his career would be finished, that was of course, if he proved lucky with injuries.

It was said that you had to be as sharp as James Bond to take Jock McAvoy for a ride. Even then all the bets wouldn't go on Bond. Nonetheless, at the height of his career he allowed a silver-tongued American con man to rob him of his hard - earned money from some of his biggest fights.

Jock's deepest strength, alongside his sheer professionalism and shrewdness, lay in his loyalty to his family and close friends. McAvoy was a fighter for the great occasion. He may have had his bad fights...and what fighter can say he hasn't? But when the crowd topped thousands, when celebrities were seated in ringside seats and thousands more listening on the wireless, he could be relied upon to deliver undiluted thrills and excitement in abundance. When the cheers had died for the supporting fighters, there was still McAvoy to come. It was like waiting for Frank Sinatra at the close of a breathless Royal Command Performance. There was only one Sinatra. There was only one McAvoy.

His eyes came in a pale, set face, and could be as chilling as chips of ice. This was what was most noticeable about Mac when you first met him. He could cut you dead with a glance. He had an air of menace which added to his attraction. This was one of the reasons he was so difficult to get to know. There was also an air of suspicion about him, a cool detached way he had of repelling invaders. He was a man so suspicious that, if someone said "Good Morning," he would first check the weather outside before answering. He always gave the impression that he believed everybody was out to deprive him of what was his. Mac had many indiscretions, barely showing a trace of emotion. He was chillingly in control of himself. Mac spoke with a strong, gruff, Lancashire accent. He was often blunt and straight to the point, calling a spade a spade. He was self - opinionated and very egotistical. When he spoke he felt no need to impress. If you didn't like what he said - hard luck. It was not wise to cross him. Those who did lived to regret it. On one occasion, McAvoy, believing he had been cheated out of a full share of his purse, took the person responsible to the window of a hotel, hung him out, five storeys up and got what he believed was his entitlement. It was said by many critics that his four strongest points were his punching power, his 'killer instinct,' toughness and remarkable physical condition. Jock was notorious because he had a short fuse for a temper and he was, at times, a violent man both inside and outside the boxing ring.

Over the years the British Isles have produced some of the greatest and certainly most colourful fighters who went on to become world middleweight champions. Bob Fitzsimmons was the first British born boxer to win the world middleweight title in 1891. Randolph Turpin was the second in 1951, when against all the odds he outpointed the brilliant Sugar Ray Robinson. Since the 1960s, Terry Downes, Alan Minter, Nigel Benn, Chris Eubank have been world champions at the middleweight poundage. Putting aside my obvious admiration for Jock McAvoy, and being totally honest as well as unbiased, while staying detached about the situation, and having been privileged to have seen every British middleweight champion following McAvoy, I state without any doubt whatsoever that McAvoy was the best 11st 6lb fighter that Britain has ever produced. What's more, he would be a top candidate as one of the world's greatest ever middleweights. His record alone informs us of that, but there was so much more to this fellow than mere figures in a record book. As I look back over the years I am convinced Mac was born years before his time. I can imagine the huge amounts of money he would earn today with the event of satellite television. He would have been the biggest attraction this century with his exciting all-action style of fighting.

While boxing is rightly referred to as the Noble Art of Self Defence, and nobody appreciates that more than myself and other connoisseurs of the sport, I have to admit that in boxing it is the knockout punchers who draw spectators through the turnstiles and have promoters rubbing their hands in glee. It is the sight of watching a fighter flatten his opponent with one pulverising punch which creates thrills and adds tension and drama for the paying customers. Just glance through the pages of boxing's history, and the names of Jack Dempsey in the 1920s through to the likes of Mike Tyson of recent vintage are forever being written about. And their exciting encounters are forever glamourised by a media who seem anxious to embellish the achievements of the big punchers. This doesn't just apply to heavyweights either. Fighters who could wallop such as our own Jimmy Wilde, Stanley Ketchel, Harry Greb, Rocky Graziano, Sugar Ray Robinson, Roberto Duran and Ruben Olivares to name but a few are revered and still idolised because of their ability to dispatch opponents into dreamland.

At one time the Americans seemed to have a monopoly in this department. English fighters were scorned and laughed at by those hard-nosed American reporters who

McAvoy in a wheelchair at Belle Vue to watch Peter Kane fight Guido Ferracin in 1948.

seemed to be forever dismissing British fighters' credentials. It was seldom that British boxing fans could boast about one of our own fighters who actually could, and did, strike fear into the top American champions and their connections.

In the early years of this century, Jim Driscoll, Jimmy Wilde, Ted Kid Lewis and Jack Kid Berg did a great deal to boost British prestige while fighting in American rings. But the one English fighter who stands out like a beacon on a foggy winter's night and is still acclaimed by those hard-to-please American journalists is a fellow from Lancashire named Joe Bamford, better known as...Jock McAvoy!

This is the true story of one of world boxing's genuine hard men of the ring, a fighter who could hold his own in any fighting company throughout the entire boxing establishment. A fighter who all through his long career gave undiluted thrills and excitement with his own special brand of mayhem. Here was a man who could take the hardest punches thrown at him without flinching, by not only fighters in his own middleweight division but from renowned punchers in the light-heavyweight class and even in the 'dreadnought' division of the heavyweights. He possessed that intangible thing known as the equaliser in either fist...a knockout wallop!

McAvoy was regarded by many as the uncrowned middleweight champion of the world; the outright winner of the Lord Lonsdale Challenge Belt; 11 years undefeated British middleweight champion; also British light-heavyweight champion; scored 91 victories inside the distance; never knocked out in his ring career which lasted 18 years. How's that for credentials? But there was so much more to Jock McAvoy.

When McAvoy managed to recover his much coveted Lonsdale Belt in 1967, a presentation was arranged to be held in the Champness Hall on Drake Street in Rochdale. Jack Peterson and Nat Fleischer were among the guests as was McAvoy's close friend, Norman Hill. Mac was absolutely ecstatic about the whole affair. When the ceremony was over, and the guests made their way out of the building, McAvoy shuffled to the top of the stairs, placed one hand on Peterson's shoulder and lifted his callipered leg over the banister with his other hand, and with a wild yell of triumph he slid down the banister and landed in a sprawling heap on the floor. Everybody was concerned but Mac was laughing like a child with a new toy.

What did the boxing experts think of McAvoy? Desmond Hackett, with his trademark brown bowler, was one of the biggest names in sportswriting. He wrote for the Daily Express: "In the 1930s, the area of Collyhurst in Manchester contained the greatest fighting combination in the world. They were Jackie Brown, Johnny King, and Jock McAvoy. And of all these Lancashire larruppers, the most lethal fighter was Jock McAvoy, whose nickname 'The Rochdale Thunderbolt' was the boxing understatement of all time. I am a devout coward, but I go down in the records of having survived two rounds in a sparring session with McAvoy, later the doctors consoled me and said I would still live. McAvoy was the most lethal thing at his weight, perhaps even more so than Rocky Marciano. Only world boxing politics prevented McAvoy from being a world champion. This man was a great, great fighter."

Frank McGhee was the chief sportswriter on the northern edition of the Daily Mirror from the 1950s until becoming chief sportswriter for all editions of the Daily Mirror in 1972, before retiring in 1985. McGhee got to know the Lancashire fight scene quite well during his time in Manchester. In his book England's Boxing Heroes, he wrote of McAvoy: "A fight against Jock McAvoy must have been a little like going to war against the Chinese Army. Punches never stopped coming at you from a man who seemed to feel a sort of primeval joy at the thrill of combat.

No English fighter, at any weight, ever punched more devastatingly -and that officially recognised. Statistics place McAvoy at the top of the records."

Mr McGhee goes on to state that out of 133 victories from 147 contests, Mac won 88 inside the distance and 53 of those stoppages were by clean knockout. On this point the journalist was mistaken. "He hit like a heavyweight and, though not much more than a middleweight, fought in that division as well," added Frank, while expressing the opinion that McAvoy was a genuine throwback to the bad old days when two fighters fought until one dropped. He, like many others, was of the opinion that with any kind of justice Mac would have become the first Englishman since Bob Fitzimmons to win the world middleweight title. "New York fans were in love with McAvoy. He was their kind of guy, a very different sort of Englishman."

Ron Bailey wrote in the now defunct Boxing World: "There have been many memorable ring immortals in the history of British boxing, one of the greatest was the legendary Jock McAvoy, undoubtedly our finest fighter never to win a world title. In his younger flamboyant days, McAvoy was a person of controversial characteristics, thus being frowned upon as a difficult person. He had his differences with authority and was often involved in happenings of a kind whether non-fiction or amusing fiction." Mr Bailey once cycled 60 miles to chat to Mac. "Jock sadly suffered more set-backs in the trying struggles of his social life than he ever encountered inside the ring. There were years of matrimonial discord in which three marriages failed. Surprisingly, the latter one to his attractive wife Renee, lasted for almost thirty years. They had a daughter Pat."

Jeff Dickson, the American promoter who was based in Paris, and promoted on the continent with success while also staging big time tournaments in London, said: "Jock McAvoy was one of my favourite fighters. In my opinion Jock was one of the best fighters Britain has produced for many a year. He showed my countrymen in the States that Britain could breed good fighters. By rights he should have been a world champion. Only bad luck has robbed him of the highest honours. From the beginning of his career I was sure the Rochdale lad had what it takes to become a world champion. I watched his progress as he battered his dynamic way right through to win the British middleweight title from Len Harvey. He was a promoter's dream and could always be relied upon to give the fans what they paid for - excitement. He was one of the hardest punchers I ever saw and I saw plenty of them in all my years in boxing. He lacked for nothing - only a little bit of luck."

Jack Bates, who trained McAvoy in his glory years, was always gushing in his praise for the Rochdale Thunderbolt. "When myself and Harry Fleming fist saw Jock he was with Joe Tolley and doing his fighting at Royton," said Bates. "Winning titles was far from our thoughts on that first sighting. Jock was just a slugger. He paid no attention to the finer points of boxing. He just waded in and fired away in all sorts of directions with all sorts of punches. We felt that if we had him in our gym he had the right sort of material for us to work on. His strength, stamina and his love of a good old-fashioned punch up was amazing. In those early days his idea of winning a fight was to go in and blast the living daylight out of his opponent. And he never cared where his wild haymakers landed, so long as they hit the other fellow. After one particular contest Mac had, I turned to Harry Fleming and remarked that Jock would suffer from hand injuries. He would throw punches with his full weight behind them and, often these punches would land on top of his opponent's head and bust his hands! When he joined our stable I often treated his damaged mitts. We got him to cut out the wild stuff and place his punches correctly, and he developed perfect and deadly hooks. We also taught him to dodge and 'ride' punches beside teaching him how to use his enormous strength by working on the inside of his opponent. From a novice, McAvoy quickly became a live proposition and packed the halls wherever he fought. The only thing Mac retained from his early wildman days was his wonderful guts. Jock's capacity for absorbing pain and getting over setbacks made him out to be a marvel among he-men."

In 1954, Jim Ruck was a veteran of 55 years connection with professional boxing. He had actually seen the majority of the world's greatest fighters from Jack Johnson to Rocky Marciano. Mr Ruck was taking part in a conversation about the merits of that great Australian fighter Les Darcy, who died tragically. In a discussion about Les Darcy, a fan said that Darcy weighing 11st 6lb would have beaten Jess Willard. Mr Ruck had seen Les Darcy in action and said it was ludicrous to even suggest that Darcy could have beaten the giant Willard. "I could name a number of fighters who would have defeated Darcy at his own weight," said Mr Ruck. "I am definitely of the opinion that Jock McAvoy, at his peak, would have defeated Darcy if they fought at the middleweight poundage. Don't get me wrong, Les Darcy was a good middleweight."

Henry Cooper, a brilliant left hooker in his own right, said when discussing McAvoy he could feel a chill run up his spine whenever he talked about the Rochdale man. "He was so ruthless," remarked Henry. "In all but name McAvoy was a world champion. He was totally fearless, he didn't care who the man in front of him was or about his reputation. I had many conversations with Harry Levene, the famous London manager and promoter who for a period managed McAvoy, and he never ended without telling me what a great, great fighter McAvoy was. The days have long since gone when fighters like McAvoy fought at the drop of a hat, they were very hard times. Imagine McAvoy against today's middleweights?"

Jack Petersen was the British and Empire heavyweight champion in the 1930's. "Jock McAvoy was the best British middleweight ever," he said in a 1960's interview. "He would have beaten Turpin and Terry Downes. I don't wish to belittle these champions, but McAvoy was a special breed of fighter, his style of bobbing and weaving was very effective. They say his best punch was his right, however, he could wallop equally hard with his left hook. He fought from welterweight up to heavyweight. Yes, a great, great fighter".

This was what boxing writer and television analyst Reg Gutteridge had to say about McAvoy: "Jock McAvoy is the only fighter who regularly bit the hand that fed him. When he grunted and chewed the thumbs of his gloves, opponents were usually doomed. He was the most tigerish British middleweight champion and, arguably, the strongest puncher. It was no exaggeration that he was capable, and often proved it, of lifting an opponent clean off the canvas with a punch from either fist. McAvoy shares with his old foe Archie Sexton, whom he knocked out in 1933, the distinction of being the highest ranked Englishman in a world list of knockouts scored in major competition. McAvoy was never given sufficient praise for his ability, though nobody ever doubted his crushing power, even at an elderly age when his hands were buckled with arthritis. Nobody ever took liberties with McAvoy, in his prime or past it. He had a barrel chest, a powerful neck and blacksmith's sinews up his arms. A striking-looking man with black curly hair parted in the middle. Today, he would be a sensation." Charley Harvey, who managed Ted Kid Lewis, Peerless Jim Driscoll and Owen Moran, said of McAvoy, "He's a throwback to the old timers. He feared nobody."

"Once upon a time, and believe me, this is no fairy story, Manchester had three boxing champions," said John Kay the boxing writer for the Manchester Evening News, while talking to me a couple of years before he sadly passed away in 1999. Mr Kay was in his late eighties but remembered events from the 1930s as if he was discussing events that took place the night before. "They were great days for the city of Manchester and for Belle Vue. In the King's Hall ring I actually paid for my seat to see Jackie Brown take the world flyweight crown from Young Perez. And to see Jock McAvoy snatch the middleweight title from Len Harvey, and to watch Johnny King and Dick Corbett in their several battles with first one and then the other claiming the bantamweight crown. Yes, those were the days! Every other Monday there was boxing at Belle Vue, and it was always value for money with Harry Fleming's masterful trio topping the bill in turn. Speaking specifically about Jock McAvoy, well, in my humble opinion, he was the most exciting fighter I have ever laid eyes on. And I was a regular at Royton, the Adelphi in Salford, Churnett Street Public Hall in Collyhurst, and Harpurhey Baths, the various boxing booths, yes, those were the days! When I was young, I could see a boxing show every night in the week and I didn't have to travel beyond a twenty-mile radius to satisfy my love for the noble art. I saw fighters of every shape, weight and size and unquestionably McAvoy was the most fierce I ever saw."

Jock McAvoy's Fighting Record

1927

Nov 6.	Billy Longworth. (Royton)	Won KO 2. Royton.
Nov 27.	Bert Hilditch. (Shaw)	Won Rsf 6. Royton.

2 Contests. Won 2. Lost 0. Inside the distance wins. 2.

1928

Jan 27.	Billy Chew. (Darwen)	Lost Ret 8. Haslingden.
March 19.	Teddy Cox. (Todmorden)	Won KO 7. Todmorden.

2 Contests. Won 1. Lost 1. Inside the distance wins. 1.

1929

July 4.	Frank Ormerod. (Nelson)	Won KO 1. Burnley.
July 14.	Jack Ogden. (Chadderton)	Won KO 3. Royton.
Aug 6.	Billy Chew. (Darwen)	Won Pts 10. Burnley.
Aug 14.	Eric Basher Bargh. (Morecambe)	Won Rsf 4. Morecambe.
Aug 28.	Jack Jukes. (Tyldesley)	Won Rsf 6. Morecambe.
Sept17.	Tiger Bob Ennis. (Halifax)	Won KO 1. Burnley.
Sept 25.	Seaman Douglas. (Warrington)	Won Ret 6. Morecambe.
Sept 29.	Billy Chew. (Darwen)	Won Pts 15. Royton.
Sept 30.	Jack Ogden. (Chadderton)	Won Pts 10. Fleetwood.
Dec 2.	Jack Harrison. (Hanley)	Won Ret 4. Hanley.
Dec 5.	Soldier Jones. (Rhyl)	Won Rsf 2. Rhyl.
Dec 6.	Ted Abbot. (Doncaster)	Won Ret 6. Blackburn.
Dec 15.	Lud Gresvig. (Norway)	Won Ret 2. Royton.
Dec 20.	Billy Horner. (Leeds)	Won Ret 4. Preston.
Dec 27.	Griff Williams. (Denbigh)	Drew 10. Rhyl.

15 Contests. Won 14. Lost 0. Drawn 1. Inside the distance wins. 11.

1930

Jan 30.	Marine Davies. (Portsmouth)	Won KO 6. Royton.
Jan 24.	Sid Aldrige. (Bath)	Won KO 4. Preston.
Feb 7.	Jack Ogden. (Chadderton)	Won KO 2. Haslingden.
Feb 9.	Andy Ross. (Barrow)	Won KO 5. Royton.

Feb 14.	Fred Oldfield. (Doncaster)	Won Pts 12. Preston.
Feb 27.	Bill Lee. (Wrexham)	Won KO 3. Rhyl.
March 7.	Bill Shockerí Bowman. (Penrith)	Won KO 3. Penrith.
March10.	Fred Blything. (Wolverhampton)	Won Pts15. Stourbridge.
March 16.	Jack Wilkinson. (Warrington)	Won KO 2. Royton.
March 21.	Fred Oldfield. (Doncaster)	Won Ret 8. Haslingden.
March 28.	Jim Pearson. (Bamber Bridge)	Lost Pts 12. Preston.
April 13.	Ted Lewis. (Wigan)	Won KO 6. Royton.
April 14.	Dai Beynon. (Merythr)	Won KO 5. Blackburn.
April 25.	Joe Rostron. (Heywood)	Lost Pts 12. Preston.
May 25.	Eddie Strawer. (Rochdale)	Won KO 10. Royton.
June 11.	Billy Green. (Pontypridd)	Won Rsf 2. Manchester.
July 26.	Eddie Strawer. (Rochdale)	Won KO 6. Manchester.
July 30.	George Porter. (Nottingham)	Won Pts 15. Nottingham.
Aug 10	Farmer Jackson. (Doncaster)	Won Pts 12. Royton.
Aug 27.	Seaman Jim Cox. (Wigan)	Won Pts 12. Morecambe.
Sept 14.	Jim Pearson. (Bamber Bridge)	Won KO 7. Royton.
Sept 30.	Billy Delahaye. (Pontypridd)	Won Rsf 2. Manchester.
Oct 3.	Patsy Flynn. (Lambeth)	Won KO 3. Preston.
Oct 14.	Joe Rostron. (Heywood)	Won Pts 15. Manchester.
Oct 22.	Joe Lowther. (Leeds)	Won Pts 15. Morecambe.
Nov 2.	Seaman Jim Cox. (Wigan)	Won Pts 15. Royton.
Nov 4.	Tate Evans. (Maestag)	Won Rsf 15. Manchester.
Dec 14.	Jim Johnson. (Newcastle)	Won KO 2. Newcastle.

28 Contests. Won 26. Lost 2. Inside the distance wins 18.

1931

Jan 11.	Bill Shocker Bowman. (Penrith)	Won Pts 15. Royton.
Jan 22.	Charlie McDonald. (Sunderland)	Won Pts 15. Liverpool.
Feb 16.	Dick Burt. (Plymouth)	Won Ret 8. Manchester.
March 8.	Charlie Keeling. (Nottingham)	Won KO 3. Royton.
March 30.	Paul McGuire. (Sunderland)	Lost Disq 4. Manchester.
April 3.	Seaman Jim Cox. (Wigan)	Won Pts 12. Bolton.
April 15.	Sonny Doke. (Battersea)	Won Pts 15. Morecambe.
April 19.	Johnny Seamarks. (Bedford)	Won KO 3. Royton.
May 11.	Fred Shaw. (Shipley)	Won Pts 15. Manchester.
May 24.	Sonny Doke. (Battersea)	Won Pts 12. Royton.
June 21.	Con Van Leowen. (Holland)	Won Ret 5. Royton.
July 11.	Jack Bottomley. (Leeds)	Won KO 1. Rochdale.

If there is anything happening in the boxing world Norman Hurst knows about it. He keeps you right in touch with the latest big fight moves.

Norman Hurst
IS HERE TO-NIGHT

Read his
Straight-from-the-shoulder Opinions
in To-morrow's

Daily Dispatch

BEST FOR BOXING AND ALL SPORTS.

Advertisement from the 1933 edition of the Belle Vue Boxing Gazette, for Norman Hurst and his influential column inches in the Daily Despatch.

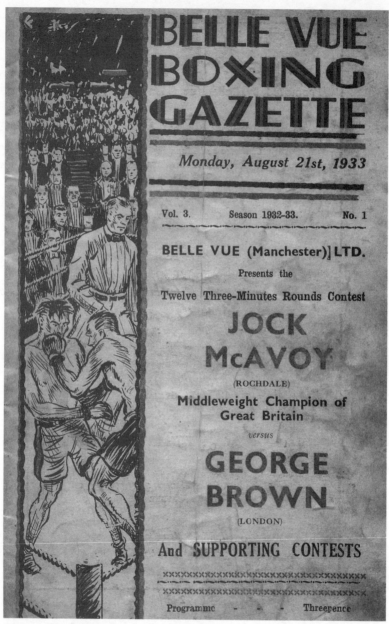

Defending his middleweight crown against the Londoner, George Brown, August 1933

| July 19. | Jack OfBrien. (Belfast) | Won Ret 3. Dublin. |
| Aug 10. | Joe Lowther. (Leeds) | Won Ret 8. Manchester. |

(Won The Northern Area Middleweight Championship)

Aug 30.	Jack Hyams. (Stepney)	Won Dis 8. Leeds.
Sept 7.	Jerry Daley. (Penigraig)	Won KO 2. Manchester.
Oct 12.	Alfred Pegazanno. (France)	Won Rsf 3. Manchester.
Nov 6.	Paul McGuire. (Sunderland)	Won Ret 2. Blackpool.
Nov 16.	Billy Adair. (Bethnal Green)	Won KO 2. Manchester.
Nov 22.	Sonny Doke. (Battersea)	Won Ret 5. Royton.
Dec 20.	Ernie Red Pullen. (Cardiff)	Won KO 1. Royton.

21 Contest. Won 20. Lost 1 by disq. Inside the distance wins 13.

1932

Jan 17.	Jack Marshall. (Accrington)	Won KO 1. Royton.
Feb 2.	Ex-Seaman Albert Harvey. (Chatham)	Won Pts 15. Manchester.
March 1.	Jack Etienne. (Belgium)	Won Pts 15. Manchester.
March 21.	Len Harvey. (Plymouth)	Lost Pts 15. Manchester.

(British Middleweight Championship. Harvey, the champion.)

May 9.	Edwin John. (Chelsea)	Won Rsf 6. Manchester.
May 29.	Bill Hood. (Plymouth)	Won KO 2. Royton.
June 19.	Sandy McKenzie. (Glasgow)	Won KO 1. Royton.
June 28.	Billy Thomas. (Deri)	Won Rsf 3. Blackpool.
July 4.	Carmello Candel. (France)	Won Pts 10. London.
July 18.	Jack Cast Iron Casey. (Sunderland)	Lost Disq 14. Manchester.

(For The Northern Area Championship)

Aug 1.	Tom Benjamin. (Wales)	Won Ret 5. Blackpool.
Aug 31.	George Brown. (Stepney)	Won Pts 12. Morecambe.
Sept 11.	Billy Roberts. (Bishop Auckland)	Won Ret 3. Royton.
Sept 30.	Phil Green. (Bath)	Won Rsf 2. Rawtenstall.
Oct 12.	Tommy Moore. (Royston)	Won KO 3. Morecambe.
Nov 7.	Ted Coveney. (Highbury)	Won KO 4. Blackburn.
Nov 25.	Mihail Fubea. (Rumania)	Won Rsf 4. Manchester.
Dec 7.	Hans Siefried. (Germany)	Won Pts 10. London.

18 Contests. Won 16. Lost 2 ñ1 by disq. Inside The Distance Wins 12.

1933

Jan 30.	Glen Moody. (Pontypridd)	Won Rsf 6. Manchester.
Feb 13.	Les Ward. (Woking)	Won KO 6. Royton.
Feb 20.	Ernie Red Pullen. (Cardiff)	Won KO 3. Blackburn.

Feb 27.   Leonard Steyaert. (Belgium)   Won KO 8. Manchester.
April 10.   Len Harvey. (Plymouth)   Won Pts 15. Manchester.
(Won British Middleweight Championship. Harvey was the champion.)
May 14.   Jack Hyams. (Stepney)   Won Pts 15. London.
June 12.   Oddone Piazza. (Italy)   Won Pts 10. London.
Aug 21.   George Brown. (Stepney)   Won Pts 12. Manchester.
Oct 9.   Archie Sexton. (Bethnal Green)   Won Ko 10. Manchester.
(Defended the British Middleweight Championship.)
Nov 12.   Jack Forster. (Norwich)   Won Pts 12. Royton.
10 Contests. Won 10. Lost 0. Inside the distance wins 5.

1934
Jan 29.   Eddie Peirce. (South Africa)   Won Pts 12. Manchester.
Feb 28.   Al Burke. (Shepherds Bush)   Won K0 5. London.
March 19.   Eddie McGuire. (South Africa)   Won KO 2. Manchester.
April 30.   Ernie Simmons. (Dublin)   Won Pts 12. Manchester.
June 18.   Teddy Phillips. (Canada)   Won KO 8. Manchester.
Aug 13.   Battling Charlie Parkin. (Mansfield) Won KO 1. Manchester.
Oct 8.   Jack Etienne. (Belgium)   Won KO 1. Manchester.
Dec 3.   Kid Tunero. (Cuba)   Won Rsf 7. Manchester.
8 Contests. Won 8. Lost 0. Inside the distance wins 6.

1935.
Jan 14.   Marcel Thil. (France)   Lost Pts 15. Paris.
(European Light-heavyweight championship. Thil was the champion.)
April 8.   Garcia Lluch. (Spain)   Won Pts 12. Manchester.
June 24.   Al Burke. (Shepherds Bush)   Won Pts 15. Manchester.
(Defended British Middleweight Championship.)
Oct 7.   Marcel Lauriot. (France)   Won Pts 12. Manchester.
Nov 29.   Al McCoy. (Canada)   Won Pts 10. New York.
Dec 20.   Eddie Babe Risko. (U.S.A.)   Won KO 1. New York.
6 Contests. Won 5. Lost 1. Inside the distance wins 1.

1936
Feb 17.   Jimmy Smith. (U.S.A.)   Won KO 2. New York.
Feb 27.   Anson Green. (U.S.A.)   Won Pts 10. Philadelphia.
March 13.   John Henry Lewis. (U.S.A.)   Lost Pts 15. New York.
(For World Light-heavyweight Championship. Lewis was the champion.)

April 23.   Jack Petersen. (Cardiff)   Lost Pts 15. London.
(For The British and Empire Heavyweight Championship. Petersen was the champion.)
Aug 3.   Bob Simpkins. (Bridlington)   Won KO 7. Blackpool.
Sept 14.   Albert Barjolin. (France)   Won Ret 2. Manchester.
Oct 26.   Bill Wainwright. (Swadlincote)   Won KO 3. Manchester.
Dec 1.   Rienus de Boar. (Holland)   Won Pts 12. Manchester.
8 Contests. Won 6. Lost 2. Inside the distance wins 4.

1937
March 8.   Cheo Morejon. (Cuba)   Won Pts 12. Manchester.
April 27.   Eddie Phillips. (Bow)   Won KO 14. London.
(Won British Light-heavyweight Championship. Phillips was the champion.)
May 3.   Dai Jones. (Ammanford)   Won Pts 10. Bristol.
Oct 25.   Jack Hyams. (Stepney)   Won Ret 11. Manchester.
(Defended the British Middleweight Championship.)
Nov 23.   Alban Mulrooney. (Macclesfield)   Won Rsf 3. Hanley.
Dec 6.   Vasile Serbanesco. (Rumania)   Won Ret 4. Manchester.
6 Contests. Won 6. Lost O. Inside the distance wins 4.

1938
Jan 24.   Billy Hardy. (Leicester)   Won KO 6. Leicester.
Feb 28.   Jack Strongbow. (West Hartlepool)   Won KO 6. Manchester.
April 7.   Len Harvey. (Plymouth)   Lost Pts 15. London.
(Lost British Light-heavyweight Championship.)
May 6.   Marcel Lauriot. (France)   Won KO 2. Dublin.
Nov 2.   Jack Strongbow. (West Hartlepool)   Won Rsf 5. Birmingham.
Nov 21.   Joe Quigley. (Sligo)   Won Pts 10. Derby.
Nov 28.   Frank Hough. (Battersea)   Won KO 6. Manchester.
Dec 6.   Jack Robinson. (Nottingham)   Won Rsf 2. Leicester.
8 Contests. Won 7. Lost 1. Inside the distance 5.

1939
Feb 27.   Emile Lebrize. (France)   Won KO 1. Manchester.
March 9.   Tino Rolando. (Italy)   Won Rsf 9. Liverpool.
May 22.   Arthur Ginger Sadd. (Norwich)   Won Pts 15. Manchester.
(Defended The British Middleweight Championship.)
July 10.   Len Harvey. (Plymouth)   Lost Pts 15. London.

(For vacant World Light-heavyweight Championship recognised only by the BBB of C. Also the British and Empire Light-heavyweight Championship. Harvey was the champion.)

| Nov 20. | Jack Hyams. (Stepney) | Won Pts 10. Manchester. |

5 Contests. Won 4. Lost 1. Inside the distance wins 2.

1940

April 29.	Jim Berry. (South Shields)	Won Rsf 6. Manchester.
Aug 8.	Freddie Mills. (Bournemouth)	Lost Pts 10. Liverpool.
Aug 26.	Battling Charlie Parkin. (Mansfield)	Won Rsf 6. Nottingham.
Oct 28.	Eddie McGuire. (South Africa)	Lost Pts 10. Nottingham.

4 Contests. Won 2. Lost 2. Inside the distance wins 2.

1941

| Oct 20. | Jack Hyams. (Stepney) | Won Pts 10. London. |
| Dec 8. | Jim Berry. (South Shields) | Won KO 6. London. |

2 Contests. Won 2. Lost O. Inside the distance wins 1.

1942

| Feb 23. | Freddie Mills. (Bournemouth) | Lost Ret 1. London. |

(Final Eliminator for the British Light-heavyweight Championship.)

1 Contests. Won O. Lost 1. Inside the distance wins O.

1943 Inactive.

1944 Inactive

1945

July 17.	George Howard. (Finsbury Park)	Won KO 2. London.
Aug 7.	Johnny Clements. (Coatbridge)	Won KO 6. Portsmouth.
Sept 10.	Tommy Davies. (Cwmgorse)	Won Pts 8. Swansea.

Retired

Summary of Contests: Fought-147. Won-132. Lost-14. Drawn-1.
Inside the distance wins 91.

Also available:

For King & Country
The Life and Times of Johnny King,
Bantamweight Champion of Great Britain, 1932/34 & 1935/47
- a biography by Brian Hughes MBE.

The British boxing scene in the 1930s was to a large extent dominated by a trio of Manchester based champions managed by the late Harry Fleming. The ring exploits of Jackie Brown (World Flyweight Champion), Jock McAvoy (British Middleweight Champion) and Johnny King (British Bantamweight Champion) made constant news, and rarely can three boxers from the same management stable have completely dominated their respective weight divisions as did the so called "Holy Trinity".

Johnny King, a superbly skilled boxer with a famed right hand punch, was an introverted personality compared to his flamboyant stablemates, Brown and McAvoy, yet was no less accomplished in a career which spanned well over two hundred contests in twenty one years. Although much has been written about the careers and turbulent private lives of Jackie Brown and Jock McAvoy, until now no one has told the story of Johnny King- the quiet one amongst the 'big three' of the Fleming stable.

Brian Hughes unravels both the private life and the lengthy ring career of Johnny King to present a picture of a man who was utterly dedicated to being the best at his weight in the professional ring. The reader also learns about a man who never let his celebrity status go to his head, who was never star struck or boastful about his many successes and was, indeed, one of the best liked ringmen of his generation. Rarely can a champion from the competitive world of professional boxing in the 1930s have been remembered with so much affection by all who knew him.

The story of Johnny King describes his difficult upbringing, his rise to fame in the boxing game, his war service, and his post boxing years. Brian Hughes, using contemporary archive materials and the memories of others around at the time, also gives detailed accounts of many of King's fights - taking the reader back in time to a period when the boxing ring was not dissimilar to the gladiatorial arena of Roman times.

Johnny King's distinguished war service in the Royal Navy during World War Two is also covered in detail, and is told here in print for the first time. A.B.Seaman King miraculously survived the sinking of the battleship *The Prince Of Wales* by the Japanese in 1942, then, having been rescued, also managed to escape from Singapore during its capture by enemy forces. This dramatic escapade is very much the stuff of fictional adventure stories, except that it true in every detail.

For King & Country is a long overdue exposition of the life and times of one of British boxing's great champions, yet also one whose name seldom crops up these days when boxing's lighter weight divisions are discussed. This well documented and fully illustrated biography, if there is any justice, should redress the situation for the sake of present and future generations of boxing enthusiasts.